HUMAN WORK

First published 1904
This edition published by Lector House in 2024

ISBN: 978-93-6138-874-3

Lector House LLP
Registered Office: H. No. 96, Block C, Tomar Colony,
Burari, Delhi – 110084, India
info@lectorhouse.com
www.lectorhouse.com

HUMAN WORK

CHARLOTTE PERKINS GILMAN

2024

LECTOR HOUSE LLP

HUMAN WORK

BY

CHARLOTTE PERKINS GILMAN

CONTENTS

I: INTRODUCTORY

SUMMARY

Common facts hard to understand. Social phenomena most important to modern life, yet least understood. Complexity no obstacle if system is known. Practical knowledge of sociology quite possible. Coexistence does not prove true association. Social rudiments cause pain. Human pain always conspicuous. "The Star of Suffering." Religions rest on conception of essential pain. Suicide a human specialty. Pain a social condition, remediable and preventable. Physical environment largely mastered, present difficulties social. Past societies died of internal diseases. Social indigestion. Human nature progressive. Language retarded by ignorance and superstitions. Civilisation retarded by same things. Economic difficulties our principal ones to-day. "The root of all evil." Innutrition, over-nutrition, mal-nutrition, wrong action in body politic. Difficulty lies in false ideas. Effect of woman labour and slave labour. Consciousness proof of power. Modern society increasingly conscious. Pain most conspicuous, pathology precedes physiology. Errors of early therapeutics, personal and social. Need of scientific social physiology, as base of treatment. Must understand works to mend watch, or society. Knowledge enough to begin. This book a study of the economic processes of Society.

CHAPTER I

INTRODUCTORY

The most familiar facts are often hardest to understand. This is described by Ward as "the illusion of the near." Because of nearness we get no perspective; because of continual presence we become used to one view and fail to perceive others.

To the consideration of new facts we come with comparatively open minds, impressed by each item and its relation to the rest; but facts long known are supposed to be understood, and we resent the slight offered to our intelligence in the proposal to reconsider. Yet the most revolutionary discoveries have been made among precisely the most familiar facts; as in the nature and use of steam, or the endless potentialities of coal tar.

We had, and used, and supposed we knew, our own bodies, through long centuries of living and dying, yet our late-learned physiology was able to show us facts most vitally important which we had never dreamed of. Social phenomena have been going on about us since we began to be human; they are as familiar as physical or physiological phenomena, but even less understood. Yet the interaction of social forces and social conditions form increasingly prominent factors in human life.

Primitive man was most affected by physical conditions, he had to adjust himself mainly to the exigencies of climate, of the soil, of animal competitors. Modern man has to adjust himself mainly to social conditions; he is most affected by governments, religions, economic systems, education, general customs. Yet the study of this especially pressing and important environment is but little advanced. The smooth-worn commonplace facts slip through our fingers, and we fail to see the meaning of our most important surroundings simply because we have always had them. Also we allow ourselves to be discouraged by the extent and complexity of social conditions. This is quite needless.

Grass may be studied in any patch, regardless of the acreage of our prairies, or the height of the plumes of the Pampas. A tree would seem appallingly complex if we tried to understand it from a cross-section taken through the branching top; but from root to leaf it is not so hard to follow. Moreover, early writers on this subject have frightened us with technicalities. Mention some patent fact about our social composition, show a relation, suggest a law, and your alarmed hearer cries: "Oh, that is Political Economy! I cannot understand that, it is too difficult!" It is really a pity that such awe should be felt in the contemplation of our social processes; as though a man were afraid to learn anything about his digestion on the ground that it was "physiology."

The statement, "Hens lay eggs," expresses a fact in Ornithology, Zoölogy, and Biology—but it is none the more difficult to grasp. The special student may, if he so desires, amass enough knowledge in these lapping sciences to appall the uninitiated; but a mere practical farmer can learn enough of the nature and habits of hens to insure a profitable supply of eggs, without overtaxing his brain. There may be fields of sociological science quite beyond the average mind, and rightly left to the learned specialist; but that is no reason why we should not learn enough of the nature and habits of society to insure a more profitable and pleasant life.

With our fertility of resource and high attainments in skill, knowledge, power, and their material product, it is strange indeed that we have made so little progress in the management of our social processes. The civilisation natural to our age is conspicuously retarded by ignorance, disease, crime, poverty, and other disagreeable anachronisms. These things no more belong to this period of civilisation because they coexist with it than do the Bushman and Hottentot because they coexist with it, or than the vermiform appendix belongs to our stage of physiological development because it still exists in it—a mischievous rudiment. Our sociological rudiments cause us increasing pain.

The growing social consciousness of our times is most keenly stirred by a sense of pain. We are beginning to feel the great common processes of human life; but we feel them, at first, only when they hurt. Our individual distresses we have always felt; and have voiced our anguish and resentment more and more loudly as civilisation progressed. Earlier man—and in particular the unhappy savage, with his unavoidable privations, dangers, and mishaps, and his ingenious systems of self-torture—had more to hurt him, but made far less fuss about it. For many an age the pain of human life has formed so conspicuous a fact that we have called the earth "The Star of Suffering." Our common illustrations of happiness are drawn from the lower animals: "as happy as a clam," we say; "as gay as a lark"; "as merry as a cricket."

The world's greatest religions have rested on a conception of general human unhappiness. Divine curses are held to account for it, Divine blessings to allay it, and a future life to recompense us for it—if we are good; but the basic proposition is the unhappiness of human life. Again, we are given a theory of reincarnation; of a slow transmigration through many lines towards a plane where we do not feel, feeling being admitted to mean pain. In Heaven, Paradise, Nirvana, from the Happy Hunting Grounds and Walhalla to our most refined conception of eternal progress, the bliss of a future life is advanced as some countercheck to the misery of this one, some hope to enable us to live.

So unbearable is the amount of human pain that we alone among all animals manifest the remarkable phenomenon of suicide—a deliberate effort of a form of life to stop living because living hurts so much. Social evolution does not proportionately abate social suffering; it improves external conditions and insures physical existence more and more reliably; but it does not make us commensurately happier. We die of different diseases, and we do not die so soon, but we continue to suffer while alive, we continue to refer to "the sea of human misery," we continue to kill ourselves because we cannot bear the pain of being alive.

All this distress, formerly borne by each man as simply his "lot,"—his personal allowance,—was yet vaguely recognised by larger thinkers as "our common lot"; even physical diseases, those most personal facts, we have generalised as "the ills that flesh is heir to." This generalising is a most legitimate social instinct; now grown keener, more accurate, felt by far more persons; and in its light we have begun to recognise many of those long-borne "ills" as not only remediable, but preventable. Yet, though we have done something, our condition remains lamentable. The general causes of our still-existing difficulties are internal rather than external.

Society has long since mastered the difficulties of adjustment with physical conditions, but cannot arrange its own intersocial conditions on a satisfactory basis. "Man's inhumanity to man makes countless thousands mourn"—not nature's. From the Arctic Circle to the Tropics man gets along contentedly enough with natural obstacles; he may be checked and modified in development, but he is not unhappy; he strikes a balance with nature and is comparatively at rest. But in his progressive social development he has not yet been able to strike a balance; his interhuman relations are uncertain and mischievous. So far as history shows us, each social group seems to have carried within it the seeds of disease; to have grown worse as it progressed; and, while conquering all external difficulties, to have succumbed in the end to its own inward disorders. The suffering of an advanced society is not that of one struggling for subsistence, or in combat with enemies, but of one in the throes of disease. Society has safety, peace, shelter, warmth, enough to eat,—and chronic indigestion!

Are these disadvantages of human life essential, as heretofore supposed; or are they merely pathological phenomena and quite unnecessary? We are now beginning to take the latter view, and a most cheerful one it is.

Instead of accepting "human nature" as a fixed condition of mingled pain and pleasure, goodness and badness, with the pain and badness preponderating, we are now recognising that human nature grows and changes like the rest of created forms; that it has already greatly changed and improved, and will continue to do so. We are learning that the troubles of any race and time are partly external and subduable; partly internal and these also subduable. See, for instance, a savage tribe in North America. Their existence is retarded by certain conditions of climate and geography; of the fauna and flora surrounding them; of animal and human enemies and competitors; but also and more seriously by their superstitions. The theory of witchcraft; the ignorance as to hygiene and belief in "the medicine man"; the contempt for women and so for productive labour—these kept the savage savage in the same region where another race is civilised. That race, dominated by larger and truer concepts, has conquered the same external difficulties and risen to far higher levels.

So we, in our present stage of civilisation, are partly retarded by natural conditions of environment. We are still decimated by wild beasts, though it takes a microscope to find them, and by still more bloodthirsty vegetables, of similar dimensions. We are still frozen to death, sunstruck, drowned, and shocked by lightning. We fight the phylloxera, the cottony scale, and anopheles; we have to tunnel mountains, irrigate deserts, bridge rivers, and cross seas; our struggle with the environment is still highly educative. But meanwhile our progress is retarded far more by conditions of social pathology—by ignorance, poverty, and crime; and these conditions are no part of our essential environment, but are due to economic errors and superstitions. If we could straighten out our internal difficulties we could get on gaily with the outside ones.

Now, since we can easily see in history how we have at given times suffered from certain popular mistakes, and how on better knowledge we have outgrown those errors and their painful consequences, why is it not reasonable to assume that we may outgrow our present mistakes and superstitions and their painful consequences? Is it not possible that the persistence in society of certain morbid phenomena is due to an equal persistence of certain false ideas? and that the one may be removed by removing the other? So long as we believe in witchcraft, or in the divine right of kings, or in chattel slavery, so long do we act from that belief, and so long is our action injurious.

Our most conspicuous troubles to-day are economic. We have reached a stage of religious freedom where the growing power of the human brain is allowed to work unchecked toward higher perceptions of truth, and beautiful results have followed. We have reached a stage of political freedom where we can express the public will in public action, as far as the great majority of one sex is concerned, and are rapidly advancing to where the whole nation will share the same position. Here, too, beautiful results have followed. But in economic development we find that whereas there is a great extension and multiplication of economic processes, and commensurately of wealth, yet there is a mighty product of evil which seems to keep pace with the advance of civilisation.

So many of our troubles are patently due to economic sources that our rough-and-ready philosophy has accepted the statement, "the love of money is the root of all evil." Some shorten the accusation to money itself.

This general observation is right in its direction, but not sufficiently accurate to be reliable. Money being a concrete fact, and in its function as representative of all purchasable goods of fascinating importance, we quite naturally attach to it directly the glaring evils we find in its company. We see the misery and sin caused by too little of it and the misery and sin caused by too much of it; we see the various villainies practised to get it, from robbery so small and direct that you catch the thief's hand in your pocket, to robbery so large and indirect that the thieving hand filches uncaught from a million pockets, via hired railroads, hired legislators, and hired newspapers; we see all this, and attach our condemnation to money itself, or, at farthest, to the love of it.

Now, knowing more of the nature of society, we can begin to classify and analyse its difficulties more intelligently and find them somewhat in this order. Let us call poverty in-nutrition—a large part of our social tissues are insufficiently nourished. Let us call wealth over-nutrition, or repletion, or congestion, or fatty degeneration—a small part of our social tissues are gorged and inflamed with too much nourishment. Then let us call our large supply of poor, false, bad things: adulterated articles of food, shoddy clothes, paper shoes,—all the flood of worthless stuff society produces and consumes,—mal-nutrition; the blood is bad and does not nourish. Back of these phenomena we find still more important conditions, having to do not with the nourishment of the body politic, but with its activities. There is wrong action in the social organism; it does not work properly. Hence this local congestion of wealth, this peculiar arrest of distribution which makes both rich and poor dissatisfied in the widest field of life—work.

Work is the most conspicuous feature of human life. In the conditions of work, in our ideas and feelings about work, in our habits, methods, and systems of work, lies the subject-matter of this book. It is held that our difficulties are to be found, not in any essential traits of human nature, and not in any essential conditions of human life, but merely in the preservation in our minds of certain ancient and erroneous ideas and feelings which act continually upon the normal processes of social economics, preventing the process and poisoning the product. See, for instance, among our American savages, how the accepted theory, that work is proper only to women, arrests their economic development and their personal progress as well. See, in the Southern States of earlier years, how the popular error, that work was proper only to slaves, arrested development in many lines. It is here asserted that we have still in the popular mind certain traditions—superstitions, falsehoods—about work, and that to them is traceable the economic distresses so conspicuous among us.

Our increasing consciousness of this distress is a most gratifying fact. Consciousness always involves power. The power to feel implies the power to act. Feeling was evolved as a guide to action; in nature's wise administration there would have been no reason for giving conscious pain and pleasure to a creature which could neither avoid the one nor seek the other. The sensory nerves are developed in careful proportion to the motory: what feels can move, what moves can feel. This law is followed all the way up through physical evolution to social, and is just as true of the social body as of any other.

A comparatively inert primitive society reacts to injury or benefit as does a plant, but shows little evidence of pain or pleasure. Modern society, however, in proportion to its rapidly differentiating organism and its increase in swift, accurate, complex activity, manifests a corresponding increase in consciousness. We are now socially conscious to an acute degree; and this proves our equal ability to act, to avert injury, and seek benefit, not as individuals, but as a society.

Naturally pain is the most impressive fact, for pleasure is a normal condition and only felt in contrast to pain. Pain is some interference with natural law, and as such makes itself sharply felt. Man was led to the study of physiology through pathology; the ache introduced us to the stomach. So society feels first and most what hurts it, and our study of sociology is prefaced by social pathology. And as men, in their first gropings after relief from pain, practised all manner of tricks with fetich-worship, with wild, noisy dances, with filthy medicines, with murderous leeches and lances and poisonous pills; and as still, among the ignorant, any wide-blazoned patent medicine is sure of acceptance if it promises to cure the pain, felt but not understood; so society's first efforts at relief are superstitious, empirical, and often deadly bad for its system.

We need the patient, scientific study of the social body, its structure and functions, anatomy, physiology, and pathology, as we have had it for the physical body; we need careful, recorded observation of the results of previous remedies, and of new ones as well, and all this is a new field of science. We have plenty of facts at hand; all history lies behind us with its glaring records; all life is before us to-day in every stage of development; but we have only begun to arrange and study those facts from the point of view of the sociologist. If a watch goes wrong, we examine its "works" for fracture, loss, misplacement, or some "foreign body"; but to do this successfully involves knowledge of what a watch is, what it is for, how it is made, and how it works. We must know the mechanics of the thing if we are to mend it. So if Society goes wrong we must examine its works, and we cannot tell if they are wrong, nor set them right, unless we have some knowledge of what Society is, what it is for, how it was made, and, above all, how it works.

This does not require all knowledge; no such complete information as Tennyson spoke of in the "Flower in the crannied wall." Flowers are sufficiently understood for us to raise them in beauty and health and profusion; and we can learn enough about this last great form of life, Society, to mend its ways, without waiting for absolute wisdom.

This book is a study of the economic processes of society, explaining the immediate causes of a large part of our human suffering, and suggesting certain simple, swift, and easy changes of mind by which we may so alter our processes as to avoid that suffering and promote our growth and happiness.

II: MAN AS A FACTOR IN SOCIAL EVOLUTION

SUMMARY

Social development affected by physical conditions. By our personal choice. We have overestimated the latter. "Natural" in contradistinction to "personal," or genetic and teleological. Conscious acts most conspicuous to man. Recognition of some other forces at work. Man's contribution to his own conduct. How individuals have promoted it, and the mass always retarded. How we retard evolution. Pterodactyls as conscious agents. Salutary effect of unconscious social processes. Our conscious behaviour always behind the times. Historic instances. Nature of the brain. Effect of education. Relative depth and size of early impressions as compared with later. Our ability to preserve and transmit ancient ideals. Folk-myth of a superior past. Reversionary tendencies, upward tendency of new brains checked by education; effect on religious progress. Should we have done better without conscious conduct? No. Enormous benefit if rightly used. Race memory, use of past. Real value of youth. Our attitude toward it. What it should be. Great advance in education in social consciousness. How to adjust conscious conduct to action of law.

CHAPTER II

MAN AS A FACTOR IN SOCIAL EVOLUTION

The contribution of the human race to its own development is the distinguishing feature in social evolution. That prompt and simple reaction to the environment by which the evolution of sub-human species has been accomplished, is complicated, with us, by a delayed and uncertain reaction, due to stored energy and to the internal environment of man's conscious mind. We are of course modified by conditions, and transmit the modification through heredity. The results in social formation and conduct are clear and startling, but if man could in no way alter these results or select among the causes, to study them would be painful and useless.

Man has, however, a limited private supply of energy, his storage battery of nerve force; not initial with him, but temporarily his to use; and he has also, in the imaged world of his mind, an environment which leads him to use that personal energy according to his separate views of life; thus he can, and does, modify his conduct to a considerable degree. His contribution varies widely in extent; some individuals living very largely from personal initiative, and some almost without; it varies as widely in value; being sometimes of a most advanced grade, and at others distinctly primitive and reversionary.

We have heretofore gravely overestimated the relative extent of this personally modified conduct or telic action, as compared with the conduct which is the result of unconsciously transmitted forces, or genetic action. In the dawn of human consciousness the field of personal conduct was most prominent to man, and he took small note of what things he did under the unobstructed action of natural tendencies.

The word "natural" is here used in contradistinction to "personal"; not as holding man's personal conduct to be un-, anti-, or super-natural, but as distinguishing between the actions resultant from general laws, and those resultant from the man's choice and will; between the genetic and the telic. Marriage, for instance, is a result of the natural laws of sex-attraction, with their deeper bases in race-preservation; celibacy is a result of personal choice and will, based on certain ideas cherished by the individual; marriage is genetic—celibacy, telic. The cerebral activity required to decide upon and enforce a given act, apart from and perhaps in spite of the natural tendencies, makes such acts more perceptible and more memorable; and man inevitably grew to overestimate that part of his behaviour which had passed muster in the front halls of the brain. In these cases he felt himself act, and assumed that the acts which he felt were the sum of his conduct. Plainly perceiving, however, that these acts of his were very irregular and unreliable, often indeed differing widely from his intention, he soon postulated other forces as working upon him, supposedly personal, for he knew no others; and gods and devils were installed in his universe as cogent factors in this perplexing mass of conduct. Some, feeling dimly the larger currents of tendency pressing upon them, conceived of Fate, Destiny, Karma, Fore-ordination—something high and invincible, governing conduct from afar. In all the history of man's conscious life he has been struggling with his conduct, and seeking to modify it to what he from time to time considered desirable ends.

That he has accomplished so much is due to the tremendous power he has to use in this way; that he has accomplished so little is due to his misapprehension of the best means of applying this power; and that he has produced such strange, peculiar kinds of personally modified conduct is due to his varying conception of the desired ends.

Overestimating his personal power, he constantly overdraws upon its resources, exhorting the individual to behave thus and thus; as if all conduct were telic. He has known little or nothing of the genetic laws of human progress which would have guided his course and lightened his task so wonderfully, could he but have understood them. Better housing for the poor does more to develop chastity than preaching it to two families who live in one small room.

As we now begin to grasp something of the position of man in nature, and of the processes of social evolution, we see how irresistibly he was urged upward by the progressive tendencies which lift mankind from savagery as they lifted the savage from the brute; and also how he has been held back by cumulative habits and earlier instincts. In this vast field of evolutionary processes, man, as a conscious, self-directing agent, flounders slowly along, now pushing violently toward a stage of development quite beyond his immediate grasp; and now as violently maintaining standards and ideals long since outgrown and become retroactive and injurious.

The extremes of his influence are most marked. Again and again has the race put forth a man with a specialised brain fitted to grasp a scheme of conduct far superior to that obtaining in his time; and, under the functional necessity of a member of society, urging this higher scheme of conduct upon his fellows with sublime faith, courage, and endurance. Social evolution has been markedly promoted by minds like these. Always someone seeing ahead and proclaiming the advance, and the mass, as they become able to grasp the new concepts, struggling mightily to modify their conduct thereto. Looking only at this side of it, we should say that man, as a factor in social evolution, worked most powerfully to promote it.

There is quite another side to it, however. The human brain, while it has the capacity to foresee future conditions, and to dictate conduct modified to such improved ends, has also memory, the power to retain past conditions, and to modify conduct upon them. If we can imagine active self-consciousness in some stage of physical evolution, it is easy to see how diversely it might have worked.

Take a high-minded pterodactyl, for instance—some poetic, philosophic, progressive pterodactyl. He might have had dim concepts of larger wings and lighter bones, of dryness and sunshine and wide spaces of sweet air; he might even have had faint visions of soft feathers, of nestled eggs, and the joyous music of love. If he were capable of transmitting these ideals among his brethren, they might have been induced to soar more assiduously and perch the higher—so sooner introducing the archeopteryx.

But if on the other hand we postulate our self-conscious pterodactyls as possessing long memories and venerable traditions, ancestor worship and a retroactive education, we should then find them forever yearning for their reptilian past; forcibly re-immersing each aspiring young generation in adhesive depths of mud, and piously destroying the would-be birds as enemies to society. It is on this side of our consciousness that man, as a factor in social evolution, is of such doubtful value.

A consciousness that works backwards, a personal modification of conduct based on the forced retention of more primitive conditions and ideals, this has been, and still is, one of the heaviest drawbacks to human progress. Fortunately for us the general mass of our conduct is resultant from natural causes, rather than personal. We are forced upward from century to century by changing conditions, whether we will or not. The tempting island and sheltered waterway evolved from us the boat, and the boat grew and spread mightily and changed the fate of nations. Under its influence man widened and thickened in social intercourse, and became wise and friendly in practice, long before his conscious ideals of conduct were anything but ignorant and savage.

Steam communication has united modern peoples faster than all religions, joining land to land in bands of iron, and the biting edges of the nations must wear smooth under the wheels. A Russian railroad track comes to the edge of Germany, with a different gauge from the German road which continues it, but the railroad is stronger than Czar or Emperor, and makes ultimately for peace.

Our constantly increasing facilities for communication are social functions, evolved in the human race on natural lines, and they bring different character and conduct long before the popular mind has understood their meaning and consciously adopted their results. As an effect of changed conditions our conduct to-day is at the grade required by steam and electric communication; but as far as that conduct springs from personal judgment and will we are still in the sailing-vessel period, some even in that of the slave-rowed galley.

Every line of social evolution makes for peace to-day, for smooth and rapid growth of international agreement; but our personally modified conduct, resting as it does on very ancient ideals and traditions, still drives us into war. Man's personal conduct has never, as a whole, been up to the level of his socially evolved conduct. Note how the development of industry and commerce lifted and lightened Europe, leading on to peace, to education, to freedom; and how all the while the dominant ideals and conscious efforts of the same people were all for war, its highly prized glories and its supposed gains. See, when learning began to lift its head as a great social factor in those dark ages, how the proud knight still boasted that he could not read or write—mere priestcraft, much beneath him. Quite late in English history it was held derogatory for the nobility to spell well, these baser arts were for their inferiors. In more recent times we can see as plainly how the advance of women, their fuller education and general development, a most important step in social evolution, has been as earnestly opposed by the great majority of persons, acting under the dominance of long-held lines of hereditary ideas and superstitions.

It would seem here as if man were a most undesirable factor in social evolution; as if he acted solely as a brake on the wheels of progress, always seeking to maintain previous conditions, and to modify conduct retroactively. We can easily see how this deterrent position is taken by us. Our range of perception depends on our brain. The brain is an organ, transmitted with hereditary modification like any other organ, and that hereditary modification is of course resultant from earlier conditions. The older the modifying conditions the deeper the modification; racial habits of unbroken centuries are not to be offset by one lifetime's change. So we look out upon the world through an ancestral brain which is far more responsive to simple primitive stimuli than to the more subtle combinations of the present; witness the absurd delight of modern man in hunting.

By this inheritance we find it easier to enjoy, approve of, understand, and uphold that which has been than that which is; to say nothing of that which is to be. Nevertheless the brain is of most easily modifiable structure, and, of itself, shares in the uplifting pressure toward higher development. Each child should bring to the race a little more brain capacity, a little more inclination to progress, and no doubt he does. But this tendency to new power of thought and breadth of vision, which is ours in every child by virtue of social evolution, is heavily offset by the parental action, by our conscious contribution to our own conduct.

Nothing is firmer in our minds than the concept of parental duty; an instinct of primitive force and cumulative development. Parental duty involves education, and education, as previously grasped by man's consciousness, has been one of the most retroactive of social forces as well as one of the most beneficial.

It is a simple physiological law that the impressions first received are keener and deeper than those of later years. Thus each old person carries a memory of better things in his youth; not that they were better in any way, but that his machinery was fresher and took stronger impression. Owing to this the teaching of the aged has always harked back to the superiority of the past—their youth, and deprecated the decadence of the present—their age. It is the measure of personal life erroneously applied to racial life. Under its pressure has sprung one of the most universal of our folk-myths, the legend of a Heroic Past.

The diminutive size and narrow experiences of a child make the events of youth seem larger than those of maturity. The aging brain, as it weakens in recent memories of what a large experience makes small events, recurs vividly to those important records of its youth, and thus naturally cherishes this conviction of the real superiority of those early days. The long life and wide range of impression of the human being give a broad field for this natural assumption, and the power of speech makes the assumption transmissible.

An ancient bear may fondly imagine that in his youth he did more glorious deeds than the enfeebled descendants he sees around him; but if he does think so, he cannot discourage them with his delusions. An ancient man could and did!

The education of the young is necessarily in the hands of their elders; and youth, with no knowledge or experience of its own, cannot conclusively deny, or even ably criticise, the statements made by the aged. This pride of the past, so manifest in the old, is not so injurious to-day. Recognised as a physical phenomenon, offset by wider knowledge of the facts, and with accessible records to give immutable proof that our environment has not shrunk in the least since we were young, this natural tendency of waning brain power does small harm. In our racial babyhood it did enormous harm. There was no record then to dispute with grandpa as to the number of wolves he had slain, or just how big were the nuts on the towering trees of his infancy.

So the Superior Past tradition was hammered hard into the unprotected infant brain, and took fast hold of it, wore deep furrows in it, set that habit of thought so rigidly in the mind of the race that it has taken all these unnumbered ages for a shouting universe to convince us that life is Growth! Only a few of us can see it even now. Deep down below our modern learning still may be found this basic assumption that things were better once—this recurring wish to go "back to nature," or back to handicrafts, or back to something or another—so sure are we in our sub-soil minds that Heaven is behind us!

All this reversionary habit of old brains would have been offset by the "tendency to vary" in young ones; by the steady uplift of each new generation; but for the cumulative weight of our conscious efforts at education. Education, necessarily traditional at first, and instilling tremendous veneration for the ever-receding past,—especially in those earliest years when memory was the only record of events,—has steadily met the expansive tendencies of each new brain by the repressive weight of all foregoing centuries. The development of new brain tissue, and its expanding cellular arrangement, urges constantly to new discovery, and to a rearrangement of earlier impressions, but education has diligently endeavoured to enforce upon each brain precisely that mass and order of impression considered as beneficial in the past. To re-impress forever the same facts in the same relation, and to severely discourage and prohibit any reconsideration of this supply, has been for ages our method of education.

How seriously this has interfered with our progress it is impossible to say. We know that in spite of it the brain has developed in more normal lines under the beneficent action of genetic social forces. A growing industry preached peace to us while church, and state, and school were yet preaching war. Social unity and organic relation are forced upon our consciousness by the facts, while education still hands down the individualistic concepts of far earlier times.

Even in the most rigidly repressed of all lines of growth, the moral perceptions, we can see how social evolution has developed the soul of man in direct opposition to religious traditions. A given stage of brain development is capable of formulating only such and such moral concepts—of postulating only such and such a perception of God.

The current apprehension of God in a given age is accepted as final and forced upon the consciousness of each succeeding age, thus tending to preserve a necessarily inferior standard, and, in preserving it, to check any brain growth tending to its contradiction. This is one of the most conspicuous and persistent of man's efforts to modify conduct. Faithfully and conscientiously he had striven to maintain the innocent errors of his racial youth as guides to succeeding ages. With every gathered force of established religion, with the growing pressure of education, with the tremendous sanction of parental government, man has always striven to preserve the religious limits of his remote ancestors.

And yet, in spite of all the allied forces of conscious humanity, the evolution of brain tissue went on; the new brains saw larger glimpses of truth and transmitted what they saw to others; those who had ears to hear heard, and the world's religions have grown and spread under genetic forces, in the face of opposition, persecution, and execution based on telic forces. A clearer and sadder illustration of the attitude of man as a factor in social evolution need not be asked. All that he could do he has done to throttle progress and stop the growth of his own soul; and this under a sublime conviction of virtue.

In scientific progress, in artistic development, along all the lines of human growth, we find the majority acting as obstructionists; always valiantly upholding that which has been, and maintaining, as respectable pterodactyls, that mud of a proper consistency is far superior as a vehicle of life to the untried vicissitudes of air. Is it then to be supposed that social evolution would have got along faster without our conscious cerebration? That we might have slid peacefully up the ladder with our eyes shut, instead of struggling on in our toad-in-the-well fashion—up three steps and down two? Surely not. The very fact that this power to alter conduct marks the highest stage of animal evolution proves its value. Nature does not make such huge mistakes as to introduce and maintain an injurious function.

We must remember, too, as against the deterrent drag of the majority, the grand uplift of the few; the power never yet measured by which the conscious life of one man can inspire and lift and stimulate the others. Again and again we see the whole race seized and pushed on by some dominant individual life, the currents of whose action vibrate unceasingly through the mass, and stir it to better growth.

When man does by some blessed chance go with the forces of evolution, and uses his conscious power to resist the downpull of old habit, and the opposition of his past-ridden fellows, he becomes an immense accelerating power. By the aid of his racial memory he can see where a new age brings us to the same danger-signals that we ignored in the past, and learn to avoid them. Man's vast stretch of consciousness, made permanent and accessible to all by the arts, especially the art of literature, gives him the advantage of well-nigh limitless experience.

Our irrevocable past, exposed before us all in the increasing light of knowledge, is not a thing to worship and to follow, but a record of splendour and of warning, of deep humility, of patience, and of hope. Our power to postulate a future, to erect hypotheses on which to work, gives us another advantage over the unconscious products of evolution. We have yesterday to learn from, and to-morrow to plan for, and these two give a far broader basis of action than the passing experience of to-day. Our ability to modify conduct, so painfully proven by our successful repressive measures, will have even greater effect when we work with the upward tendencies, instead of against them.

So far the attitude of the race towards its own vanguard—the young—has been that of a heavy old gentleman throwing himself solidly down on an active child, and seeking to smother him and pin him to the earth. Being larger and heavier than the child, he seriously interfered with his normal activity. But when this size and weight is turned to account to help and not hinder, when, instead of piling the dead years on the quivering young brain of the child, we set ourselves as a bulwark to keep the past off him—then we shall see surprising progress. We have but to gain a clear idea of what the natural lines of social evolution are, and cease our opposition, to make large and healthy increase in our growth.

Nowhere is this better shown than in the rapid improvement of education to-day. Instead of a mere transmission of what people used to believe, the young mind is set to find out what is to be known, helped by a large array of carefully tested facts, and the best machinery of latest inventors. The laboratory method, to learn by experiment, to test by proof—this is the modern system; as against the blind belief in changeless traditions that held us back so long. The educator of to-day seeks to develop the brain by exercising all its powers—not to fill and seal it like a preserve jar.

That superstitious respect for the aged which distinguishes China is giving way to a respect for wisdom, for knowledge, for judgment, and ability wherever manifested; and if we swing too far toward honour for the young, it is a healthy extreme to counterbalance the huge and heavy back action of the past. The mind of man is now being opened to perceptions of facts as he finds them, rather than the retention of old stories, and is exercised more in free, responsible action during its early years.

We are beginning to learn now something of the true history of our race—what we rose from, and how we have risen; what forces urged us most, what conditions helped us most. We are seeing with increasing clearness the desirable lines of action, and how best to follow them. Alert, intelligent, and active among the great currents of social evolution, we can do much to promote their effects. Here we can let them alone, there we can oppose our allied wills against some eddy of reversionary tendency, or check the growth of some disadvantageous excess; we can use our consciousness to choose between the varying forces, and such individual power as we possess to steer among them.

To see our line of progress, to see the tremendous currents that push us upward and take advantage of them; to see also the pitfalls and stumbling-blocks, the reaction and inertia to which mere genetic progress is exposed; and then to use our telic energy to assist nature and go farther—that will make man a far more useful factor in social evolution.

III: CONCEPT AND CONDUCT

SUMMARY

Human evolution. New faculties and instincts. Egoistic concept useful to individual animal. Disadvantage of outgrown ideals. Persistence of social rudiments explained. Need of social scrap-heap. Social relations psychic. Despot only a concept. Concepts internal environment. Shipwreck and character. Maternal and sex instinct and concepts. Negro hero, power of concept on conduct. Man's efforts to check his growth. Prejudice a physical brain condition. Healthy brain must be used. Virtue of "believing." Natural organic tendency to consistency,—how perverted. Belief in luck. Charades. Basic concepts wrong. Superior past traditions. Ancestor worship. Fanaticism. Forced inconsistency. Concepts antedate facts. French Revolution. Slavery. Undertow of old brain habits. Increase of social convenience. Brain as developed by natural selection, by social selection. Apparent injustice. Individual hunter. On his own head. Mistakes most possible in highest grades. Peasant grade always preserved. Rub out and do over. Society the best culture for fools. Present concepts in economics, primitive, false, injurious. Ego concept. If bees were "idiots."

CHAPTER III

CONCEPT AND CONDUCT

Human evolution involves the development of a number of individual animals into specialised functionaries of organic social life. This requires the gradual assumption of new faculties, new desires, new instincts, and new activities; and the gradual disuse and discarding of older ones. The egoistic mental make-up of a solitary animal, of a low savage, of any reversionary self-supporting human hermit, is advantageous to him as a separate creature; but disadvantageous to a society to which he might become attached, and, if he was so attached, to himself.

A given society, in any age, possesses certain dominant ideas and feelings proper to it; and the individuals manifesting most of those ideas and feelings are most beneficial to that society and so to themselves. But if members of a given society persist in maintaining and acting upon social ideals of a previous age, they are injurious to their society and so to themselves. Social evolution, in any given place and time, is visibly checked by the number of persons who do not keep up with it; but insist on feeling and thinking after long-past standards, and trying to act on that basis.

This peculiar persistence of social rudiments in all stages of our progress requires some special explanation.

When a given social process, once useful, then useless, then increasingly injurious, continues to force itself upon a growing civilisation, there must be some strong agency to account for it. Naturally, it would have been gradually eliminated by proven undesirability, as cartwheels of solid wood were eliminated. In our material development we have moved steadily on, growing into ever newer and better methods, simplifying, cheapening, quickening, easing, following nature's methods exactly—the conservation of energy—the line of least resistance. Our American industrial supremacy is attributed to precisely this willingness to grow, to discard the old things, to our constant resort to the scrap-heap. But in social development we seem to have no scrap-heap, or never to use one unless compelled to, making history a sort of sacred junk-shop.

In business life, that is, in its material processes, we eagerly accept the new. In social life, in all our social processes, we piously, valiantly, obdurately, maintain the old.

Why?

Because of the peculiar effect of the human brain on human action—the relation between concept and conduct. In adaptation to our physical environment, whether the original face of nature, or the latest inventions in mechanics, we have material relations to deal with, and have learned how.

Social relations are psychic. That a steel spade is better than a wooden one is easily proven to the hand and eye. That a democracy is better than a despotism is not so simple a proposition. The laws of the hydraulic press are established by visible experiment; but the laws of the distribution of wealth work in another medium, and are more difficult to establish.

Society is a psychic condition; all social relations exist and grow in the human mind. That one despot can rule over a million other men rests absolutely on their state of mind. They believe that he does; let them change their minds, and he does not. As a human animal the despot is of such size, weight, colour—he is a physical fact. As a Despot—he is but a psychical fact—he exists as a Despot only in the minds of men. (This is not Christian Science, but sociological science.) He is a concept, a common concept, acting under which all men do thus and thus; outgrowing which, they discard their Despot and adopt some other political belief.

In pre-social planes of evolution we do not find this factor in determining conduct. Earlier forms of life reacted directly to conditions and were modified by them. Man reacts to external conditions as do other animals, but also he acts according to these special inner conditions—his ideas. The power to form and retain concepts, and act under their influence precisely as if they were facts, is what gives the element of special progress and also of perversity to human conduct. This internal environment, the general furnishing of a man's brain, and more particularly its basic concepts, do more to determine his action than does external environment. His reaction to external conditions is modified by these internal conditions; unless you know them you cannot predict the result; unless you change them you cannot change the result.

Present the same conditions of shipwreck to sailors of different nationalities, and see how widely they differ in conduct. A crew of Chinamen, wild with terror or in a stupor of fatalism, show no discipline or courage, they can scarce save themselves. A crew of the Latin race, as was so lamentably shown in the wreck of the *Bourgogne,* seek frantically to save themselves, at the expense of passengers, women, and children. A crew of English or Americans show self-control, resource, courage. They save first the women and children and the passengers, last themselves. If there is no escape they preserve their discipline to the last, as in the crew of the *Victoria* going down to death in perfect order, to the sound of music.

Even under that imminent pressure, the most direct modifying force in nature, the fear of death—the action of the human being depends more upon his character, that is, upon the sum of his concepts and consequent habits, than on the present environment. Maternal instinct is one of the strongest and most deep-seated in nature, but under the action of certain religious concepts, mothers have given their babies to Moloch or to the Ganges. The sex instinct is of incalculable force, but under the action of certain concepts men and women have been known to stultify it absolutely in voluntary celibacy.

An excellent proof of the power of concepts compared with conditions is given in the heroism of William Phelps, the Indianapolis negro. Two coloured men were at work in a great boiler, riveting. Some person by accident turned on the steam. Hot steam as a material condition is quite forcible, and the two men started for the ladder. But Phelps, who was foremost, was arrested by a concept. He stepped back, saying to the other, "You go first—you're married!" Even in that comparatively undeveloped brain, a group of concepts as to Duty and Honour were stronger modifiers of conduct than boiling steam.

This power of directing action by concepts is at once our great advantage and disadvantage. If the concepts are true, if they are founded on fact and in accordance with law, they promote advantageous conduct; if they are false, they promote disadvantageous conduct. Even if once true, that is, as true as the brains of a given period, acting on the knowledge of that period, could comprehend, they become mischievous if not changed to suit the larger brains and larger knowledge of a later time. As shown in the previous chapter, this is precisely our difficulty. We are always being hindered by our back-acting brain. Society progresses far more rigidly than our recognition of it. The acts and facts of to-day continually diverge from the concepts of yesterday.

History exhibits an endless series of man's efforts to check his own growth. Patient, persistent, ingenious, devout, he has laboured incessantly to stay where he was—where he used to be; and is continually astonished to find himself still in motion and going upward. In dealing with the average human brain, these deterrent forces are constantly met; the mere physical resistance to a new process of thought; and a conscious, yes, and conscientious, resistance to a concept not in accordance with the previous supply.

That common resistance to progress called prejudice is a physical brain condition. Certain ideas are early formed, usually under strong pressure, and no further action is taken on that subject, no admission of new ideas, no examination of what is already there. This inactive area dwindles in disuse, is ill-nourished because unused, becomes stiff and feeble; and it is exceedingly difficult to make any fresh impression on the neglected part. When another person does try to arouse thought in that locality, to explain, convince, persuade, enlighten, he is confronted with this thick, inert mass we call a prejudice.

Prejudices are stronger and more extensive among the ignorant, because the brain is so little used in any part that the clogged areas spread and thicken undisturbed for generations. The lumpy brain is transmitted in turn to the young, and the false ideas promptly reinserted during each child's defenceless infancy, so that in time a formidable obstacle to progress is developed, called race-prejudice. The more learned are not absolutely free from prejudice, only relatively so in comparison with the more ignorant. In whatever portion of the brain we do not actively think, we find an accumulating tendency to prejudice.

A healthy and active brain, used to free movement and clear connection, is affronted by any inert mass among its vital processes, as a housekeeper is affronted by some mouldy heap in a disused closet and cleans it out energetically. Old and familiar subjects are more heavily clogged in this way than those more recent and less known, yet prejudices will form, if allowed, even on the most recent of sciences. A brain, like any other organ, must be frequently and fully used to keep it healthy.

These natural tendencies of the brain, the inertia of habit and the local stiffening of prejudice, would not be so injurious if left to the healthy counteracting influence of equally natural tendencies to growth. But the passive resistance has been rendered active and infinitely multiplied in power by the conscious brain action which has so mistakenly exalted its worst faculties, and choked the growth of its best ones.

We very early made it the highest test of virtue to believe what we could not understand; *i. e.*, to hold by main force an unassimilated idea, like a stone in the stomach; and an equal test of sin to presume to examine this irritating mass.

The organic method is to relate each perception to those previously received. The brain is of its own nature logical. Impressions made upon it are sorted and stored in definite connection. This may be noted in ordinary conversation, as when the hearer discovers that the stream of talk he understood to concern Jane was really about Mary. "Oh!" says he, with a sense of physical un-ease as of one who has stepped down where there was no step, "I thought you were talking about Jane!" and there is a pause while he hastily pulls out all those statements from group "Jane" in his mind, and rearranges them in group "Mary."

By this natural power of relating impressions, called consistency, we are able to form a connected scheme of things and work rationally thereunder. If any of these impressions are incorrect, it leads to further error; and if the false impressions be those of main importance, the whole fabric of mental association will be wrong.

Thus a belief in luck necessarily tends to underrate mere knowledge—study, accuracy. The woman who says she "has no luck with her bread" is not likely to go to a cooking school. Take the full extension of this same concept about luck—chance—fate—and you get fatalism, the logical consequence of which is seen in those backward and inert nations where it rules. They may make good fighters, but never good inventors—discoverers—creators; they endure life, but do not promote its development. Religious history gives us plenty of "awful examples" of the power of one radically wrong concept to fill the mind with error, and the world with blood and tears.

Our disinclination to accept a statement which does not agree with those previously held is the brain's physical rejection of an impression claiming to belong to a certain group, but finding no connection there. If forced to accept it as incontrovertibly true, we must then throw out all the others and wholly rearrange that group of concepts. This is where we say "Ah! that alters the case," when some patent fact forces us to "change our minds."

If forced to accept facts indisputably true, but as far as we can see irreconcilable, there can be no mental action whatever on that subject. They are held by force in the brain, but do not grow there and do not lead to any further grouping of concepts. This state of mind is familiar to the guessers of charades. "My first is this," "my second is that"—"my whole is so and so"—and the brain seizes these detached assertions and seeks for some possible arrangement in which they will "make sense" as we call it—or else "gives it up." If the riddle has been misstated, it is impossible to guess it. And this is the first great difficulty in what has been so long called the riddle of human life—it has been misstated. No wonder we have had to give it up.

The value of that proper relation of ideas we call consistency is this: A brain with all its concepts in natural sequence and order transmits energy in a smooth, continuous stream. The brain with inconsistent concepts, lodged in thought-tight compartments, loses energy in cross-currents, contradictions, *culs-de-sacs;* and the resultant conduct is weak and uncertain. Each root idea tends to modify conduct its way; and if the root ideas do not agree neither does the conduct. Often it results in mere inhibition—we see this act to contradict that—cannot reconcile them—and so do nothing. The basic concepts of early man were wrong. His observation was necessarily narrow, his deductions most partial, his whole position one of repeated errors, as is so generally true of all extreme youth. These errors of the undeveloped brain would have given way in course of normal development to better thinking, as the child's missteps lead on to better walking, but for the ill-founded Grandpa theory.

The traditional superiority of the past, on the authority of statements open to no examination and no criticism, rapidly developed into ancestor worship and that whole great retroactive tendency of thought which is still so heavily dominant among us. In it we have deified inertia, as best instanced in China. Assuming that the crude theories of humanity's youth were true, the brain tried to correlate them; to form some connected scheme of life based on such premisses. This was functionally impossible. No healthy brain could "make sense" of such postulates as these. As a consequence, normal brain action on such lines ceased. Abnormal brain action developed freely, its extreme being what we call fanaticism. Those who attended to the maintenance of ancient concepts soon found that any increase of mental activity led to the unsettling of their supposed truth; and so, with the best of intentions, used every possible means to discourage such activity.

And as the average mind found itself forbidden to think on certain of the most important lines in life, and unable to think logically on such bases as were allowed, it simply accepted them as "unthinkable" and so admitted in the common stock of ideas these disconnected heaps of arbitrary statement. Our natural tendency to relate and connect our percepts and concepts in logical sequence, so as to form a rational collection agreeing with itself and with our behaviour, has been not only neglected but prevented; and this arbitrary disconnection of mental processes has been so thorough and universal that we have grown to expect what we call "inconsistency" in human action.

Yet consistency is one of the brain's most essential laws. We expect things to be consistent, we demand it. Talk disconnectedly to the most ordinary person and he soon cries, "What on earth are you talking about? I don't see what that has to do with it!" And we all know how busy our brains are, trying to make out to ourselves that our own conduct is consistent. We are naturally consistent, but the unbroken centuries of violent insertion and compulsory retention of irreconcilable statements in the young brain have perverted natural action and trained us in an artificial inconsistency.

This enforced maintenance of older concepts has for its result this: At any given period in history the ideas of the common mind are found to antedate the facts. The facts of the twentieth century are approached with the ideas, feelings, prejudices of the tenth. And as our conscious acts are modified by those ancient concepts, our acts are necessarily behind the times. Changing conditions constantly demand revision of the conduct of society, but if that conduct—so far as it is consciously ours—is based on unchanging ideas, there must be conflict. There has been, always. Take some well-known historic instance, as the French Revolution.

Here was a long-established social relation, that of feudalism, lineal descendant of still remoter patriarchal grouping, producing in the conscious mind a highly developed concept or group of concepts, described in the phrase, *"l'ancien régime."* Meanwhile the conditions which made feudalism an advantageous form of social relation changed intrinsically. The natural basis in fact was gone, but the idea remained firmly intrenched in the mind. Acting under the idea, feudalism was maintained, but the change in conditions proceeded irresistibly.

Some few there were whose minds consciously perceived the change in conditions, formed new concepts, and sought to transmit those concepts. But this effort was on the one hand too limited in range, and on the other too vague and varied in form, to really bring about the change, or wisely guide it. The action of the cruel facts on a no longer normal social relation, resulted in a vast reaction, quite uncontrollable by the newer ideals.

The endeavour to reconstruct society on the theory of the "social contract," or any other then advanced, naturally failed, as the endeavour to maintain an outworn system failed, and the carnage and confusion, the partial reaction to the old basis, the slow, irregular, fumbling progress toward a better state were the results, as we have seen. That conduct which led to the improvement of the social system in France was resultant from conditions and not from concepts.

In our own recent experience with the system of human slavery we have another marked instance, both in the irresistible trend of progressive conditions which brought the change and in the splendid effort to alter those governing concepts on which the system rested in the minds of men. In the abolition movement we have the conscious human effort to alter conscious conduct. The physical extension of our national boundaries and the mechanical extension of economic processes was the unconscious pressure of conditions which also modified conduct. And against both stood the vast weight of brain inertia, and the unending array of false concepts, dating back to the historic period when slavery was a useful relation, and buttressing itself with the crudest quotations from ancient religions.

The power of the freely developing brain to keep pace with new social relations and proclaim newly perceived truth is offset by the tremendous undertow of the undeveloped brain and its power to compel acceptance of ancient errors.

In a long-range view of social progress it would seem that in early times the conscious mind had a very small share in our development, and that conditions did almost all, even while man fondly thought that he did; but as society grows and the brain grows in spite of itself, the balance of power swings steadily toward conscious conduct. A broader religion and a fuller education make the formation and transmission of ideas continually easier; and personal freedom so accustoms us to handle our own conduct that the power of humanity to consciously improve its world is now a large and growing factor in social evolution.

This carries its visible proof in the increasing activity of our interest in social phenomena, and of our efforts to alleviate the distress of humanity and better those conditions within our reach. We have the power and the desire to help, and the main obstacle to a swift and orderly improvement is in the brain; both in its passive ignorance and prejudice and its active maintenance of mistaken or long-outgrown ideas.

The position here taken, that the human brain has not kept pace with the development of society, and has acted as a deterrent rather than an assistant to our growth, may be questioned from the point of view of the evolutionist. Natural selection, he will assert, develops in each animal a brain capacity suited to his needs, and speedily removes him from the field of contest if he does not manifest it; man in the struggle for existence must similarly develop the kind and amount of brain that is necessary to him, and if he does not he will perish. Therefore the human brain to-day is all that can be expected, and it is useless to talk of any wholesale and sudden improvement in social conditions from that source.

This would be true if man were a creature whose existence was conditioned upon his own individual activities. While the human animal remained at that stage of development where he was directly reached by the consequences of his own personal conduct, his brain power was cultivated in this simple way; if he was not smart enough to live, he died, and was well out of the procession.

But so soon as any social relation was established, when our gains and losses were fused in collective action, this method of brain culture was no longer reliable. Once firmly established as a living species through the process of agriculture, the degree of intelligence necessary to the maintenance of this process was sufficient to sustain life, while the further development of intelligence rested on other activities less instantly important to the life process, and not so sharply brought home in personal consequences.

The individual hunter, if he failed to show the grade of ability necessary to supply his wants, promptly died of his own inferiority, but man, in social relation, is maintained by the collective effort, prospering or suffering with his society, and his pooling of abilities is so far-reaching and hopelessly intermixed that it is impossible to pick out the consequences of one man's action and pile them neatly on his own head. Naturally, selection acts on the society rather than the man, and must needs act slowly and with an appearance of injustice. Incipient errors are not met by the sharp reproof of individual consequence, and wide ranges of eccentricity are possible, so that they do not touch those basic economic processes of society on which all our lives rest.

Gross mistakes in agriculture would be soon punished by the extinction of the mistaken society, or errors in mechanics, in navigation, in any part of our work which deals with the primal necessities of life, but errors in astronomy, in religion, or education do not result in such immediate destruction.

Thus the human intellect on the lower stages shows a certain solid average ability, built up by natural selection acting on societies as it acts on individuals, but the human intellect in its higher grades is painfully irregular and defective, making our higher social manifestations as questionable, uncertain, and often mischievous as our lower ones are clearly good.

Man has stayed alive because he knew enough to plough and sow, to kill wolves and steer a ship, but in later social development he has been as open to destruction as any poor beast below him. In the long lesson of history we may see him again and again killed down to the level of his intelligence. Nations have been conquered, civilisations destroyed, kings decapitated, but the peasant survived.

The problems we have really solved do not have to be done over again; the downfall of past societies is but the wiping off the slate of a mass of elaborate failures. "Rule it all out down to that first line and begin again!" says the teacher.

We are quite clever at simple examples in units, but very weak on fractions. We could see how one man affected another in the short radius of a limited early group, but the long-range effects of our widening interhuman activities have been beyond us, and we are slowly working out in heavy centuries those problems of liberty and justice, of honesty and love, the mastery of which is as essential to our further progress as was the early mastery of metallurgy and mechanics.

A mistake in short and simple addition is easily seen, but as the examples grow more complex the errors are more difficult to trace.

They spread wider and last longer, and by the time a society begins to meet the punishment due to the behaviour of its misguided constituents, those worthies have long since died in the odour of sanctity and a new generation is piously producing the incipient errors which will destroy its grandchildren. The vigour of our basic life processes sustains us through wide reaches of experiments and mistakes.

A flourishing society can maintain more fools than any savage period could afford.

We have to do in this book with several of the basic errors in our common concepts as to economics. We shall see how different are the facts of our economic life to-day from that inner world of concepts we carry in the brain and always take for facts while they remain there. The world is, to us, the sum of our concepts concerning it; and while the real facts relentlessly affect us, our supposed facts are of deadly importance because they modify our conduct.

In the field of economics we maintain to this day some of the most primitive ideas, some of the most radically false ideas, some of the most absurd ideas a brain can hold. They do not fit the facts; they are not provable as true, but very promptly provable as false; they do not agree with such true ideas as we have, nor even with each other; but all this gives no uneasiness to the average brain. That long-suffering organ has been trained for more thousands of years than history can uncover to hold in unquestioning patience great blocks of irrelevant idiocy and large active lies.

In the face of every century's accumulating facts of organic social relation we have peacefully maintained our original animal theory of individualism—the Ego concept. If bees had brains like ours, and the exquisitely organised modern bee could consciously maintain the state of mind of her remote prototype, the solitary bee, we might have some parallel to comfort our lonely height of foolishness. Well did the Greeks call an "idiot" the man who behaved as a separate individual and considered his personal advantage first. Consider the ruin and disorder of the hive if bees were "idiots." That type of industry, of harmony, of peaceful wealth, could never have arisen under such misconception.

We have many more root concepts, some basic, some collateral and derivative; all working, discordantly enough, against social progress. Several will be touched upon here; those most patently connected with the subject of the book, our Human Work. In pursuance of which subject it is necessary to lay down some of the facts as to the nature of society, its structure and functions; and to show how perverse, how inadequate, how deadly mischievous are the ancient theories which still stand in our minds in place of those facts.

IV: SOME FALSE CONCEPTS

SUMMARY

The ego concept, based on pre-human status. Our separate consciousness not human. Human consciousness collective. "We" human, "I" animal. Absurdity of individualism in organism. Pleasure-in-impression theory. Animal basis. Pleasure through motory nerves as well as sensory, and in us far greater. Pay Concept, animal basis, logical extremes in Heaven and Hell. Other forces also operative. Woman labour. Slave labour. Shame and agony resultant in concepts of eternal torture. Wage labour. Want theory. Self-interest theory. Self-preservation not nature's first law. Race-preservation. Pain concept: "Sweet uses of adversity." Action and reaction equal. "Good to be born poor." Pain only a message, always indicative of wrong. Defensive torture. Hazing. Evils of poverty. Abraham Lincoln. Illegitimate wealth. Dumbbells not dinner. Contempt for work, how derived. Veblen. Paradox of "independence." Law of demand and supply.

CHAPTER IV

SOME FALSE CONCEPTS

As we shall frequently have to refer to certain major errors in popular thought, it will be as well to clearly enumerate and describe those selected. The field is wide,—each of those mentioned connects with many others,—and there may be serious question as to which antedates which; but difference on that point will not invalidate the actuality of their influence on conduct. The group mentioned in this chapter will be further described and elaborated later; this is merely to introduce them in some order for reference.

The first, and here assumed to be the basic error in the human mind, the parent of almost all the others, is the Ego concept. This is the universal assumption, based on a pre-human status when it was true, that human beings are separate entities, like the lower animals.

As animals we are separate, and, when we first began to think, the animal life was so enormously preponderant, and the human life so weak, so vague, so intermittently realised, that it was quite natural we should carry over the sense of personal entity into the social entity. That we have a separate personal consciousness is not denied, but it is not humanity. The human consciousness is collective, as we shall see later.

Our mistake has been, not in retaining the Ego concept, which is as necessary in its place as the concept of a leg or a liver, but in failing to grasp the larger inclusive Social concept. All the complex organic phenomena of social life we have continually tried to construe in terms of the individual. The distinctive features of human life are invariably social. No one trait or power of our great race but what must be accounted for in its development and understood in its use as a social factor.

"We" are human, "I" am an animal, save as "I," being part of Society, embody and represent it. The discord and mischief which would be wrought in a physical organism by any absurd pretence of individual life and interest on the part of its organs, is precisely the discord and misery wrought in our social organism by the persistence of this archaic idea.

Another error, most deeply basic in its logical relation, though perhaps not so early recognised by the conscious mind, is our general belief that pleasure lies wholly—or even mainly—in impression. Like the first, it dates from a pre-social status, is the governing theory of personal animal life, and has not been removed and replaced by truer views as social life is developed.

The individual animal having no functions but those of maintenance, reproduction, and improvement, and accomplishing his improvement only along lines of personal heredity, acted only toward those ends, and remained at rest when those ends were served. Pleasure led and pain drove him to the attainment of the means to these ends of this fulfilment, so he early learned to associate pleasure with getting what he wanted,—pain with the lack of it,—a perfectly true concept as far as it went. But as the individual animal's activities are promptly reactionary, and not matters of conscious judgment and volition, he never took into account the pleasure inherent in action, in the discharge of energy, and the pain equally inherent in the prevention of such discharge.

The nerves bring to us sense of pain and pleasure: certain currents feel good to them, certain others bad. An inflow of warmth is a pleasure; increase the vibration, make it heat, it becomes pain, agony, torture. The sensory nerves bring to us their burden of impression, the consciousness we call enjoyment or dislike; but have the motory nerves no burden? Are the currents of energy going out not as perceptible as those coming in? To the individual animal they are not; he does not "feel himself work" particularly. His consciousness is in his income, not in his output.

But the social creature comes under different conditions. His range of activity increases, both in complexity and power; he has an enlarging fund of energy to discharge and a thousand complicated avenues to discharge it through. Moreover, this discharge is no longer a personal affair of his own arms and legs, but involves concurrent action of many others.

To adjust rightly this intricate mutual activity requires consciousness, and consciousness involves pleasure and pain. The whole field of distinctively human activities is under this law. We have a vast fund of energy, a vast field of exercise, and a constantly increasing consciousness of this exercise. Meanwhile the income of man, as a separate animal, remains the same. He has, as before, the pleasure of the intake, the attainment of the means to his separate welfare. He has, beyond that, his share of pleasure in the larger collective intake also, the gratification of his social desires; but he has, pre-eminently, the pleasure of action; of the conscious expression of energy.

This is the largest field of human delight, but has not been so recognised. We still commonly associate pleasure with impression, with things we are to get, to have. Whereas, in fact, our pleasure depends far more largely upon what we do.

Closely derived from this basic assumption is our general theory of return as an incentive; what we may call the Pay concept. This was one of man's earliest generalisations. He observed the excito-motory action of the individual beast; under the influence of hunger or fear he acts; not influenced, he does not act, sleeps in the sun, and accumulates energy for the next jump.

The beast, seeing his dinner running before him, ran after it; having caught his dinner, he ceased to run. Seeing his enemy running behind him, he ran away from it; having escaped from his enemy, he ceased to run.

"Aha!" cries that astute observer, Early Man, "Exertion depends on pleasure before you or pain behind you!" and he forthwith produced his grand primeval generalisation of Reward and Punishment.

This is still exclusively held by almost all of us. We have used it to account for all human actions, with the bitter conclusion that "every man has his price." We have spread and lengthened and deepened it to cover our waxing field of action, till out of its logical extremes we have built both Heaven and Hell.

It was a tremendous concept for the early brain to achieve, and it was true—as far as it went. These two forces do modify action. They were very strong upon individual animals, and they act upon us yet—to a degree. That is, there are still some of us so near the plane of individualism as to be readily and strongly influenced by these agents.

The error of early man lay in not observing other forces even then operative; and the error of modern man lies in not observing that these others have grown continually, and the primal ones have dwindled in proportion.

Right beside our rashly generalising ancestor laboured the primeval squaw, working patiently, working eagerly, working most efficiently, out of the overflowing energy of the mother instinct, with the power of recreative love. Not because of anything to gain or anything to fear, but because energy must have expression; and the expression is in proportion to the energy, not in proportion to the return. Later, in the fall of the matriarchate and the inception of our dramatic androcentric period, the woman was made a slave and her labour became slave labour, not to its improvement. Later again men were made slaves; their activity was coerced by these two primitive stimuli, the fear of punishment, the hope of reward; mainly the former.

In that first period of co-ordinate activity among men, the irreconcilable male energy was forced into service by the immediate pressure of pain and fear. Slavery was one step short of slaughter, as such accepted, as such hated. All that deep-rooted aversion to labour—sense of scorn for it, shame in it, honour in being free of it—was superimposed upon humanity at this period, and has never been fully outgrown. This terrible period, its wrong, its shame, its agony, its hopelessness, deeply impressed the growing brain of man, and, as this period was of great duration, it made possible to our minds the prodigious concepts of eternal torture.

Later, in the second stage of coerced action, that of wage labour, we have the reward used instead of the penalty. We will not whip the man if he does not work, but we will not feed him unless he does.

Our governing concept being that action is produced only by these means, we must needs use one or the other. Since we believe that if the slave were not in fear of punishment he would not work, or that if the employee were not in hope of pay he would not work, we act upon our belief consistently enough. We have outgrown the period where we believed we had a right to enforce labour by inflicting punishment; but we have not outgrown the only less primitive belief that we have a right to enforce it by withholding the reward. We do not yet, to any extent, recognise the other forces under which human beings act.

Closely allied to the Pay concept and following it, a more concrete expression of the same general thought as applied to industrial activity, comes our universal economic fallacy, the Want Theory.

This is repeatedly defined and opposed in later chapters, and here need only be stated as that basic proposition in Political Economy in which it is assumed that man works to gratify wants, and that if his wants are otherwise gratified he will not work. This fundamental theory of economics rests, as will be readily seen, on the foregoing, on the Ego concept and the Pay concept. Part of it, more generally applied, is our general Self-interest theory, usually expressed in solemn tones: "Self-preservation is the first law of Nature." Men say this as if it were so, and other people believe it simply because it is said to them so solemnly. Our brains, trained for all time to bow to authority, have a treacherous trick of believing whatever is advanced by those in authority or even by the scribes. The present scribe asks no such gulp, but that the reader use his own active thinking power on the propositions here advanced. Now, this self-preservation theory is contradicted on its own doorstep by the fact of the race-preservation instinct, the individual counting for nothing, absolutely nothing, in the unbroken stream of racial life of which he forms so small a part.

If we were solemnly taught "Race-preservation is the first law of Nature," we should be nearer the truth. Even in the purely individual animals the good of the race is paramount to that of the member, and in the collective animals the social instinct is so highly developed that self-preservation is not even thought of. Break an ant-heap, and watch "the first law of Nature"! Immediate, instinctive, unquestioning, they rush to save the eggs and young, to guard the queen, to preserve the group—not the individual.

"Nature" develops whatever faculties are required in a given form of life, and if the life-form is collective the collective instincts appear in force. Now "Self-interest" as a motive does act upon the human being, but it does not compare in weight and value with the larger later motives of social interest. We assume that the visibly social processes we see going on about us are best governed by self-interest in the parties concerned; that efficient service is best commanded under this pressure. We are wrong.

Social processes were initiated primarily along lines of self-interest, in orderly development, from existing instincts to higher ones, but the further developed are these processes the less useful is the early motive, the more needed is the later motive of social interest. Self-interest, preserved too long in social growth, becomes a deterrent force. The more wide and complex the process, the greater the distance between producer and consumer, the more injurious is the action of that essentially limited force. This is why in small, early societies there is more honest and efficient service under this motive; and in large, modern societies, unless the social instincts of duty, honour, and the like are operative, we find such infinitely ramified dishonesty and inefficiency.

Another stumbling-block of progress is an extremely ancient belief of ours, not derived from the preceding five, but in flat contradiction to some of them, which the popular and poetic saying calls "the sweet uses of adversity." We very generally believe that pain and difficulty are good for us, and the logical consequence of this belief—so far as practical life allows such an absurdity to have any consequence—is of course that we do nothing to remove pain and difficulty. The further logical consequence, that we should deliberately add pain and difficulty to our lives in order to improve them, is seldom allowed; it is too ridiculous even for our brains.

Now what is the fraction of truth in this peculiar piece of idiocy? At its very base lies the law of physics: "action and reaction are equal." As hard as you push against a wall does the wall push against you. Following this comes the early observation of the effect of environment. Where the channel is narrowest the stream is deepest; where it is widest the stream is shallowest; and if you dam the stream the water rises to the height of the dam.

So in the action of the human forces we observe that, if you hinder and obstruct a man, he resists your pressure and rises against it—sometimes! Sometimes he does no such thing, but is crushed instead. However, we perceived numbers of cases where opposition called forth resisting energy where action and reaction were equal, and we made our easy generalisation as to the beneficent effects of difficulties.

Applied to human life, in the concrete environment which we call good and bad according to our lights, we observed further that this law seemed to work backward; that where a person had no difficulties, where all was made easy for him, he did not manifest energy. Then we felt sure we were right. We produced a lot of popular expressions of this general thought, a religious phase of it being "whom the Lord loveth he chasteneth"; its application in education leading us to believe that it is good to make the child labour and struggle in learning—bad to "make it too easy for him"; and in economics we apply it in our sad comments on the disadvantages of wealth, our cheerful assertion that "it is good for a man to be born poor."

Of course no one ever thinks of staying poor because of its benefits; no one foregoes being rich, or trying to be rich because convinced of its evils; above all, we do not seek to work out this theory on our children. Its main mischief is in preventing us from trying to remove the obstacles to human progress in general. So long as we even partially believe that obstacles promote to progress, that the hurdles add to the speed of the racer—why, if we do not really give extra hurdles to aid the man we want to win, we at least do nothing to clear the track.

Now where does the essential error lie in this loosely hung together bunch of foolishness? In the first place separate "pain" from difficulty. Pain is merely a message; it is a telegram to headquarters to say that something is wrong. It always means that. Normal action does not hurt. It may be "good," as the sentinel is good who gives the alarm so that you may save yourself; but his alarm is a warning of evil. It may accompany a "good" process, like that of resuscitating the drowning; but that is not a normal process, the pain is conditioned upon water in the lungs.

If a person is so situated that he must bear pain, then it is good to get used to it, if possible. On this basis the early savage used self-torture to help him bear the incidental miseries of life, and from that practice dated our views on the subject.

The most unblushing survival of this gross savagery is seen in our practice of hazing, calmly defended by its perpetrators as "it makes boys manly," "it develops character." The savage had at least the grace *to do it to himself,* and it was not practised upon children. Our imperfectly educated children maintain in this the customs of the lowest savages, in a rudimentary form. There are times in life when pain has to be borne for a greater good, but that does not make the pain good.

As to the other and a little more legitimate branch—difficulty. Here we feel more assurance. We do see the poor boy making tremendous struggles, and rising above his difficulties hardened, bruised, belated, but triumphant. We do see the rich boy making no struggle at all, and rising above nothing. Hence—but wait a bit. Do *all* poor boys thus struggle and rise?

Do the slums produce the best citizens? Is a well-bred, well-fed, well-educated boy so hopelessly handicapped in life by those advantages? Is our ceaseless attempt to provide for our children the best advantages all folly? We may not be logical, but have horse sense enough to know better than that.

We know that poverty coarsens, weakens, stunts, degrades; that under its evil influence "the dregs of society" are steadily and inevitably produced. We know that where one person of phenomenal capacity can rise *in spite of it,* thousands of ordinary capacity are ruined *because of it.*

Abraham Lincoln was a rail-splitter. Yes. Were there no others? There were and are many poor boys splitting rails, and yet the crop of Abraham Lincolns remains limited to one.

Our error is a very simple one. We confuse a coincidence with a cause. Most people are poor. Therefore most great people have risen from poverty. How many more great people we might have had under better conditions we shall never know.

As for the effect of wealth, great wealth in private hands is not an advantage; it, too, is a morbid condition, and under its evil influence the scum of society is steadily and increasingly produced. It is perhaps as hard for a great nature to overcome the difficulties of our illegitimate wealth as those of our illegitimate poverty. Still some do it. We have but to study the biographical dictionary to find that the proportion of great men to rich and poor is about the same as the proportion of those two classes, that is all.

Meanwhile the healthy truth under this is the physiological law that exercise develops function. Whatever power you have is increased by exercise to a certain extent. But you must first have your power. A punching bag helps develop your muscles if rightly used, but it does not make them. Your daily food is the prime factor.

To get the best results from people they must first be born in good condition—starved mothers and exhausted fathers are not advantageous; then kept in good condition;—good air, good food, good clothing. Does anyone wish to claim that poor air or poor food or poor clothing is advantageous? When you have good stock, and give it all the advantages of true education, bringing out and correlating all its powers, then the strong and active creature can maintain and develop those powers by exercise. But dumbbells in place of dinner do not strengthen.

One more very common attitude of mind with regard to work, not as fundamental as the foregoing, and not founded on any law whatever, but on arbitrary and evil conditions, is our general contempt for it.

Regarding it, as we must under the Want theory, as done only to gratify a want; regarding it, as we must under the Ego concept, as done by the individual for the individual, it does seem a poor thing enough. Why should we honour and approve the never-so-ingenious efforts of a person to keep himself alive, so scornfully described in a poem of Robert Buchanan:

> "Struggle, speculate, dig, and bleed,
> Reap the whirlwind of Venus' seed,
> O senseless, impotent human breed!"

But beyond the legitimate scorn of a social creature for what he estimates as an individual activity, comes our illegitimate scorn based on lamentable, evil conditions.

The work of the free mother in the matriarchal period was never despised; when men enslaved women their work became contemptible. So when the despised captive was made to labour, his work also was held contemptible. And then, as Veblen shows so irrefutably, this primitive attitude was retained through all the centuries in the stagnant pool of leisure-class life, that singular medium wherein the active modern world may find preserved a sedimentary deposit of most ancient times. This class and its customs and habits of mind, being revered by us, we have made permanent and constantly reinforced the scorn of work which else would have been contradicted long since by every fact of progressing civilisation.

With this mixed foundation the feeling remains in full force. It serves to check the normal activities of those who "do not have to work," and to belittle the importance of those who do. It shows, for one result, this pretty paradox: a human creature absolutely helpless, doing nothing whatever to maintain himself or anyone else, depending for the meanest service as for the greatest, on the assistance of others; and then calling himself "independent," and believing that he "supports" those who keep him alive, by "furnishing them employment"! And—still more paradoxical—the active and valuable persons who so laboriously maintain this ornament believe it, too.

A minor fallacy in our popular economics, but one doing much mischief, is that familiar phrase "the law of demand and supply." It is in part a logical derivative of the want theory; in part based on a true natural law, and for the rest weakened and confounded by the conditions of our own artificial "market."

Spencer refers to this with great solemnity in "The Man vs. The State"; showing how smoothly and beautifully great London is provided for by the working of this "law." He points out the immense numbers of people to be supplied daily, and the immense amount of materials brought in daily, by ship, by rail, by horse and cart, under the wise guidance of individual self-interest and this governing "law of demand and supply." It sounds very attractive! and when stated by so great a thinker it seems as if it were so. But is it? Are the millions of inhabitants in London thus accurately provided for? Do none starve and freeze? Do none dwindle and sicken, and become hopeless cripples and invalids for lack of proper supplies? Or again, do none waste and spoil, receiving far more than they need? Are the demands of the human body, of the human mind, of the human heart, really supplied in London, or anywhere else, by this alleged law?

What do the words really mean, if they mean anything? For "demand" read "purchasing power"; "the law of supply and purchasing power." What does "supply" mean? It means the product of human industry. The product of human industry is equal to the purchasing power. This does not sound so smooth, but is more accurate. And what does it mean now? That those who have purchasing power can get what they want. Can they—always?

Why, yes—*if there is any*. But if all the purchasing power in the world should happen to demand a few more of the works of Phidias—they would not be forthcoming. There is frequent complaint even among the very rich of their inability to get some things they want; such as ideal servants. This is a very common demand, and the air is filled with protest because, at any price, the supply does *not* equal the demand. This law is a common vagrant—"having no visible means of support." All it amounts to is that if you demand a thing—and can pay for it—and there is any such thing—the previous owner will sell it to you—if he wants to.

On the other hand, nothing is more frequent than our upsetting this supposed equilibrium by what we call "overproduction." If the supply were equal to the demand the demand is certainly not alleged to be equal to the supply. "It's a poor rule that doesn't work both ways."

What does govern the supply, if demand does not?

"Supply" is human production—the output of our social energies. If it can be called "equal" to anything, it is equal to the combined action of heredity and environment, modified by our volition. The product of a race depends on its stock, its inherited characteristics; on its education, physical and mental, on its nutrition and stimulus, on its governing concepts.

To make such and such a product forthcoming you must have such and such a producer; he must have the capacity and the wish to produce such a "supply." If he has not the capacity, no power on earth—be it a reward of the princess and half the kingdom, or a penalty of thumbscrews and boiling oil—can get it out of him.

Turn your "supply" round and apply it to the producer. Supply him with all the necessary conditions for rich production. Then we might say in a general way "the supply is equal to the supply." But "demand" is not a producing agent. It does not make people create, invent, or discover. It does not make them sell unless they want to—see Ahab demanding Naboth's vineyard—or Frederic and his Miller of Sans Souci. It does not make them work even, unless they are able and willing. Demand what you please of the tramp and pauper—he cannot produce it.

A natural law is a series of observed phenomena. Such things always happen, so we say it is a law. The observed phenomena in this case are those of a past stage of economic development; and at no time "natural" but purely arbitrary. A parallel may be drawn from similar observed phenomena in the system of slave labour. The "supply" then was the work of the slave. The "demand" was a command, and was enforced by the whip; no whip no work, more whip more work, and behold "a law"! The work equals the whip! So it did, in most cases—granting the man was a slave. But it was no law of social economics; it was a law of slavery. Neither is this theory of ours that "The work equals the pay" a law of social economics—it is only a law of wagery.

Among free men, the whip would not produce work but merely a fight. Among independent gentlemen an offer of pay does not produce service of any sort—it is regarded as an insult. The crucial condition of the work-and-whip law is that you shall hold the whip and have power to use it; in the work-and-pay law, that you shall hold the pay and have a right to withhold it.

These are the root errors most especially discussed in this book:

1. The Ego Concept.
2. The Pleasure-in-Impression Theory.
3. The Pay Concept.
4. The Want Theory.
5. The Self-Interest Theory.
6. The Pain Concept.
7. The Law of Supply and Demand;

with the derivative scorn for work; here only enumerated and briefly set forth for convenience in reference.

V: THE NATURE OF SOCIETY (I)

SUMMARY

Idea of social organism, not new. Proposition stated. Proof advanced on three main lines. First, nutritive processes of collective and organic society. Men do not support themselves. World-wide production and distribution of food. Individual could not become baker or tailor, they are social functionaries. Organic evolution along line of modification to food supply. Man the only creature who has mastered his food supply, he makes that which makes him, he produces food. Production of food a collective function, never found in individual animals. Physical conditions of agriculture essential to social progress, agricultural unit a village. Second, specialised activities of society collective and organic. Social evolution of trades, arts, businesses. Increasing interdependence. Instance of teacher. Evolution of social functions. Third, the brain a collective organ, a social organ, thought a social function. Effect of isolation on human brain, partial or complete. Difficulty of retaining mental stimulus. Individual animal's brain in relation to his own activities. Human brain in relation to common activities.

CHAPTER V

THE NATURE OF SOCIETY (I)

The concept that society is an organic form of life is not new to the world.

The popular mind, confronted with many conspicuous proofs of human solidarity, admitted the idea to one of those thought-tight compartments in which we keep such concepts as we are unable or unwilling to *think through* and hold in logical relation to our others. There it has remained, enlarging somewhat in course of time and loud events, and tending to modify such conduct as came its way to the social benefit. But since a much larger brain era was governed by the egoistic concept, and vital affairs far more directed by it, we still consciously act as individualists, and still construe Human life in terms of the individual. Let us now use the temporary power of the brain to think in defiance of its own previously held ideas; and study the organic nature of Society.

The proposition is that Society is the whole and we are the parts: that that degree of organic development known as human life is never found in isolated individuals, and that it progresses to higher development in proportion to the evolution of the social relation; that a man is, individually, a complete animal, with sufficient ability to attain the necessities of an animal existence; but that as a human being he is but a minute fraction of a great entity, the necessities of whose existence are only to be attained by the complex interdependent activities of many men.

That this relation is strictly organic, involving the high specialisation of the individual man to the social service in activities which are of no possible benefit to his separate animal life—(as the activities of a dentist or a teacher); but which are of visible benefit to his community, his community in turn supporting him.

That these common and composite activities have developed a life-form quite above and beyond that of its constituent men; with a structure and functions outside of and including theirs. That whereas the life processes of the constituent individuals must of course be insured and improved by the higher life inclosing them; yet that a greater or less sacrifice of individual interests may at any time be necessary—and is naturally made—the greater including the less.

That this Social Organisation tends to make safe and happy its constituent organisms in their separate animal lives, yet their greatest happiness lies in their recognition and fulfilment of the social life.

That an increasing social consciousness and social activity is the most healthful and happy growth for the human race; and further, that "the riddle of human life" is made quite simple by this purely natural and evolutionary position.

In proof and illustration let us consider certain facts, most of them commonly known to us all, but not commonly considered in this connection. We will observe in turn the organic nature of Society as shown in its nutritive processes, in its high and personally sacrificial specialisations, and in its patently collective mental life.

First, and most visible, come the physical life processes; those daily activities in which our energies find expression, by the products of which our lives are maintained. Among facts suitable for nursery education is the glaring one that in plainest economic relation "no man liveth to himself nor dieth to himself."

Each man does not support himself by his own efforts, as an individual animal does, but pools his efforts with those of others and shares in the common good as a collective animal does; as the bee or ant. This does not refer to any consciously advocated plan of collectivism; but to the present fact that our coffee comes from one country and our tea from another; that the Californian gives us oranges and the Kansan beef; that the carpenter and mason build our houses and the tailor makes our coats.

The daily necessities of one man are met by the activities of countless other men. If they were gone, the one man could not supply himself with any of these things; but would, if he lived, sink to the level of the savage hunter,—who is indeed "self-supporting." We have, it is true, a system of exchange in which it is endeavoured to make each man's share in the common product proportionate to his personal efforts; but even if this system worked successfully it would not alter the fact that the supplies are really made by the others—and the one—alone—could not make them.

Lay aside for the moment the confusion of idea naturally arising from our system of interpersonal exchange and its convenient medium, money.

Suppose that money were entirely out of the world; or that we were so flooded with it that it lost its value as a medium of exchange. Great confusion as to how much of anything should be demanded for something else would of course ensue; but the most conspicuous result would be the unavoidable perception that it was *the thing* we needed to live on—not the money.

The purchasing power of money varies continually, but the nourishing power of wheat or the heat-retaining power of wool does not vary. We eat the bread and are kept warm by the coat; and the wheat and wool are prepared for us by many strangers. It may be for a moment supposed that an individual man could, if he chose, make his own bread and coat from his own wheat and wool, but follow back the evolution of these processes and see if he ever did.

The more nearly alone you find a man—as the Bushmen—the more nearly naked he is, the more absolutely a hunter and an eater of raw food. To raise wheat and bake bread requires a stationary group of long standing. It is a social process. So with the coat—the man who lives really alone wears at most the skin of another animal.

To keep sheep, to shear, and card, and spin, and weave, and cut, and sew—all these processes require a stationary group of still longer standing; they are social processes. A man alone can catch another animal, can "eat his fat and wear his hair"; but the baker and the tailor are slowly evolved social functionaries. Everywhere we see the present proof that the wants of man are not supplied by his own efforts and cannot be; that his life processes are essentially collective.

Now let us approach these facts from behind, watch their inception and growth, and see how unavoidable is the conclusion.

The life of any creature is primarily dependent on the regular renewal of its constituent particles. The process of living uses up the materials lived in. Living involves dying, and to postpone the dying the structure is continually supplied with fresh materials. This continuous supply of fresh materials we call nutrition. It is an increasingly elaborate process, with "many a slip 'twixt the cup and the lip"; and the main line of organic evolution is in development of these nutritive processes.

Conditions of the environment modify a creature, as in hide and hair; conditions of inter-animal competition modify him, as in horns and stings; conditions of reproduction modify him, developing an elaborate physical mechanism and a more elaborate scheme of decoration; but the most distinctive modification of a creature is that produced by its nutritive conditions. "Order Mammalia," with all its towering superiority, is founded merely on a new way of feeding the baby. The food supply of the world is subject to fluctuating influences—climatic, geographic, and other; and as we watch the widening panorama of animal forms changing and growing up the ages, we see the whole procession to be moving always in one line—in pursuit of its dinner. We think of our dinners as a pleasing series of events, but we do not appreciate their awful importance.

The life of any creature absolutely depends on getting together a certain group of chemical constituents and keeping them reinforced. While those constituents, massed in certain proportions, are cunningly poured through a certain small orifice called a mouth, the creature lives. A procession of dinners passing a given point—that is the physical condition of life. *We* are the given point. If the procession goes another way—or stops awhile—"we" cease to live.

And since there is no law of nature calling on the proper constituents to arise, to detach themselves from their undesirable comrades, to form into rightly proportioned groups, appear at proper intervals and to enter the "given point,"—therefore the principal machinery of every living form is developed to discover, pursue, seize, and gather in these constituents. To obtain what we want from the air, gills and lungs are invented; that supply is so instantly imperative and so plentiful and easy of access, that an unconscious organic motion sucks it in. If food were as simple and common as oxygen we should be spared much exertion.

But food is anything but this. In its crude forms it is thinly scattered in the water, and small early beast-lets float around and grab it as they can. "You get food when it drops and you die when it stops—you helpless free agent of sorrow!"

Food in vegetable forms is also widespread and thin. The creatures that live on grass have had to develop the most cumbrous and involved of alimentary canals; huge barrels filled with many stomachs, supported by sturdy legs, as of tables, to hold the eating machine up, and carry it eternally about after its plentiful but highly diluted dinner. A concentrated vegetable food, like the fruit, brings out quite other qualities; as seen in all light swift arboreal animals, as the monkey; and between ground and tree rises the long neck of the giraffe—stretching, ever stretching, after his ascending dinner.

The humming-bird has slowly acquired a very special tongue to get his dinner, so has the butterfly; the tooth of the squirrel is necessitated by the stubborn nut; and the poor thirsting camel has his private portable food-and-water supply to meet the demands of life between far-scattered oases.

But when it appeared that food in predigested ready-to-eat packages was specially desirable; when the carnivorous habit was developed, then indeed we find a wild variety of adaptation to one's dinner. Food in this form was not only widely scattered and difficult of access, but actively reluctant, sometimes even contentious. But means were found to encompass it. Was it small and hidden like the ant, yet numerous enough to pay for eating? Lo! the ant-eater's slender snout and slenderer tongue pursue and capture it. Is it a fat grub, deep boring in the bark? The ingenious Javan monkey develops a special finger for his extradition. Does the insect fly waveringly from flower to flower? The bird flies more accurately and swiftly from insect to insect, and the hawk swoops still more efficiently from bird to bird.

Whatever form the dinner took, wherever the dinner went, there followed the fluent, ever-changing animal organism, producing tooth or claw, tongue or proboscis, seven stomachs or a private fish-pole—whatever was necessary to lure, catch, hold, inclose, and assimilate, this ever-receding and sometimes actively resisting, but always indispensable dinner. The evolution of animal organisms is conditioned mainly upon the food supply.

How does humanity figure in this transformation scene?

Man alone, of the whole animal kingdom, has attained a complete new stage in this imperative process of nutrition. Where the most primitive ameboid cell can but receive food; where the whole machinery of later organisms can but seize food; man, and man alone, produces food. Through all the ages, through every conceivable modification of structure and function, the animal has pursued its dinner. Man has caught it.

Man alone has permanently mastered his food supply; instead of an endless chase it is a closed circle—he makes that which makes him. That is why physical evolution stops with man—and psychical evolution begins. No longer at the mercy of thin grass, man makes the fat-grained corn; no longer endlessly chasing the buffalo, he raises the big steer. His prairie in the garden, his prey in the barnyard, the animal can rest at last, and man can grow. By what strange new power is this immense step taken, which has enabled this one out of all created forms to apply productive force, instead of mere destructive force, to his food supply? By the power of organisation. By entering upon that new life, the social life, which raises us above all lower forms.

The cell groups with others into the organ, the organs group again and form organisms; the organisms, once more combined, form an organisation. Society is the fourth power of the cell.

A low and limited form of social life began with the temporary union of hunters; loose fluctuating hordes, like those of wild dogs or wolves.

When cattle were kept instead of killed, were milked and sheared and bred with care and forecast, there arose a higher group form, the family. With an insured food supply at hand man sat quiet, watching his cattle; and with food to spare and time to spare, he began to grow. The family, our physical nucleus, grew too; grew as it had never grown before.

The limits of cattle-fed life were sharp and clear. There was no permanent home, no village, no extra-familiar intercourse, only warfare over pasture and water between tribe and tribe. But the hour came when corn was planted and eaten; and then our human life was indeed established.

The conditions of permanent physical juxtaposition, so essential to social growth, were met for the first time. The Hunter, requiring forty square miles of land per capita to chase at hazard his laborious prey, had no chance for social growth. Any other man on his forty miles was a competitor and reduced the supply of food, so he killed him if possible; and this habit also did not conduce to social growth. Families, too, were small when each man "did his own work" as these did. When came the Shepherd and his plenteous food, came larger families; but there was still a need of some five square miles per capita to feed the beasts; as the family grew the miles increased; and on the "free land" with its "equal opportunities" the families met at the edges and warred with one another as competitors. This, again, was not conducive to social growth.

But the Farmer, with far more food on far less land, food more richly and rapidly reproductive, and taking far less time to mature; with the family growing faster than ever, but taking up less room for its food supply; the Farmer is the base of the true social structure. Surplus nutrition and surplus time meant accumulated energy and frequent opportunity which, with the permanent home, allowed the birth and nurture of the industries and arts. The physical nearness of the people—acres instead of miles for their nutritive base—allowed of larger growth of language; and so in and with and following these conditions the social life became possible.

Note the absolute collectivity of this productive food process. The lowest food-producing unit is a village; not a separate man, or even a family. Agriculture is not found below a certain human group form. Social life is born with agriculture. The distinctive food processes of humanity are collective.

A second field of proof of our organic relation, and one as patent as the first, is the complex specialisation of humanity.

If you find a lump of protoplasm you cannot tell whether it is a whole or a part; if you divide it, its parts make wholes and prosper as before. Very low life-forms may be cut into fragments, and each develops whatever it lacks and makes a new whole. There is little differentiation here. But if you find an eye, a tooth, a claw, you are at no loss as to whether it is a whole or a part.

If it were a whole, it would be able to maintain and reproduce itself. Being a part, it can do neither. The eye is a remote, highly developed special organ, *of no use to itself*; able only to serve the complex organism of which it is a part; and nourished and maintained only by that organism. This condition is absolute proof of organic life as distinguished from individual.

Apply this proof to society. Society consists of numbers of interrelated and highly specialised functions, the functionaries being individual human animals. Society develops them—they could never have been evolved in solitude. As easily conceive of independent eyes, rolling around and doing business by themselves, as of independent teachers, carpenters, dentists. Society maintains them, as the body does the eye; intricate labours of many others feeding, warming, housing, protecting the teacher, while he teaches.

Alone he might hunt, and "support himself" as a separate animal; as if, conceivably, the eye could return to a protoplasmic condition and soak up a living somehow; but as an eye it would cease to exist; and he would cease to exist as a teacher. The teacher, teaching, cannot support himself. His time, his strength, his enormously specialised skill, are spent in teaching, and the society which made him and which needs him, necessarily supports him. Teaching as an activity is not predicable of individuals. It is a power to transmit the social gain in intelligence and knowledge among the social constituents. No solitary individual could have attained this knowledge and experience; and, if he had it, he could *not teach it to himself*. Teaching is a social function; a very elaborate and long-developed social function. The teacher is an extreme instance of the social functionary. Other than as a social functionary he does not exist.

This test may be applied far and wide, in every trade, art, science, or business; no human occupation escapes it. Whatever a man can do separately for himself, an ape can imitate. Whatever a man does which is worth calling human is done collectively and for others, it is a social function. He may work alone at his business, but the tools he works with are the fruit of slow social evolution, and the work he does is done for others. He may retire to the forest and think alone, but he thinks on the problems of human life; no personal affairs can occupy the energies of a human brain; and the brain he thinks with is a slow social product too.

The evolution of the interdependence of social function is as clear as that of the interdependent physical functions of our separate bodies. As early animal forms have few and simple functions, gradually evolving those more delicate and complicated, so do early societies have few and simple arts or trades, and similarly evolve them. As society progresses the trades flow wider, dividing and subdividing as they go, until we have the exquisitely sublimated special skill of the modern worker; and at each step of the process the organic relation tightens as well as widens; the specialist is less able to "take care of himself," and the others are less able to do without the specialist.

"Every man to his trade" voices our popular recognition of this law, and "Jack-of-all-trades and master of none" shows the true merit of the "all-around-man."

We now come to a third, and in itself a fully sufficient proof of the organic nature of society—not of the social organism as a useful figure, an illustration, an analogy, but as a literal biological fact. Here are a number of separate animal bodies. Each is a group of interactive organs, each does business for itself with no need of combination with another, save in the temporary union of sex with sex, and of mother with child. These creatures are individuals. Here again is a number of apparently separate animal bodies. But each has in his head an organ *which cannot perform its functions alone;* an organ which for its healthful use requires contact and exchange with similar organs lodged in other bodies.

This organ is the brain. That degree of brain development which we call "human" is only found in creatures socially related; it is not individual brain power, but social. The human brain, for health and usefulness, for its normal life, requires a number of human beings with whom to feel, think, and act. We can, it is true, physically isolate a human animal, and maintain his animal life; but his human life—*i. e.,* social life; his "feelings" and "thoughts," the whole field of brain activity—is injured.

The human brain is *the* social organ; it is our medium of contact and exchange. Set a man in absolute solitude and his brain is affected at once. Cut off from the contact which enables it to freely receive and discharge its supply of social energy, its action becomes increasingly morbid. In proportion to the completeness and duration of the isolation the brain is injured, and ultimately ruined.

We know the effect of solitary imprisonment, or of being cast away alone on some remote island. Short of this we know the progressive effect of degrees of isolation. The lighthouse keeper knows—they put two men in lighthouses most removed from social touch; and even that is a dangerously "short circuit" for the social organ to act in. The solitary shepherd knows, on the wide waste plains of Australia or Texas. The hermit or recluse of any age, the separate dwellers in old houses in the country, any human creature who lives alone, is injuriously affected in brain action.

This is not saying that mere privacy is harmful—that is a necessity for the social brain; such temporary solitude as shall enable it to work out its special contribution to our common thought, and to rest from the forceful social currents. But however solitary the student or author, the product of his labour is for others, and must reach them; his brain must connect with the others, though at long range.

In this is another side of the proof of our mental collectivity. The poet feels for humanity, the student studies for humanity; the discoverer, inventor, all work for humanity. (This does not refer to the pay they expect, and their attitude toward it, but to the work itself.) All through our history we see the great-brained men who thought for the world, moved by a quenchless impulse to transmit this thought to the others, to pour out into the common stock the product of their brains. This they did because they *must*—even when loss and injury, ostracism or martyrdom followed. It is the compelling functional necessity of the brain to discharge into other brains, as well as to seek from them its vast and varied stimulus.

In more immediate and commonplace instances we see the same law. The difficulty of "keeping a secret," *i. e.*, of voluntarily retaining stimulus; the necessity of "relieving one's mind"—a perfectly fit phrase, as much so as its familiar physiological analogue; the value of the confessional; and, commonest of all, the vivid interest of each human brain in the affairs of the others; all these show the collective nature of that organ.

The most ordinary woman, gossiping with her neighbours, manifests this social necessity for contact and exchange, however low. "Mind your own business!" we cry, and cry in vain. No brain advanced enough to be called human can possibly find full use and exercise in contemplation of one person's business. It must concern itself in the business of the others, their common business.

The human brain is a social organ. Human thought is a social function.

Approach this fact along lines of evolution. The brain, like all other organs, is called for by conditions and developed by exercise. Simple conditions, simple exertions—low brain. Enlarge and elaborate the conditions—increase the exercises—and the brain develops. Observe here, within human history, how we have developed the brain of the dog by such change of condition and action.

In every form of animal life you find an exact relation between the range of activities of the creature and his degree of brain development. This is necessarily so, as the increase of activities is what produced that degree of development. The simple activities of the clam need no brain, and have none. The complex activities of the fox need a complex brain, and have it. Everywhere this exact proportion is found until you reach the human animal.

There is no relation whatever between the individual human being's brain and his individual activities. But there is the same inexorable law of development by which alone to account for this highest of all brains, and the same relation is plainly to be seen between the social brain and its social activities. No conceivable activities of one biped, through however many generations, could have developed the brain of the architect, for instance. He has the power to think a church. He cannot build a church—never could—never could have even wanted one!

The growth of many men, for many ages, brought their common needs, their power of common action, and their brain power to co-ordinate it. You need no power of co-ordination to run one individual animal; the need for social activities developed the social brain. The single human animal could have only needed a single shelter; could have so only built a single shelter, and so have only thought a single shelter. The power of one man to think for many men to do, is a distinctly human power, and evolvable only by the common doing.

In our collective relation we have developed a capacity to think, focussed perforce in some individual brain, for the working point of Society is the individual; to think, to the advantage of thousands of people for thousands of years. This organic capacity cannot be accounted for on an individual basis.

The laws of natural evolution work to develop in each organism the powers which it most needs; steadily raising the efficient type. The human animal manifests powers of no earthly use to himself, relatable in no way to his personal needs, inexplicable on any individual hypothesis, but plainly useful to Society, relatable to the Social needs, perfectly explicable by the Social hypothesis.

VI: THE NATURE OF SOCIETY (II)

SUMMARY

Social organism a natural life-form. Confusion from arbitrary and superficial distinctions. Social functions not physically hereditary. Village type. Earth-limits. Social life in Individual. Natural law under "imperialism." Mistakes of social functionaries. Why society was developed. Tendency to revert. Wider consciousness and activity of Society. Social Soul. Race memory. Joy a social quality. Size of social feelings and actions. Early decoration. Fund of power. Social consciousness in young persons. Happiness of right social relation. Social nourishment, rest, exercise. What are limits of social organism. No material really solid. Human connections. Detachment of human individual only temporary. Apparent paradoxes. Ex-man. Smaller human relations. Family, Church, Army, City, Nation. Appearance of world-consciousness. Order of importance of function. Change in relative value. Ethics the physics of social relation. Egoism right for individual. No basis for ethics in individualism. Collectivism of Christianity. Social life immortal.

CHAPTER VI

THE NATURE OF SOCIETY (II)

The Social Organism is as natural a life-form as fish, flesh, or fowl. It has been naturally evolved, its processes and appearances are as natural as those of any other part of creation. We do not recognise it because of the interference of that ancestral brain; and we are further confused in looking at it by our arbitrary classification, resting on old and false ideas.

As physical geography is confused to a child's mind by the demarcations and contrasted colours of the map of political geography; so is the natural organic relation of Society confused in our minds by our superficial and artificial "social distinctions." We have established social distinctions and relations on lines of physical connection, such as birth; whereas physical relationship has no similitude with social relationship; or of political connection, as nation or party; whereas, again, there is no resemblance; or on even more fantastic lines of sex, of caste, of creed, or of the amount of money possessed.

These arbitrary distinctions are no more social and legitimately organic than Indiana is yellow and Ohio blue. Legitimate social relationship is functional. It is that relation in which we serve each other. Its classification is on lines of industrial evolution, together with the gradual development of those later functions of government, education, art, and science which follow the industrial. In the evolution of government the king was a normal functionary; his kingship being his power to act as general chairman of his assemblage of people, and, in very early days, as leader in battle. To make kingship hereditary was an arbitrary classification; social functions not developing in lines of physical heredity. You can no more make "a line of kings" than a line of poets or surgeons. If you do it, arbitrarily, you injure society by inferior service. That was the conspicuous result in the king line.

In pre-social times there was merely the protoplasmic mass of undifferentiated human stock. Arising from this we have first the sporadic growth of villages, resting on their common food activities, and then the appearance of larger groups, and more and more diverse functions, elaborating in mutual dependence.

The natural limits of an organic social relation are the limits of its essential functions. These were once quite narrow—each little community being self-supporting. To-day we are rapidly approaching a social organism limited only by the earth. Our interdependent functions are now international; and natural development on those lines is only prevented by our false classification on unnatural lines, with the resultant endeavour to maintain the self-supporting independence of the smaller unit.

The more highly organised a society, the more range and force have its component individuals. America is in the American. Athens was in the Athenian. Where else? A member of some tiny social unit on a remote island does not carry the same amount of social efficiency as a member of a larger unit. This is the underlying natural law which makes for general human unity, but which finds its misguided and injurious expression in our doctrine of "imperialism."

The normal line of enlargement is simply *an extension of functional exchange*, a sharing of the highly specialised activities and advantages of the larger society by the smaller. Every step of this really beneficent process has been accompanied throughout history with the utmost injury to all parties, by conquest and carnage, by insane pride and cruelty; because we did not understand the process in which we were the actors, but governed our conduct from ideals of egoism, localism, and rapacity. This is especially plain in our time, because of the enormous growth of industrial functions, and their inevitable spread around the world.

The process is natural and in itself means increasing benefit to all society; but, being grossly misunderstood by the highly specialised individuals who carry out these processes, the beneficent results are mingled with terrible evils. The social functionary who is evolved to distribute some food, oil, or other necessity to a larger radius of consumers than ever before, takes advantage of his position to sequestrate a larger share for himself than was ever before possible. The "master minds" who are able to manage these giant industries are social products, called for and produced to meet the larger social needs of our times, but they are still governed by economic theories suitable to a South Sea Islander, and so we have that "malfeasance in office," in social office, which so shamefully blackens the face of nations to-day.

It is a fair inquiry to demand of the organic theory of Society a reason for its development. Why should independent individuals have been led into a combination which inevitably involves some personal loss and injury, and has been made to involve such an enormous amount?

How are we to account for this higher life-form, in the iron economy of nature? Many have seen the visible benefit to individuals which comes of the Social relation. The fact that we help one another is plain enough; but even that sum of benefit does not seem sufficient to justify the social sacrifice; the loss of individual liberty, the life-long labour at one thing; the growing distance between social man and the free, simple, contented individual animal.

"I think I could turn and live with the animals, they are so placid and self-contained.

"I stand and look at them long and long.

"They do not sweat and whine about their condition.

"They do not lie awake in the dark and weep for their sins.

"They do not make me sick discussing their duty to God.

"Not one is dissatisfied; not one is demented with the mania for owning things.

"Not one kneels to another, nor to his kind that lived a thousand years ago.

"Not one is respectable or industrious over the whole earth."

—WHITMAN.

This reversionary tendency is strong in us all, the easy backsliding to the physical freedom and independence of the hunter and fisher. The immediate stimulus, the immediate action, the supply of one's own needs by one's own efforts,—this is a delight to almost all of us; and some are constantly straggling and dropping behind the procession, to revert to the wood life of primitive man and his pre-primitive forbears, to "turn and live with the animals." Current literature is full of this social reversion to-day, this "call of the wild," this tempting invitation to give it all up and go back to the beginning.

It is so much harder to pour your life's energies a life long into the Social pool, and perhaps get very little out—and then not what you want. What deep inevitable gain has been at work for which relentless nature has slowly driven us up the path of Social Evolution—a steeper, bloodier, more agonising road than any other creature has had to tread?

The gain is this (and observe that it is precisely of the same nature as that which has driven the contented annelid up to all the excitement, difficulties, and perils of the higher mammalian): the Social Organism manifests a wider range of consciousness and activity than any other life-form. The human animal, alone, is but a beast; and has but the narrow egoistic range of consciousness and activity. As part of Society the human animal becomes the organ of a consciousness and an activity so vast that in its limitless expansion we have been able to conceive of Life, Death, and Immortality, of Time and Eternity, of Humanity, of Liberty, Justice, and Love. What we call the human soul is developed in the social relation. It is Human indeed, *i. e.*, Social. It is Ours.

In the organic division of labour of a physical body, the life processes are so developed that more exertion can be made and more sensation received, than in the same amount of living matter in lower forms. A hand, taken separately, would have a certain contractile power; but as connected with the arm it has far more, as connected with the general nervous system more yet.

In that transmission of energy which seems to be the business of the universe an increasing complexity of mechanism is evidently called for because it has been produced and maintained. Society is the most complex mechanism of all. It can receive, store, and discharge more energy than could its constituents in equal number, but unorganised.

The social consciousness is the widest and most sensitive receiver and transmitter so far produced. "We look before and after, and pine for what is not." This is a social quality. As man grouped and grew together came that development of race memory which gives to family, to nation, to Humanity itself, its dignity and power. It is "Our" past, "Our" present, "Our" future. The life of Humanity is one, and it is that life which we as individuals feel; which makes us able to suffer more, enjoy more, and do more than any other kind of living thing.

In failing to recognise the real nature of society and put ourselves in right relation to it, we have largely checked the flow of social energy and perverted the social instincts and social processes; therefore, to our morbid egos, social relation often seems to bring us more pain than pleasure. We admit that we cannot live out of it—the sufferings of the hermit are greater than those of the misplaced social constituent; but we live in it blindly, in cramped and distorted positions, rendering our social service under the crushing pressure of the egoistic concept, and getting but a faint and occasional sense of the potent joy of true social relation.

The transcendent happiness possible to Humanity, to all humanity, by virtue of its humanness, is a thing of which we practically know nothing. Consider the range of sensation in an individual animal. This is most strictly limited to his physical activities and such psychic impressions and expressions as pertain to his narrow field of being. The female animal has the joy of the maternal function, that great first step beyond the Ego-consciousness; a pleasure and a pride partly physical and partly psychic, but limited forever to the individual young. The male animal sometimes shares a fraction of this parental feeling. In certain creatures which live in groups or herds there seems to be a very vivid common consciousness on some lines, as shown by the instantaneous nervous transmission in a stampede; and in the highly socialised bee and ant there appears as highly developed a collective sensorium. But, though collective, it is on a low plane; the impressions it receives and the expressions resultant all pertain to the physical wants of the individual constituents, however elaborately these wants are met.

With us, in our social relation, there is an enlargement of the sensorium past any measurement we can yet make. The *size* of our sensations increases as more and more individuals are tuned to respond to the same stimulus. There is room in what we call "the human heart" for a passionate exaltation of feeling that finds no parallel below us. This immense influx of stimulus prompts us, yes, forces us, to a commensurate expression; and if this expression be true, it puts in concrete form the intense feeling and then continually transmits it to as many people as are sensitive to that form of expression.

Take an illustration on a very early and simple plane. A happy, primeval squaw, not hungry, not cold, not afraid, and feeling in her already growing social consciousness both the pleasant memory of these conditions and the pleasant assurance of more, has more stimulus coming in than her body can sit quiet under. No human being can ever be as stationarily contented as a ruminating cow, his income of sensation is too great. That small, perfect circle of life of the individual beast,—hunger, effort, gratification, rest,—is changed to an endless upreaching spiral in our social relation.

It is not only that our hunger is greater because one can hunger for all; because no human being can be really satisfied till all are satisfied; but that our stimulus is greater, and calls for endless discharge. So our happy squaw is moved to transmit her press of feeling; she must discharge it in action; and she does so in some decoration of her jar or basket. This decoration is an embodied joy, and, being fixed in visible form, it then transmits that joy to as many as behold it. It is a little fountain of social energy.

A society, from its inception, multiplies the range and depth of sensation, and commensurately, the working expression of its members. From age to age, as this great common fund increases, is the power to feel and the power to do increased. More and more people thrill to a common impression; the rising wave of force prompts to ever greater expression, reaching more and more people.

Thus, in a normal society, the individual life increases in sensation, in power, and in joy in an ascending line that as yet suggests no limit. In pain and degradation also, the pessimist will protest. Of course, as an accompanying possibility. *But not as an essential condition.* Such as exists is merely owing to our wholly unnecessary and mistaken action. The pain is a transient and needless thing; the immense joy is in the real nature of society.

The young human creature, as he begins to grow from the individual animal period into social life, feels this intense current of force, the vast and varied desires, the vaster energies; but he does not know what it is, nor do his teachers. Ego-bound systems have cradled and nurtured him, an egoistic family, an egoistic economy, an egoistic religion cut off every avenue of growth; and the stimulus of the whole world throbs and beats in vain, forced finally into some dog-trot routine, wherein he thinks to "earn his own living," to "support his own family," to "save his own soul."

The tremendous thirst for happiness which the young human being feels is perfectly natural. Young individual animals show no signs of such disproportionate desires. The tremendous ambitions of young people are equally natural. Human life is in them the multiplied and accumulated life of all humanity for all time, and all it needs for the same peace and poise which is the portion of "the lower animals" is free expression.

The nature of Society is no mystery. Our relation to it is no mystery. It is simple, orderly, healthy, and in its largest manifestations either peacefully unconscious or sublimely happy. Every person who has by blessed chance found his right place in social service, who has the range of contact with his kind which he needs, and the range of activity which he needs, may be as calmly happy as any browsing cow, as ecstatically happy as any soaring lark.

What does any creature need for right growth?—nourishment, rest, exercise. Society needs these too. We, in social relation as social beings, need the social nourishment, rest, and exercise. Social nourishment comes through contact with the world's supplies, permanent and current. We need to "stock up" in our common heritage of information, of beauty and use and power. Whatever we need which lower animals do not need is social nourishment. The desire to know of the healthy young mind, the desire to travel, the desire to see people, these are forms of our undying hunger for that which belongs to us as human beings. When all of us, from our youth up, are put in easy connection with the unlimited supplies of Society, we shall all be socially nourished. Observe that these things *are not consumed* while they nourish, but remain continually refreshing as many as can partake of them. Every member of Society should have free access to all social products: art, music, literature, facilities of travel, and education; and would so absorb his preferred nourishment as unerringly as do the cells of the body from the whirling profusion offered by the blood.

Social rest is another imperative need of human beings, in proportion to their humanness. The more highly specialised and intense the service of the individual the more he needs to break off the connection and rest; rest from being social; go back and be animal awhile; find in pure ease and relaxation, in irrelative physical exercise, and in the beautiful family relation (one of the safest and loveliest life-forms sheltered by society), that complete rest which will enable him to return to his social relation with renewed vigour.

Vacations of all sorts—the country home, the hunting trip—tell of this need, and the nervous collapse of highly socialised types when denied it is a common occurrence. Simple and primitive trades, if not excessive in hours of labour, are far less exhausting. Breathing goes on continuously, digesting with regular frequency, but thinking has to rest. A healthy social life will allow for the natural periods of rest for all its members.

Social exercise is but the use of our best and highest faculties to the largest end. A Gladstone confined to directing envelopes would not be exercising his social faculties to their full extent. Napoleon as a *chauffeur* might have killed quite a number of people, but would not have been really satisfied. Exercise is life's first law, and full exercise is required for full development.

This is where in our imperfect degree of socialisation we suffer most, for lack of this full use of our social powers, especially women. We are frequently overworked as individuals while underworked socially, another condition accounting for morbid, nervous states. A man with capacity for managing a high-grade department store would lack exercise to a most injurious degree if he were kept as a country grocer's clerk, though he might ruin his eyes with bookkeeping and his back with lifting barrels. The full use of our largest faculties in the largest relation—that is social exercise.

Another thing which prevents us from recognising the nature of Society is our almost unavoidable mental limitation to the perception of the stage of development represented by the animal organism.

"If Society is an organism," we say, "where are its feet and hands, its eyes, nose, and mouth? Where is its skin? Where does it begin and leave off?" And not seeing any large beast stuffed with persons like the Trojan horse, or some vast man-filled man like the wicker-built sacrificial cage of the Druids, we deny the existence of the alleged organism.

Organic life is not limited to existing forms. As it has developed so far, it has been in the line of increasing freedom and fluency of relation. The constituent cells of vegetable matter are held together less rigidly than in the pre-organic mineral formation. In animal matter the relation is more fluent yet. And in social matter, so to speak, it is yet more free and movable. Yet, if you look down upon the earth as one with some vast microscope studying the life of mould, or monads, you will find that the human particles are connected inexorably. Remember that even in minerals—if you can see largely enough—the atoms whirl alone. They are held in relation by laws of attraction and repulsion, and that relation is close enough to form to our senses a solid body.

Human beings are not webbed together like frogs' eggs, but they are held together in definite relation by laws of attraction and repulsion, like the constituents of any other material body. The stuff that Society is made of is thickest in great cities, and as it develops these dense and throbbing social ganglia grow and grow. In wide, rural areas the stuff is thin—very thin. But watch the lines of connection form and grow, ever thicker and faster as the Society progresses. The trail, the path, the road, the railroad, the telegraph wire, the trolley car; from monthly journeys to remote post-offices to the daily rural delivery; thus Society is held together. Save for the wilful hermit losing himself in the wilderness, every man has his lines of connection with the others; the psychic connection, such as "family ties," "the bonds of affection," and physical connection in the path from his doorstep to the Capital city.

The social organism does not walk about on legs. It spreads and flows over the surface of the earth, its members walking in apparent freedom, yet bound indissolubly together and thrilling in response to social stimulus and impulse.

Before Society grew at all we were but human animals, maintaining and reproducing ourselves like any other animals, but with no *connection*, no common life. They were of no faintest use to one another, but quite the contrary, being legitimate competitors for a free supply, and so naturally hating and destroying one another. As Society grows the connection between its members grows and thickens and differentiates. Men are of increasing use to one another, no longer competitors in any legitimate sense, but combiners in common production and distribution, and so naturally helping and loving one another. Those who still compete and destroy are but survivals from the earlier period, mischievous relics and back-numbers. All Social evolution is the story of the development and improvement of the connective tissues of Society, from language, the great psychic medium, to steel rail and wire, the infinitely multiplying physical medium. This connection and interaction of the human animals is the most conspicuous fact about them, and that connection is by every test organic.

Another and similar reason for our denial of the social organism is the fact of the temporary detachableness of the individual human being. Men visibly walk about on their own feet, going apparently where they will, and no examination discloses a Siamese band between one man and his brother man. So when the sociologist says there is no such thing as a separate human creature,—that a solitary human creature is a contradiction in terms,—the average individualist replies, "See Robinson Crusoe!" This answer shows great lack of biological knowledge. The splendid growth of education in our day, which is beginning to teach our children dynamics as well as statics, laws as well as facts, will soon remove this ignorance.

If I say, "There is no such thing as a tree without roots," it might be replied, "But there is! See my Christmas tree?" Yes, it is there for a little, but it is not really a tree, it is timber; it cannot last, nor grow, nor reproduce its kind.

I may say, "There is no such thing as a man without a head," and someone reply, "But there is! See this gentleman on the dissecting table and his head on the tray yonder." That is not a man, it is a corpse. I may say, "There is no such thing as a finger without a hand," and it be replied, "See this one here in alcohol!" That again is not a finger, it is but a corpse. If you join a severed finger quickly enough, it will grow on again. If you return a severed man to his society soon enough, he will grow on again. So in this perfectly true statement, "There is no such thing as a solitary human creature; it is a contradiction in terms"; the presentation of a man on an island or in a prison cell is no answer.

Though cut off like the finger, he does not instantly deliquesce and disappear. His connection with the society which evolved him being severed, he may continue to live as an animal, but is in process of decay as a human being; he is an ex-man. Our connection is so subtle, so fluent, each human brain being so large a storage battery of social energy, that we can separate for a time with no loss. But make the separation complete and the humanness dies.

We have been deterred also from seeing the larger and more vital human relation by the smaller and more arbitrary. Perhaps the most conspicuous of these is the Family, often called the Unit of the State.

Now the family is not a distinctively human relation at all; many varieties of animals, especially among the higher carnivora, have families, with monogamic union, too, where devoted parents strive and suffer to provide for and protect their young. A perfectly normal and necessary group is the family, and one proved best for successful reproduction of the species, but not a social unit at all. The individual is the social unit, combining to develop the structure and functions of Society.

Families never combine, they can't. Families take no part in social relation. Each family has its own structure and functions, its own interests, its own purposes, and these are frequently in direct opposition to the social good. Just as Society offers a surer, safer, higher life to the individual, and thus makes possible that inordinate egoism which is so serious a danger; so it gives the same opportunity to the family and allows of a wider, deeper, and more intense familism than is possible among sub-social animals.

It is most interesting to watch the slow struggle of the true social relation to establish and extend itself against these natural obstacles, as in the successive overthrow of Patriarchism and Feudalism by the State. The City as a social group has much easier recognition with us than larger entities. Civic consciousness began early and found its splendid flower and fruit, as well as its iron limitations, in Greece. National consciousness is now quite well established, having the same advantages and disadvantages as the Civic, only on larger scale. To-day we are beginning to feel the largest consciousness of all, the truly Human, in whose unbounded growth and beautifully progressive development the petty limitations of all earlier forms are slowly disappearing. "What are your national distinctions?" an inquiring Englishman asked me. "The time is past for national distinctions," I replied. "The time is coming for the people of the world, and Americans are the first of them."

Then, too, we have been so occupied in the specific local function of Society as to miss that general grouping and balancing which made them all possible. Take that vast and varying social function the Church,—organised religion,—appearing very early in the dominance of savage priestcraft, finding its height in the resistless Hierarchies of Egypt and Palestine, and struggling ever since to hold its failing sway.

Take the Army, another very early, very strong, and very hard-dying social form. It is still with us, brilliant and loud, an increasing evil in the fast-growing industrial life of to-day. See the Soldier scorning the Merchant in the Middle Ages. See the Merchant directing the Soldier to-day. His time of pre-eminence is past.

So in course of social evolution one and another organic group has been developed, each tending to excess by the law of inertia (and social inertia is the most long-winded we know), yet all inevitably sinking into place in the smooth, complex interaction toward which we are moving. Men, specialised to the social service, in their several lines, yet knowing not what they served, have limited their enthusiasm to their specialty, and striven to make the Church, the Army, the Law, Art, or what they call Business, their supreme end.

The real social organism includes them all, and relates them all in order of importance. This order of importance may as well be laid down here, as quite essential to an understanding of the nature of Society. The standard of measurement used is that of evolution, "lower" or "higher" being marked in that line of progress which leads always from the less to the greater, from the simple to the complex. Relative importance may perhaps be measured downwards: a stomach is more important than an eye, because you cannot live without it. But the eye is "higher" than the stomach, a later developed and more specialised organ.

So in social evolution agriculture is more important than literature, because we cannot live without it; but literature is higher than agriculture as being later developed and more highly specialised. The social organism has followed in its evolution the same path as earlier life-forms, developing first the simpler and more immediately vital processes, and later those more delicate and finer organs which are needed to fulfil the uses of its progressive life. And as, in physical evolution, we find now one and now another function of dominant importance to the creature, so in social evolution we can trace the varying value of social functions, the military and religious processes of early societies gradually giving way in importance to the industrial and educational processes of our own times.

Most valuable of all, to our so long religiously moulded minds, is the effect of this recognition of the nature of society upon Ethics. Vague indeed, complicated, mystical, difficult to understand, have been our gropings after this great science. Ethics is the Science of Social Relation; it could never be understood by individualists.

There is no ethics for an individual except to maintain, improve, and reproduce himself. A consistent and remorseless egoism is right for the individual animal; through it he fulfils the law of his being; through it he improves his race. So we, wishing to improve a breed of cattle, consistently and remorselessly select and train and breed from preferred individuals, neglecting or destroying the inferior ones. So do mistaken men, not appreciating the nature of society, urge a similar stern stirpiculture upon us, and would have us neglect or destroy our defective members and breed only from the best.

But when we have a social animal to deal with, as the bee, different laws operate, or, rather, the same laws on a larger scale, a higher plane. It is the best swarm now to be selected; and the value of the swarm depends not so much upon the size and vigour of its individual constituents as on *how they work together*. There is ethics in a hive, laws of collective behaviour. There is ethics in Society, because it is a collective unit.

Ethics, to Society, is what physics is to matter; ethics is the physics of social relation. Physical law holds material constituents together in those combinations and relations which make the material bodies we know. Ethical law holds social constituents together in those relations which make the social bodies we know.

But we, not knowing the social body, could not know its laws. We have striven in vain to predicate ethics of individuals. You "ought" to do so? Why "ought" I? Because it is "right." What is "right"? Whatever God said. And what did God say? What these ancient gentlemen have written in their ancient times. And if I do not believe what the ancient gentlemen wrote? There is no answer to this except the somewhat fatuous one of "so much the worse for you!"

The writings of the ancient gentlemen were not susceptible of proof.

Then came Christ, talking sense. He grasped the nature of Society and preached its laws. Ye are all members of one body and of one another. You shall love your neighbour as yourself; that is, recognise him as really part of what you are part of—all one self; and the love of self becomes mutual love as we see what Self is to a Human Creature—Our Self. Christ saw and said all this, and did it, which is more; lived,—as far as one individual could,—true to his social relation, faithfully fulfilling his function to that great living thing, though its immediately surrounding constituents very naturally killed him.

That great Christian concept of mutual love and service is good ethics; it is scientific; its truth and value can be proved; it works. Had we grasped and applied it a good many painful centuries might have been saved us.

But we, our minds still darkened by the beast-concept of Egoism, trying to personally own the human soul and save our piece to all eternity without caring what became of the rest of it; we, with our personal God and his personal Son, and our personal damnation or salvation to consider, have very generally ignored the theory and practice of Christ, and made of him merely an article of faith by which to maintain our precious Egos forever and ever. And this in the face of his "Whoso saveth his life shall lose it; but whoso loseth his life for my sake [man's sake, the sake of the whole] shall find it!"

When we realise the nature of society we shall come nearer to understanding the teachings of Christ than we have done in twenty centuries of sublimated self-seeking. In recognising it we rise at one step from the dark and narrow limits of the personal life, that poor animal existence, with its common animal wants and their fulfilment; with its animal loves and hates, hopes and fears, pains and pleasures; with its brief period of animal life, cut up into changeful patches of infancy, childhood, youth, maturity, and age, and take our true place in social life, which is immortal. Whether it dies off the earth in a million years or so we do not know yet; since it was born it has not died, but grown and grown continually. This wide, rich, glowing field of consciousness includes the animal life and maintains it in a higher and better condition than ever before, but its real distinctive range of feeling is far beyond that.

All noble and beautiful emotions we call "Human" are social and immortal. All the distinguishing abilities, the power and skill and ingenuity that we call "Human," are social and immortal. "I" am born, grow up, and die. "I" am a transient piece of meat, enjoying food and sleep and mating, hunting and fighting.

But "We" are more than that. We together constitute another "I," which is Human Life. That was born gradually, many long ages back, and is now slowly growing up. In that human life, that common, mutual, social life, are all things that make us human. When we enter consciously into that great life we are indeed immortal, "saved," indeed, from primeval limitations of the animal ego.

VII: THE SOCIAL SOUL

SUMMARY

Our "common sensorium" the "human heart." All human feelings common. Action and reaction between body and spirit. Cat and Sheep. Mob spirit, civic spirit, etc. Effect of institutions. Effect of industries. Confusion from Ego Concept. Prominence of painful processes. Widening social consciousness. Collective pleasure greatest. Team-work. Effect of position of women. Sex combat in industry. Altruism and Omniism. "Self" an extensible term. Organic relation. Progressive injury of egoism. Effect of special industries on altruism. Sailor, farmer, miner. Household labour. Men more altruistic than women. Religion has not understood altruism, which is a natural social instinct. Man with tail. Nature of "charity," transfusion of blood. Selfishness and socialness. My soul, our soul. Social needs. Inefficiency of personal gratification. Longitudinal extension of the soul's life not satisfactory. Must widen our life, our soul. The Social Passion. Names do not affect facts. Social life evolves social love. Social instinct in duty, in work. Social ascetics. Human nature Social nature.

CHAPTER VII

THE SOCIAL SOUL

Some deny the organic concept of society on the ground that we human beings have no "common sensorium." But we have. The most conspicuous and distinctive fact in our psychology is precisely that common sensorium. We call it in ordinary speech "the human heart," or "the human spirit," or "soul," and quite correctly. It is human, and "human" is "social"; it is the social soul.

The individual feels it, inasmuch as the brain, our medium of sensation, is lodged in an individual head; but what he feels is a common feeling, not a personal one. He has of course his purely individual range of sensations, emotions, promptings to action; but these are felt also by any other animal, they are not "human."

All our distinctive human feelings are in common, are transmissible, belong to us collectively, not individually. So markedly true is this that we have labelled our most visibly collective feelings "humane." Common feeling is human feeling, and that great sum of higher consciousness we call the soul is the human soul.

Psychological terms are all vague and slippery to handle; but we can clearly observe in any living thing these two departments—the spirit and the body. While they are together the thing lives, works, goes; when divided the body gradually disintegrates.

We observe, too, that once a specific allotment of spirit makes to itself such and such a form, that the form continually reacts upon the spirit and modifies it. Each animal as we know it has a spirit exactly suited to his body, evidently the result of long lodgment in it. The sheep has a spirit suited to his body, the cat has a spirit suited to his body. Each can do what he wants to and wants to do what he can.

If we can imagine the two transformed and trans-spirited,—the spirit of a cat in the body of a sheep and the spirit of a sheep in the body of a cat,—it is plain to see how grievous would be the condition of that beast. It would want to do what it could not, and could not do what it wanted to. Spirit must fit body, or body fit spirit, or the two disband and that creature is dead.

This relation holds in the life of Society; but as that life is large, complex, enduring, and comprises within it not only the lives of its constituent individuals, but the lives of its constituent institutions, the facts are not so easy to follow. Taken historically it may be observed thus: from the small, early social forms of the tribe and its villages up to the nation and its cities we see this relation of body and spirit.

"A body of men" of any kind that lives, *i. e.*, works, must have a common spirit or it cannot so live and work.

The loosest mob must have some transient but compelling spirit to hold it together, else no mob. The smallest village has its common spirit; and the largest city—the largest nation—must have its common spirit, to live, to grow, to work. We are familiar with some terms of these facts; we know, appreciate, and condemn the absence of "the civic spirit." We admire and reward "public spirit." We *have* to deal with the facts of Society's organic life, even while those graveyard brains of ours are still crowded with the monuments of dead concepts.

In popular literature and oratory we freely handle such terms as "animated by a common spirit," "the national spirit," the "spirit of our institutions," *"l'esprit de corps"*; but we have not set our minds to work to grasp and relate these terms in their full meaning. We are familiar also with the reactive modification of social forms on the social spirit; seeing men of all characters enter some definite institution and come out all more or less altered to one distinctive character, the academic, the military, or whatever; and to us the largest, newest, most gratifying proof of this is the effect of our American institutions on the people of all nations. In organising this nation we embodied the best spirit of the time in a certain form of government and invited all men to come and enter the new national body. They did, and a more marked and rapid modification of spirit by form history has never shown. Come from wheresoever they may, their children enter our educational, their parents our industrial and political institutions; and they forthwith become Americans, manifesting our virtues—and our faults—with startling rapidity. The effect is strongest on the young and composite races, and weakest on the older established stocks, as the Chinese and Hebrew, but it is perceptible in all.

In smaller instance we all know the effect of a given school or college on those entering it,—either teacher or learner, but especially the learner, as more young and impressible,—as shown in "the Harvard spirit," or that of Oxford, or of Yale. When fighting was the dominant activity we had the natural growth of fighting bodies, elaborately organised, and of a common fighting spirit which completely overmasters the individual spirit of its constituents. If specific religious practices are pursued we have the appearance of a religious body and its accompanying spirit.

Once more, a small and literal instance: if a charitable body is founded,—an "institution" in that limited and unlovely sense,—in the "inmates," both officials and beneficiaries, speedily appears the spirit of that body, and a very disagreeable one it is. Wherever interdependent functions are established appears organic life; a common body to perform these functions, a common spirit to co-relate them.

The social spirit is a common consciousness developed by common activities, and appearing in us in proportion to the extent and interrelation of those activities. To share in it demands of the individual, male or female, a share in the collective activities which constitute human life.

Activities performed by one's self alone, for one's self alone, or one's immediate physical relatives, are not distinctively human, and do not develop the human spirit.

An agricultural population manifests certain traits in common the world over. Distinctions of blood and of religion are in abeyance before the unifying force of a common industry as a modifier of character. Fishermen, or sailors, or miners, or traders invariably show marked traits in common, however otherwise differentiated.

If all men followed one industry we should have one principal character; but fortunately our social processes are increasingly varied. There does arise, however, a steadily widening field of common character as the traits demanded by all industries alike increase among us. All industries require peace and self-control; a regard for law and for organisation; and these tendencies steadily improve the social spirit as we leave savagery farther and farther behind.

Commerce requires honesty and accuracy, and steadily develops them, though commerce is more open to certain retroactive influences than the directly productive processes. Productive industry, being the economic necessity which brings us together, is the source of our social spirit, and that spirit is constantly modified by changes in the forms of industry.

Our social consciousness is of slow and partial development, as is easily explicable. The highly developed personal consciousness which the most primitive savage brought with him into social relation, and which occupies the same field of sensation as the wider social consciousness, has operated to prevent easy recognition of the latter. The social pleasures and the social pains we took to be personal and sought or avoided them as such. Even the most sublimated and morbidly acute social consciousness, as shown in a passionate philanthropy, is still diagnosed by some as a form of self-gratification, so persistent is the dominance of the egoistic concept.

Another reason is that as our external activities, requiring conscious cerebration, are more perceptible than our internal ones, so we were far more easily impressed by the external activities of Society than by its deep-seated organic processes; these external ones were more telic, partook more of the nature of personal actions, and were readily thought to be such.

A third and very strong force operating against our recognition of social consciousness is that it so generally hurts. So long as our organic social processes went on normally they were unconscious. Individual man, well fed, well guarded, reproducing the race in peace and comfort, sported in the sea of social well-being and failed to observe that there was such a thing. But let any industry become inflamed, or paralysed, or arrested, and the pain is felt far and wide. No one likes to be hurt. The more socially we felt our pain the more it hurt, of course, being bigger. To be hungry one's self is one thing—to *feel a famine* is another. People with the most social consciousness suffered most, so long as social processes were not healthy; and, therefore, our effort has been to resist the increase of social consciousness.

We say "mind your own business"—"don't concern yourself about other people," "let the other man walk." We try *not* to feel the famine in India, the flood in

China, the ignorance in Russia, the cruelty in Armenia, the crimes and casualties, the deformities and diseases of our own great cities. But in spite of our natural reluctance to a widening of the sensorium that thrills most to pain, it is widening in spite of us.

More and more every year we are feeling common evils, and seeking to remove them. It is not that "I" am seeking to relieve "my" distress and improve "my" conditions, but that "we," in institute and association, club, congress, and convention, are rousing more and more to a consciousness of "our" distress, and seeking methods by which "we" may improve "our" conditions. This marks the growth of social consciousness. A pleasant thought here is that as fast as social conditions improve so fast does social consciousness become an avenue of pleasure instead of pain, and so we shall encourage instead of oppose it; thus the improvement will widen more and more rapidly.

Something we see already of the larger joy obtainable in social consciousness, in our pleasure in one another's work. I do not mean in personal consumption of it, so to speak, but in our satisfaction in the achievements of "our" business men, "our" "scientific men," "our" inventors, mechanics, artists, discoverers, teachers, and the like. "We" take pleasure and pride in what "we" do—requiring social consciousness.

Children's games show the natural development of this feeling in the human being. A child likes to play alone if he has to; but children like far better to play together—the excitement and joy of co-ordinate activity being far greater than in individual activity. This delight in collective expression increases from age to age. As measured merely by popular sports and amusements, the game involving a contest of team with team is more enjoyed than the older sport of individual race and contest, both by spectator and player.

There remains one more strong cause for our slow-born recognition of social consciousness, and that is the position of women. Their activities being confined to an excessive development of sex functions, and industry on the low stage of solitary disconnected performance, or at most the first step of group labour, personal service; and this industry, too, confined to self or family interest altogether; it is not to be expected that any high degree of social spirit could be attained by this inchoate mass of individuals in society, but not of it, taking no part in its processes economic or politic, and no share in its growing responsibilities; nor is it to be expected that men, though increasingly socialised by themselves, could avoid the influence of this unsocialised half of humanity, both through its daily companionship and the tremendous effect of maternity.

We are still further affected by the result of the position of women in maintaining an abnormal degree of sex-tendency, and we have seen how anti-social an influence is the natural belligerence and destructiveness of masculine energy in excess; therefore, it is no wonder at all that our social development has been slow, erratic, and liable to extremely morbid forms and processes. Nothing will conduce so much to the right growth of society in body and spirit as the progress of women from their position of prehistoric sex-bound egoism and familism, to their rightful share and place in the vital processes of Society. They, as half the component individuals of Society, will then contribute their share of modern social feeling and action; they, becoming more human and less disproportionately sexual, will reduce the influence of morbid sex-tendency in both male and female; and they, as mothers, will rapidly fill the world with full-blood human beings, instead of the present half-bloods,—half socialised through the father, but held in prehistoric individualism through the mother.

The social spirit is as "natural" as the individual spirit. It is conspicuously visible in action among us, but we have hidden it under false names.

"Altruism" is one of these. This in its very assumption of "others" preserves the ego intact, and that ego has never yet been convinced of any rational cause for surrendering to those other egos. We have only been able to urge it under our equally mistaken Pay concept, trying to show that we should meet reward either from the other egos, or from God. And as our nobler instincts have always revolted from the Pay concept, the progress of Altruism has been retarded.

We need merely to understand it to withdraw all this opposition. What we call altruism should be called—has been called[1]—"omniism"; it is a feeling for all of us, and *includes* the ego. It is, if you please, an extension of self-consciousness, a recognition that my self is society, and my "ego" only a minute fraction of the real me.

This omniism is as normal a growth as egoism. The preservation of the individual by individual action required egoism, and developed it. The preservation of society, by collective action, requires omniism and develops it. That it is not more generally developed is due to the resistance and confusion of our brains.

The superiority of omniism to egoism is in its being a later and more complex development, an organic superiority. As the single cell is lower than the organism, so cell-consciousness, if there be such, is lower than self-consciousness, and as the single organism is lower than the social organism so self-consciousness is lower than social consciousness. Egoism is common to all beasts, is perfectly natural, useful, right; but omniism is a human distinction, progressively developed as we become socialised.

My "self" is my conscious area of working machinery, wherewith I receive impressions and produce expressions, and if I were a tenfold Siamese twin—if I felt, and thought, and worked with the bodies of twenty men—those twenty men would be my "self," and to care for them would be as "selfish" as it is for a solitary animal to care for itself, and as perfectly right. Not to care for them, to be only actively conscious of my twentieth part "self," would be a condition of arrested development, pitiable rather than blameworthy. In a social condition of existence, the life and prosperity of each member is absolutely interwoven with that of the others, of the whole, and not to recognise this, and act accordingly, is to manifest an inferior plane of development.

Organic relation of any sort is mutual, involving mutual obligation, duty, and, if necessary, sacrifice. When a physical body is starving to death, it is impressive

[1] By Mr. J. G. Phelps Stokes. Article in *Wilshire's Magazine,* March, 1903.

to note the gradual surrender of its constituent parts in the order of their importance. First, he calls in all his savings,—the fat. Then the muscles slowly feed in their store. Lastly the "vital organs." And all this is unconscious, managed by the long-established mechanism inside, without any dictation from the cerebral consciousness the man calls "self."

Our internal social functions, the immediately necessary economic processes, may proceed unconsciously to quite a degree of development under the direction of egoism, because, as the social life is the main protection of the individual, so the interests of the individual and of society are in many ways identical, and the individual may serve society very fully and never dream that he is doing anything more than to "take care of himself." But Society cannot proceed far in development before the interests of the whole may involve a temporary subversion of the interests of the past, and here a beneficial social conduct requires social consciousness.

Our carefully preserved ego concept acts mischievously in proportion to the progress of society. The more complex the social process, the larger the social interests involved, the more injurious is this primitive spirit of egoism. The selfishness of a peasant is far less harmful than the selfishness of a railroad-owner. In the orderly development of social economics this would have been taken care of by the natural extension of feeling accompanying the extension of action, but that has been checked, as usual, by our mental heirlooms. Nevertheless we can observe this natural relation of action and feeling in spite of our opposition.

The growth of altruism in certain special industries is most instructive to study, as showing precisely what conditions most regularly and rapidly develop it. Look, for instance, at the distinctive characteristics educed by the industries of agriculture and navigation.

Sailors, as a class, are generous, quick in heroism, licentious, intemperate, and profane.

Farmers, as a class, are by no means generous—frequently stingy; you never heard of a sailor who was a miser, but often of farmers who are such. The farmer is not quick to heroism, but, on the contrary, is slow to recognise his class-needs, hard to organise, prone to the most primitive individualism. On the other hand the farmer is comparatively chaste, and temperate, and guarded in speech.

Why these obvious distinctions, in men of the same race, class, and time, often of the same families? As obviously from the difference in their industries.

The farmer is engaged in our most remote and ancient industry, the one nearest the bottom, in fact it is the bottom of real social growth; only the cattle-keeper stands between the farmer and the savage. The farmer is more nearly self-supporting than any other member of society. He is still in the short-circuit activities of the self-feeder; while his surplus product does in truth feed the world and give us all a chance to grow, he sees nothing of the world he feeds, and, blinded by our customs of exchange, thinks that in selling corn he is but feeding his family. Therefore the farmer is naturally egoistic—inevitably so unless he recognises the social nature of his function.

But as the farmer marries early and easily; woman, too, on that plane of economic activity being a valued co-agent in living, like the squaw; so the farmer is under no strong temptation to unchastity. His life of out-of-door muscular exertion is another help here. Lacking other forms of association, the church is a welcome social ground for the farmer and his wife; so he conforms easily to the current standard of morality. And with this moral tendency and lack of startling events, we find the reason for his temperance in speech and other habits.

In the sailor's life, the opposite conditions obtain. His is a late and highly socialised industry. He combines with other men in elaborately specialised labour for the benefit of innumerable widely scattered people. His combination is absolute for considerable periods of time, and physically isolated from all other social forms. The dangers of the profession are great, requiring constant watchfulness and the most prompt and perfect interdependence. From the seamen singing and hauling together to the quick co-ordination between the captain on the bridge and the uttermost sailor on the yards, there is this constant interplay and conspicuous interdependence. Of course, they develop a high degree of comradeship—of course, they stand by one another to the last degree of danger. It indicates no greater nobility in Jack Jones, who went to sea, over Jedediah Jones, who stayed on the farm; it is a quality of his industry, that is all.

So with the other traits. The sailor is communally fed while engaged in these common activities. The ego is not called out in any way. Then, his private share of wealth being given him at the same time when he is turned loose to provide for himself, he naturally pours forth the money freely; a trait well known by all the barnacles and borers who infest the sailor ashore, as others do the ships at sea.

The sailor has no wife; he cannot marry as early as the farmer, because Jack has to support his wife at long range out of his earnings; she being of no service in maintaining the family. Or, if married, he must be away from his wife for long periods. Thus denied the natural relations of the sexes and exposed when ashore to the instant swooping down of the parasitic female animal in her frankest form, he is, inevitably, "immoral." Let Jedediah go to sea and Jack stay at home, and you reverse the characteristics of each.

The intemperance comes under the action of these last conditions, long-enforced abstinence and sudden profusion; and the profanity is coincident with the sudden shocks of excitement in his work, with all the jars, difficulties, and dangers involved. For similar reasons ox-drovers are less given to profanity than mule-drivers. Thus we see the vices and virtues of a given profession inhere in its conditions. Individual character may fight against it, and there is a difference always in the personal expression, but as industrial classes the farmer and the sailor manifest certain distinctive characteristics involved in their form of industry.

Miners furnish another conspicuous instance of this force. In no class of men—not even in sailors—is altruism, even to heroism, more prominent. Given death and danger well-nigh certain, but comrades to be saved, and the miners always volunteer at once. If valour and self-sacrifice among miners were rewarded as they are in some sporadic rescue of the drowning, we should need to run a factory of decorations. The miner, like the sailor, is engaged in a highly socialised industry. He works at great personal sacrifices to promote the social welfare.

The farmer, in his corn, sees tangible immediate food for himself and family. The miner sees no such prompt advantage in his coal. The farmer, safely and alone, pursues his individual labours. The miner, in danger and in company, pursues his group labour. They are cut off from the rest of the world, the mining group, and easily develop a common consciousness. Their danger is a common danger, only to be met and overcome by common action. Hence they act in common and for each other.

This may be studied in varying degree in all industries. The effect of household labour on the growth of altruism is even worse than that of farm labour. The farmer does in truth connect with the whole world, serve the whole world through his products. The domestic labourer connects with nothing but the family, serves nothing but the family. Absolutely the most primitive form of human labour surviving among us is that of the woman "doing her own work" like the squaw. The only enlargement admitted is that of domestic service, being a survival of the next lowest form, slave labour. This industry, in its shortest of short circuits, develops no social spirit whatever; nothing but egoism and familism grow from it.

Altruism, due to other causes, may be felt and manifested by the domestic worker, but the work does not conduce to it. Conversely, when this stage of labour is at last abandoned; when we have socialised these antiquated industries; an immense increase of altruism will appear. We are so accustomed to think of men as egoists, and women as altruists that it will be a blow to many to advance this position, but seeing that altruism, the social spirit, is but the essential condition and result of our social co-activities; that only men take part in these activities, and that women have been arrested in this natural development and forced to remain as they began, working in solitude and utter disconnection, for their own families solely; it is plain that the world's growth in altruism comes through men as a class, and that women as a class contribute to the social spirit only an exaggerated familism and egoism. That animal instinct shown in "the maternal sacrifice," or the devotion to one's mate of exaggerated sex development, have nothing to do with the larger human love—with omniism.

The two are constantly blended through heredity, but the industrial influence of the sexes is as above stated, and it is through industrial development that our altruism comes. Observe that the nations most "humane" are those most advanced in industry, and those least "humane" are those most primitive in industry, down to the savage who has only the rudiments of either industry or humanity. Altruism is recognised by religion as a virtue and urged upon us, but it appears in us only in proportion to our social progress in interrelated service. Our own principal religion, Christianity, is altruism incarnate—but it is not altruism understood. It preaches altruism as a virtue and a duty, but it does not show altruism to be a natural product of certain industrial relations and urge upon its followers their entering upon those relations as the chief means of developing altruism.

Religion has not showed us the *naturalness* of altruism. It has taught that it was natural for man to be selfish, and that to be unselfish was a continual struggle, needing the grace of God to attain it. When we learn at last that the social instincts are as natural as the personal, that they are evolved under the same biological laws, that our failure to manifest them in due proportion is due to unnecessary social conditions quite within our power to change—the burden on man's conscience will be lifted forever.

We shall learn to lay no false stress on altruism as a lofty and difficult virtue, but see it to be the spirit of civilisation; and the lack of it, the uncivilised egoism still so prominent and evilly active, we shall perceive to be merely an anachronism, which needs only to be recognised to be despised, and only to be despised to be outgrown.

A man still maintaining a visible egoism in a period of dominant altruism, would feel as uncomfortable as a man with a tail. A tail was "natural" to us once,—not now.

Another vital error, maintained by our religions, is the confusion of altruism, the social spirit, with that abnormal action known as "charity"—"benevolence," "philanthropy." We are taught to regard the expression of this rare and hard-won feeling of altruism as requiring us to "sell all we have and give to the poor."

Giving to the poor, from direct alms to the subtle ramifications of organised charity, bears about the same relation to a healthy working altruism that the transfusion of blood bears to a mother's nursing a child. There are times when a direct transfer of subsistence is called for in society, as in some great disaster, like the Chicago fire, or Johnstown flood, or awful submersion of Galveston.

So there are cases when one human being may save another's life by giving him his own blood through a syringe. But you would find it difficult to raise men to a daily level of devotion willing to transfer blood as a steady diet to their anæmic friends; and it is similarly difficult to persuade the healthy working mass of society that any such sacrificial transfer of property is right and reasonable.

They are quite correct in this position. Charity is not right. It may be necessary at times, but it is not a normal organic process. A healthy working altruism involves no sacrifice of one to another, but the common good-will, and common effort for a common good. We err in the very word—it should not be "other-ism"—but "our-ism." There is no justice or benefit in "robbing Peter to pay Paul," but there is in each giving to all—for all includes each.

Just as our foolish "business" methods deal and shuffle money among the rich without adding a cent to our wealth, so does our foolish charity deal and shuffle it among the poor, with similar uselessness. The fact that we are, and always have been, so open to the demands of charity, proves our social spirit, but proves also that we have not understood its nature and its use.

One more error that hinders our realisation of this great feeling is our persistent misuse of the word "self."

The Ego, the personal consciousness, desires for itself and strives for itself. The Socio, the social consciousness, desires for us, for ourself, and strives for society.

But we, feeling this larger desire and impulse, think it is the Ego still at work, and speak of the colossal "Selfishness" of man. It is not Selfishness—it is Socialness; and he, not knowing what it is, tries to satisfy it by satisfying himself.

The futile attempts of a modern man trying to be selfish would be funny if the effects were not so dangerous. Here he is, with this enormous area of social consciousness, this enormous stock of social energy, this enormous field of social activity, all lodged in the executive machine of one small biped animal.

He is awed and impressed by the vast currents of feeling that sweep through the social consciousness. "Dear me!" he says; "what a great mysterious thing is my soul!" It would be mysterious, indeed, if John Smith had a soul of that size. He feels the irresistible pressure of the social energy. "Ah!" he says; "how strong I am!" He launches out into the social activities, doing, it may be, his full share of social service, but *thinking* that he is doing it himself, for himself.

And then—poor hungry tortured soul—he tries to satisfy the social demands he feels by gratifying his own personal desires. The capacity for personal enjoyment is extremely limited, and mainly physical. Warmth, quiet, cleanliness, food, rest, physical exercise, and the joys of mating and rearing young; these the ego wants, and every ego ought to be guaranteed their full gratification. They cost little, they were long ago well within the assets of every civilised society. But a society wants more. All our higher needs are social. "We" want them, and we shall never be satisfied till "we" have them—all of us.

Suppose the inhabitants of a certain city need more rest, or recreation, or entertainments, or better facilities of communication. The individual citizen feels the wants of the city. He cannot satisfy that want in himself till the city is satisfied. The misguided self-styled egoist, feeling the social needs, tries to quench the demand by gratifying himself. He soon reaches personal satiety—*and is still unsatisfied*. Of course. Here is another of the alleged "enigmas" of human life cleared up.

Q. Why is man so inordinately selfish?

A. He isn't. He is social-ish and doesn't know it.

Q. Why is man never satisfied in spite of all he gets?

A. Because he hasn't found his mouth yet. He is hungry for a thousand, and tries to give a thousand dinners to himself to quench that hunger.

When humanity sees its own governing spirit, recognises its own consciousness as a common consciousness, and goes practically to work to meet its common needs, the human soul will find peace. It will not stop growing, but it will become healthy, and grow right. The upward reach of the human soul will carry always its unfulfilled aspirations, but that is but an open road, a glorious ever-spreading opportunity; the way of life; a very different thing from the wailings and convulsions of a crippled and imprisoned soul, struggling for air—for food—for room to grow.

Each human being represents humanity. Each has within him as much of the human soul as he can feel and express, and if he increases his expression he will feel more. But to call that great Social Spirit "mine"; to try to explain it by any sort of self-bound theory; to try to exercise or gratify it within the limits of the individual life—is almost too absurd for illustration. Some private pipe connecting with the ocean, and the owner of the pipe prating of "the mystery of 'my' tides," is a possible simile.

The pressure of the great thing has been so beyond our visible ego that we have been forced to account for it by the hypothesis of personal immortality. There was evidently no room for the soul—no explanation of the soul—in one human life as we saw it before us. "But," said we, "if we make a human life *long enough* there will be room for the soul! That will give us time to understand it, and to gratify these quenchless aspirations, these boundless desires."

It did not occur to us that if we made it *wide enough* it would have the same effect. Our illimitable egoism, being unable to satisfy its own demands by any earthly means, has postulated an eternal ego, with whole ranges of planetary systems to feed in, and hopes, in course of eternity, time not being enough, to satisfy Itself!

And so, postponing the problems it could not answer to a conveniently extensive after life; and considering its own agonies and contortions in this life as part and parcel of the great game between God and the Devil; it has struggled and suffered on; pushed relentlessly upward by the organic social forces, held down most cruelly by its self-made bands of iron; the rigid clamps of primitive ignorance renewed from generation to generation, in spite of the increasing agony of the growing soul.

No wonder we are more unhappy than we used to be; we are bigger, much bigger, but the ego hasn't grown at all. The social spirit of a small young society could masquerade as an ego without too painful inconvenience; but the social spirit of the world to-day is so vast, so strong, so much nearer to expression in our more developed minds, so much more commonly felt, owing to our more equal education, that its confinement to an ego is too agonising to endure,—it is simply impossible.

Therefore we see the steady growth of "public spirit,"—"civic feeling," national and international movements toward general improvement; more and more individuals, rich and poor, devoting themselves to social service; the growing objection to war; the tendency to distribute as well as to accumulate millions; the development of "the home church"; and even—most hopeful of all these splendid signs of life—even the rising current of organisation among women.

This Ego hypothesis might as well be laid aside at once and forever. We are not separate creatures at all, our life is ours, and only so to be rightly lived. It is so easy,—leaving off the ego-theory,—to observe the natural growth of the social spirit in its ever-broadening, steady pressure and in those bursts of irresistible energy we call passion.

Any intense human feeling we call a passion, using the word to distinguish certain main lines of feeling common to us all, as "the maternal passion," "the tender passion," and those broad divisions Hate, Fear, Envy, Remorse, Ambition, Grief, Revenge. Also some special gust of intensity in minor lines of feeling is distinguished by the same word, "a passion of gratitude," "a passion of loneliness," "a passion of rebellion," or of avarice.

Our words climb slowly along the facts, changing as our perception changes, and always behind. Heat as a fact we observed and used long before we knew what to call it, if, indeed, what we call it now is any more true than it was before. But, whether "a fluid" named Caloric, or "a force" named Heat, the fact which we all know and use remains the same. It did its work in the world as fully before we came as after; before we named it at all as after. But to us, to our consciousness, the thing does not exist until we see it, and, seeing, name.

"The maternal passion" is as strong a force in mother-wasp and mother-whale as in the most sophisticated and analytic mother-human. These passions are simply accumulations of stored energy along certain much-used lines, and serve to keep up a steady flow of the desired energy when there is no immediate stimulus to call for it. In the maternal passion, for instance, long ages of iron experience have developed a certain average of watchfulness and care even when the young are visibly safe, and a surprising fund of power and fury in defence of the young even when the exciting cause is comparatively small. It keeps up a safer average of care and defence than if the feeling were merely reactionary, and has therefore been developed in surviving species.

Society, the vast and varied organism in which we live, calls for a devotion more single and fearless than that even of the mother; for a steady average of service and a sudden fund of fury in defence, a love and care and courage higher than any heretofore required; and as it needs such a feeling it gets it. Those societies having it most highly developed survive. We have called it many names; let us now give it another, the Social Passion.

We are most familiar with its branches, minor and local, and with its blazing heights of expression; but the governing line of feeling is as simple as the animal mother's. She, for the sake of race-preservation, must feed and guard and teach the young, therefore she manifests the maternal passion. We, for the sake of race-preservation, must feed and guard and teach each other, therefore we manifest the social passion.

One common form is what we call "the sense of duty." A single animal has no "duty," he acts and reacts under direct stimuli, and so in large measure does the savage. But social maintenance requires a steady service without immediate and apparent cause; an even standard of merit in the work done; a reliability in the fulfilment of the allotted task, and, at times, a tremendous fervour of exertion and heroism. The "feeling" in us which urges to these acts is as deep and unreasonable as any other "feeling"; it is a genuine passion.

The irritation of a mother at any criticism of her child, however plainly merited, is perfectly paralleled by the irritation of the citizen at any criticism of his country. The instant rush to the rescue of an injured "fellow creature," co-creature, member of the same great body, is as blind and instinctive as the mother's rush to save the child. It finds its most familiar and acute form in the soldier "dying for his country." Devotion to "a cause" of any sort, a class, a club, a corps, a union, the intense "co-ability" of the human creature, this is but manifestation of the social passion.

The hero, the statesman, the patriot, the public saviour and servant of any sort are conspicuous examples of this feeling at its height; the reformer and religious leader, from the most mistaken enthusiasts to the greatest prophets and teachers, are all exponents of this mightiest of forces, the social passion. A blind, deep, instinctive pressure, a *must* in the very blood, a feeling bred of centuries of social contact and interdependence, this is what kindles the great hearts who live or die to serve the world.

Where it touches the present subject is in its relation to Work, of which indeed it is the immediate conscious cause.

The maternal passion does not manifest itself merely in bursts of wild self-sacrifice, but speaks plainest in the patient, steady labour with which it serves the young. So the social passion, while most conspicuous in Horatius at the bridge, is as valuable in the engineer at the lever, or the steersman at the helm.

The Love of Work is one great manifestation of the Social Passion. The maternal function urging to expression, this gives the rich joy of nursing one's child, and that almost inconceivable torment of the black past where the starving baby cried before the chained mother's bursting breasts. The social function urging to expression, this gives the rich joy of work accomplished and the aching, quenchless misery of work denied. Fulfilment of function, that is Work, and, forbidden, the poor functionary aches like a tied leg.

We may trace this suffering from work denied through all the uneasy contortions of "the leisure class" to the final surrender to that social paralysis, *ennui*. Healthy physical impulses, checked in natural expression, twitch and cramp the unused member. Healthy social impulses, checked in natural expression, twitch and cramp in similar agony and distortion. Always the impulse to do—the human instinct, the social passion. Then the inhibition from mistaken theories and false ideas, the individual checking his healthy social impulses as perversely as the religious ascetic checks his healthy physical impulses.

And as the ascetic, bottling his life up, froths off in wild visions and fanatical activity, so the social ascetic lives in a whirling rush of useless exertion and excitement, always seeking in what he calls "society" that true social contact and social action which he never finds. And as the body of the ascetic wastes and dwarfs and deforms under the unnatural life his gross delusions bring him to, so does society suffer under the diseased conditions engendered by this fatuous mistake.

More firmly and reassuringly we can trace the social passion in its true expression. Clear and strong it has left its mark on every age, and rises steadily with our rising socialisation. The co-consciousness with its beautiful result in love; "a fellow-feeling makes us wondrous kind"; "one touch of nature makes the whole world kin"; the co-activity and its resultant virtues and abilities; the need for expression of those "co-abilities"; the urge toward exertion, ultimately seen to be in the social interest, but pushing from within as a passion; this feeling it is which made Palissy the Potter break up his furniture to insure his glaze; which drove Galileo to his studies in defiance of the Church; which fed the fire with prohibited books and gave up martyrs by the score to die because they would let out what was in them; they must.

We see it clearest in the arts and sciences, in the inventor, the explorer, the teacher of new truth. But what drives these conspicuously specialised social servants to their work is the same force which holds the steersman to his wheel, the engineer to his lever, the sentry to his post: the power of functional expression; stronger in us than any other force, as our social nature is stronger in us than the nature of the beast.

If we would recognise our "human nature" to be our "social nature," and that what we have so scorned and pitied as "poor human nature" is not human at all, but merely animal,—ego-nature,—it would alter our whole range of thought on this vital matter.

The social spirit is not "poor," but bounteously rich and strong. It rises grandly to meet great emergencies, but is felt most continually in our impulse to work, to do what we are made for, what we are together for; that which constitutes the primal condition and line of development for human life.

VIII: THE SOCIAL BODY

SUMMARY

Likeness between spirit and form, mutual modification. Love modified by form. The soul human. The body of society our manufactured things. Bones of dead societies. The thing made. Animal's things all grow on him. Society secretes its material form. The thing marks the age. Axe-man, swords-man, pen-man, etc. Value of detachability of tools. Potentiality of human body. Value of exchangeability of tools. Vehicle of common use. Reaction of thing made on user. Body a machine we have to learn. Thing promotes further action. Growth in work. Cloth. Effect on life. Value and effect of machines. Pleasure of transmitting energy. Mistaken objection to machinery. Reversion to "hand work" foolish. Social progress conditioned by mechanical. We are now capable of far better living and have the means for it. American advance. Machine does for society what the cerebellum does for the body. Our power to facilitate social progress. "Truth in art" and "better housing." Restrictions due to false concepts, not to conditions.

CHAPTER VIII

THE SOCIAL BODY

We have seen that in every living creature there is a close and vivid likeness between its spirit and its form, between body and soul. Given such a spirit and it tends to evolve such a form. Given such a form and it tends to evolve such a spirit. The form must limit and modify the spirit.

Fortunately forms can change; and spirit, to grow, continually discards old forms and makes new. If anything succeeds in fixing a given form unchanged, so is the spirit within it imprisoned and checked in growth forever. It is for this reason doubtless that the primal force has been so busy making its endless procession of forms. First we have the universe set whirling with great suns and their spattering planets; then the planet flames, crackles, cools, crusts over, and so fringes out in all manner of soft green, and following these we have life cut looser, freer, in animal forms; lastly the social.

Imagine the sun as loving; it can but shine and glow to express that love. The dog loves, and can but leap and lick and wag his tail, fetch and carry, watch and fight to show it. The man loves, and in the manifold activities made possible by his form, by the special development of the brain, he can express that principal force more deeply, widely, fully. The spirit of every living thing is expressed through its form and limited by it.

Humanity, if a living creature, has a soul and a body. The soul we all know; we call it rightly the human soul. Where is the body of that soul? Not in our little bundle of arms and legs—we had that in full career before the human soul was possible. That is the body of an animal, capable of expressing as much spirit as any animal, perhaps a little more than a large ape. If we had no medium of expression but these physical bodies there could be no Society, no Humanity, and no social soul.

That last and best expression of creative force finds its material form in the things we make in the manufactured world. Take from a society its body, the structure of brick, stone, and iron, wood, cloth, leather, glass, paper,—all that elaborate compound of materials in which we live,—reduce it to a mere congregation of naked animals, and what would ensue? Those animals would either rebuild in desperate haste the material forms in which alone Society exists, or they would relapse into individual savagery. If too small a group, or too highly specialised to reproduce the social body to live in, they would be unable even to revert to savagery and would simply die. The Social Soul we have seen to be a common consciousness developed by common activities. The Social Body is a common material form, also developed by common activities. Both appear in proportion to the extent and development of those activities.

As house and vehicle for the spirit of an animal has been slowly evolved the cunning mechanism of bone and muscle, with all its constituent organs, in which a man lives. It is but a combination of chemicals and minerals, and when the soul is out of it they disintegrate and revert to lower combinations. As house and vehicle for the spirit of society has been slowly evolved the more cunning and elaborate mechanism of wood and cloth, brick, stone, metal—in which Humanity lives. It too is but a combination of chemicals and minerals, and when its inhabiting humanity is gone, it too disintegrates and reverts, though more slowly. The bones of dead societies remain to us in stone and glass and pottery, as do the bones of extinct animals.

An animal life, once started in the germ, goes on growing, *i. e.,* making to itself a body suitable to its soul. If you arrest the growth of the body,—if, for instance, a baby's head were cased in iron,—you would arrest the growth of the soul. It would have one, potentially; that is, it would if its brain had room for it, but actually you would have checked it. So the social life, once started, goes on assimilating material particles and recombining them in mechanical form, enlarging its functions as it enlarges the structure through which alone they become possible. Society builds its body for good or ill.

A piece of human creation—a manufactured article—is the record, the physical manifestation of our humanness. By these things, reading backward, does the ethnologist reconstruct the vanished races as the paleontologist reconstructs a vanished beast from fossil bones. A bead, a knife, a needle, some torque or bracelet, a broken jar,—and the lost people rise before us.

Man, to be such and such, requires such and such things, and evolves them as naturally as the sea-beast makes its shell. It grows from him—so do our manufactures grow from us. Society secretes, as it were, the manufactured article. We need clothes, for instance, a purely social need. The individual animal does not need clothes. He carries his wardrobe on his back. Never a solitary creature in clothes. Clothes are for other people more than the wearer. Other people are required to make them. Even in a one-generation-reversion, as of some hunting hermit of modern times,—back he goes to buckskin! He cannot shear and card, weave and spin, bleach and dye, cut and sew. Back he goes to borrow some other animal's skin; and, if he stayed a hunting hermit for enough generations, back would he go to his own skin and its natural growth of hair.

But the increasing social faculties and desires—the love of ornament, the sense of decency, the need of concealment, the demand for a more fluent and delicate expression of personality—these call for clothes, and society evolves them through a thousand trades.

A trade is a social function, and clothing is a social product as hair is a product of the individual body. In the thing made lies our social history so fully that, had we a full line of specimens, we should need no other monument of progress.

The progress of each age rests on its things: the unchipped flint and the polished; the bronze knife and the steel; the wonder-working wheel (how much of social progress goes "on wheels"!); the bow and arrow, the sword, the axe, the spade,—small things for separate use at first,—and then the marvellous, monster engines of to-day; they are at once the means and the record of progress. There is a phase of thought which despises "material things," and prattles ardently of our "spiritual nature." But in steady-marching ages of coincidence man's spiritual nature manifests itself through material things, and grows by means of them. The ships of Tyre made possible that Phœnician civilisation which has so affected the Grecian and all that follow. The roads of Rome knit and fastened her Empire to the ends of the earth.

Axe-man, bow-man, swords-man, plough-man, boatman, pen-man,—there is a steady likeness between man's things and man. As there is the same likeness between the spirit and the body of each animal, so man, having the new, wide, aspiring, endless, social soul, manifests its growth in ceaseless progression of manufacture, in developing this vast body of Society. The human soul is greater than the animal's because it has a greater body to live in—complex, universal.

One marvellous power that is ours by virtue of these things is that whereas they do not grow on us personally, we remain somewhat free of their inexorable reaction.

A beast depending mainly on digging for his livelihood, as the mole, is relentlessly modified to claws. Paw, arm and shoulder, neck and head, the body, the fur, the eyes,—he is a digger, and the spirit within him is a contented digger, too—needs must.

Once in a permanent form the spirit accepts it and stops growing.

Man digs mightily, but spade and pick do not grow on him. He takes them up, he lays them down; he substitutes the axe, the scythe, the flail. And so he does not become hopelessly the spade-holder. Too much of one kind of tool, and we have the "Man with the Hoe."

With this rich fluency of attach- and detachability we have sped up the ages of social evolution with an ease and swiftness inconceivable of any other animal whose machinery is so inalienably attached to his spirit that it takes slow centuries to change him. This is what gives the subtle beauty to the human body, its measureless potentiality. Every other animal's body is a perfect representation of its blended activities, greater or less. The hound, the cat, the stag, the horse, the swan, each speaks to us of its activities, each form is an embodied motion. But each in its degree is final; being that motion or those motions, it cannot be others; its personal perfection is its limit. Man's body is an almost limitless possibility. He is the handle of innumerable tools. The upright, balanced trunk leaves the legs free for all possible movement; the high-hung, wide-reaching arms with branching fingers are tenfold elephant trunks; he can perform more kinds of actions than any other creature.

But the distinctive power of these actions involves always the thing made. A collection of human bodies pure and simple would tell you little of their social stage. But a collection of the tools and weapons of the man would tell you what he was and where.

With the detachability comes the great characteristic of exchangeability, the "our-ness" of human things; the social body is necessarily usable by all. There is no vexed question of possession with the beast. His teeth and claws are his indeed; he cannot lend or give, and none can rob him. His "dogness" is a little bundle all his own, but our "man-ness" lies in these wide-flung tools of ours, made by one, used by another, profited in by all.

This is again our infinite advantage. If the protean change of characteristics made possible to us by tool-chest and armory were possible to any other creature we should not hold our easy supremacy. The dying leader of the wolf-pack cannot hand his superior teeth to the next one, or produce sudden wings and lend them to his followers. The distributability of our tools gives us the limitless flux of power which is human. One man makes swords for a thousand, and each sword spreads the sword-power far and wide. The needle, the pen, all individual tools, may be used by many in turn, to the advantage of all.

Even more do we see this advantage in anything which may be used by many at once. Here indeed is humanness made manifest. Men, separate men, may swim as well as some animals, or ride a log, perhaps a hollowed one. But man, the human creature, man socialised, make for *themself* the ship, a swimming body for the social soul, and in that one material product of humanity lies unmeasured share of our real growth and greatness.

Only men together can make it, with ages of gradual evolution and relentless elimination of the unfit, with elaborate specialisation and co-ordination of effort; only man together and in similar complex relation can use it. And because of this larger range of usability is its larger value. More persons can use it, and for a longer time; it is a large and lasting piece of the social structure. So of the road, the bridge, the hall,—whatever is open to the largest use by the most people for the longest time, this is of the largest value to society; as statue, picture, music, book. In direct practical result these common products for our common use minimise effort and maximise gain, and in the living miracle of their use they steadily react upon the user and make him something nearer to the power that made them. The shiny-bladed knife in the hand of the eager boy cries to him to cut, to carve, to do a thousand things; and as he uses it, skill, the human skill bred by long ages of knife-using, is born anew in him. Ward has shown this—achievement embodied in object.

The pillared temple, visible product of the human soul in purest, proudest aspiration, reacts always on those who come within, lifting their spirits to its plane, to each according to his power of receiving. In our made things lies that much of our humanness, and as we use them we grow by that much more human; in this reactive power lies the desirability of the Thing, and its importance. The power of "mind over matter" is commonly observed, but the effect of matter upon mind, the reaction of the body upon the spirit, is not so clear to us. We see the human spirit laying violent hands on clay and wood and iron, and building for itself a visible, tangible form. We do not see so well this visible form steadily and inexorably reacting upon the imprisoned spirit.

The made thing is the vehicle, record, and monument of human progress. The things we make are nearer to the human soul than is the physical body. That body is but a machine in which our nerve currents have run so long and intimately that the act is unconscious, and we say "I did this," not "my hand did it."

If a baby could express his relation to his body in plain words, we should find him getting acquainted with it, "learning it" as one learns a bicycle or a sewing-machine. He can make it work, but he has to learn how, as he would have to learn how to row or shoot.

Moreover, It has its tendencies and habits with which he has to respectfully acquaint himself that he may promote or check or change them; the tendencies and habits of a long-established animal mechanism, in which the human soul is quartered. The tools and implements in the use of which lies our humanness are scarcely more foreign to us than his hands and feet were to the baby, or than some new combination of muscular action is to the adult. We have to learn to act through sword and spear, spade and plough, knife and axe, as we had to learn to act through muscle, cord, and bone, and they become as automatically natural to us in due time.

The physical body is not an end but a means. Life is the end, action; the body is what you do it with. So these material forms we make are not ends, but means. Human life is the end, and these things are what we do it with. The expression of force through higher forms, that is life's line of progress.

Our creations are all to do something in, or with, or from. Even the most perfect form of art stands as an inspiration to other human beings, is a means to better action, better living for us all. Every human product is an instrument, in using which we can more fully express the divine spirit. A house is not a final end. We do not build a house as a crowning achievement and then sit and wait upon it for the rest of life—or at least we should not! We build a house to live in, that we may work. Human life is not a means of promoting house-building; house-building is a means of promoting human life.

Book, picture, statue, these are our fruit, our product, evolved through us as a means of further growth. Our "civilised" life to-day, the consciousness of an "educated," "cultivated" person, is developed by contact with the things in which previous human beings expressed their measure of life and passed it on to us.

Some brain is born with new cellular development which enables it to receive impressions from mountain scenery, which scenery had hitherto failed to impress the less developed brain. The brain impressed must express the force received, must transmit it in a material form. According to its capacity it works to do this, producing picture or poem or prose description. That material form continues to transmit the impression received to those whose brains are developed in comparative similarity, and the race is gradually opened to the stimulus of this aspect of nature, and by so much is greater, wiser, able to do more.

Human work, all of it, is a means to further expression. If we ask "to what end," we can only reply that as far as our lit circle of perception goes life has no end. But its direction is plain, and its method; to receive more and more of the forces of life as the brain becomes more widely and delicately susceptible, to express more and more of the forces of life in our work, and so further to develop that brain,—that is the process. The savage has not brain development enough to "see God" with even as much as we, or as little; he is but dimly and narrowly affected by the currents of divine force. But such energy as he does receive prompts him to work, and as he works he develops further brain power. In working is human growth, and in its visible forms is the permanence and transmissibility of each advance.

Take cloth, for instance, as an illustration of the value of the thing made. Imagine it out of human life. See its relation to the human skin, both in clothing and cleanliness—fancy man with neither shirt, towel, nor handkerchief! We revert at once to leather and foul habits. No carpets, no hangings, no banners and flags, no sheeted beds, no daintiness in eating, no subtle play of feeling in our dress—down would go human history backward, ravelling out to first principles. Cloth is a social tissue which enables us to come close and slip smoothly in our complex interaction. Leather means solitude and living out of doors. Civilisation is inwoven with the twisted threads; textile manufacture is a social function.

These material forms which humanity makes are not gross and ignoble, as the blind asceticism of the past supposed; they are humanity's living body, and should be lovingly and reverently regarded, most honourably and gladly constructed, as the intimate avenues of spiritual growth for us all. Human production is marked plainly higher than that of lower animals because it is in common. One makes alone for many to use; or, as we progress still further, many make together for still more to use.

Beyond even that, we construct the complex implements of further construction, and make machines. Man's first step up was in the detachable tool, though but a stick or stone. From the hand-thrown stone to the far-flung lyddite shell is a clear line of mechanical evolution, in which each thing made held the thought which made it and suggested further possibility. From the twirling spindle to the many-loomed mill; from the stylus to the press,—this is familiar ground in fact, but all untrodden in its rich significance.

Nowhere have we more misused, misunderstood, and blasphemed the laws of human life than in our attitude toward machinery. Measured by any standard you will, as low as that of individual physical comfort, as high as that of the widest social service, human progress, lying in the same line as all evolution, involves the constant adaptation of means to ends with conservation of energy. Most energy is spent with smallest result at the level where the mole digs, each for himself, with his tools growing on him. The spade is higher than the claw, and the modern earth-devouring excavator is higher than the spade. Some digging is necessary for the maintenance of our physical lives. The more human energy we spend in digging the less remains for further development. To dig is not our purpose here, but to grow. Therefore social evolution quietly relegates digging to the lower automatic functions, making the mechanical organs by which the most digging can be done by the least men, that more and more of us may leave the level of the mole.

Of all things made, the things we make things with are most vitally and distinctively human. Something of the truth of this may be seen in the larger and deeper pleasure given by the use of the higher tool, and, even more clearly, in the higher kind of man developed by the higher tool. The digger with the attached claws is but a mole. The digger with the detachable spade is but an "unskilled labourer," and even the maker of that spade but a simple smith. The digger with the great excavator is an engineer, and its maker a skilled machinist and inventor. The ox-driver is not to be compared with the engine-driver or the bargeman with the admiral.

Now the mole, or the unskilled labourer, may be as "happy," as an individual, as the skilled machinist. But the measure of their value is in this. The mole is incapable of further combinations. The unskilled labourer is capable only of a low order of combinations. The more specialised brain of the inventor is capable of higher combinations. Of such as he a democracy can be built; he is raised far along the line of social evolution. The childish, primitive pride in a "hand-made" individual product is most ignoble compared to the modern pride in a common product through complex means.

The brain to make and to use a complex machine is the brain to make and to use a complex social order; and in that growing social order lies our line of duty as a human race. In the inexorable working of our own machines we learn law newly; as in our works of art we learn beauty newly. Kipling has treated of this in "MacAndrews' Hymn."

The relation of our complex mechanical products with our minds and hearts is as clear as the relation between any animal's spirit and body. The increasing pleasure is as clear as the increasing use. "Man loves power." Of course. He loves to transmit energy, to feel it pouring through. He loves it well in his own physical exertions: to swim is a pleasure, to row alone is a pleasure, but to row in a racing eight is a greater pleasure. To sail a catboat is a pleasure, to command the flagship a greater pleasure. The captain loves his ship, and loves to work her, to feel the complex mechanism move in answer to his thought and will, and the prompt co-ordination of all the men whose combined efforts move the great machine. And the kind of man who can be a good captain or a good sailor is a higher social constituent than a South Sea Islander, though the latter could outswim him.

Our general feeling of condemnation for machinery is a kind of social asceticism, a reaction from our misuse of the social body, just as the personal asceticism of earlier times was a reaction against misuse of the personal body. In our blind ignorance of the real social life and its laws, in our persistent maintenance of a rudimentary egoism, we have claimed private ownership in these exquisitely social products, and have striven to restrict their mighty multiplication of wealth to private consumption. Such sublime treason has roused instinctive reaction in the public consciousness, and we blindly include the machine in our hatred of its vile abuse, as did the early Christian in his condemnation of the body. Partly owing to this, and partly owing to our cruel form of specialisation, we associate evil with machinery, and, with our usual helpless reversionary tendency, look back fondly to the time when each man or woman worked alone "by hand."

These theorists should be set down in some wilderness for a while with only their hands to help them, as a lesson in social chronology. The hand is at its best in the early Palæolithic period, or even back of that, when it could do duty as a foot on occasion. As the hand made and mastered the tool, society has grown. As the tool became the machine, society has grown better. In the vast machine, moved by tireless natural forces, and guided by the specialised brain and hand, we find the highest expression of nature's steady tendency to minimise effort and maximise results.

When we appreciate the true use and nature of all this machinery, realising that by means of its measureless service we can now apply almost all our power to the conscious development of society, we shall find it to be an unmixed blessing, of value beyond our dreams. Seeing that the social soul needs such and such a body, and is developed with it, and that we have at last the means of evolving that body at a speed hitherto impossible, we can now utilise these unlimited forces to facilitate our growth with results that will make previous historic progress seem stationary. It is not as if we were required to force long cycles of evolution, to hasten the steps of nature, and hurry mankind over slow steps of necessary ascent,—we are there now!

Society being an organic whole, social progress being ours in common and exquisitely transmissible, the material forms of that progress and vehicles of transmission being ready to hand, we can, by our present means of rapid production and distribution of these material forms, open the way to such swift advance of civilisation as the world has never seen. The spirit of modern society is capable of a plane of life far beyond the present conditions wherein we find that spirit gagged and blinded by the fossil Ego concept, that body inconceivably dwarfed and twisted by the efforts of each ego to occupy it all himself.

The right relation of spirit and body in the animal gives health and beauty and power, and in our human life the right relation of the social spirit and body is as important. A healthy, growing, social life constantly re-creates its body as does the physical life, and our American civilisation shows this beyond all others in its rapid adoption of new material forms and processes. The constant demand for easier and swifter mechanism is as natural and healthful in society as it is in a physical body, and physical evolution has moved on that line continually.

The passing over of individual effort to the automatic action of machinery is analogous to the constant passing over of conscious cerebral action to the less expensive automatic management of lower brain centres—the development of "habit." The body is not the man, and brick and mortar are not Society; but their connection is as intimate and vital. And as the soul of a man is grievously injured or equally benefited by the condition and use of his body, so is Society affected for good or ill by the mechanical forms in which it lives, their condition and their use.

Recognising as the first quality distinguishing the social body from the physical, that it is made by common action and open to common use, and recognising that the proper use of the body has a reactive effect in developing the soul, we have here a means of promoting social growth so prodigious in its scope and speed as to be fairly dizzying. We have, as usual, felt this great social truth, even though not understanding it, and our groping efforts in its pursuance are seen in two main lines: that which urges to "truth in art" in our common crafts; to making things beautiful, true, good, that all may be improved by them, and in our blind but earnest effort to provide "better housing for the poor," with all that that implies.

We have seen that the slum tends to make the criminal, and that the school, bath, playground, museum, library, art gallery, free access to the best products of society, tend to make the better citizen; but we have not seen the large and simple principle involved.

Each thing made is an embodiment of social energy, and transmits it to the user, be it a fork or a fiddle. A noble and beautiful work ennobles and beautifies the beholder, listener, reader, occupant,—the user. All especially general social structures, or those glorious deposits of energy known as works of art, as well as all the materials of knowledge, are valuable in proportion to their free and public use.

The more people circulate in their great social body the more socialised they become. This we are doing much to promote in our free schools, libraries, museums, etc., but we do not begin to appreciate the possibilities involved, being impeded, as usual, by our prior concepts, Want theory and Pay concept in particular. The increased facilities of travel of our time, for instance, which should be enlarging the mind of the public as well as increasing its wealth, are greatly restricted in application by these errors. The people who administer our railroads are allowed by popular consent to "own" them, and as owners, regarding their property as bound in the first instance to "pay" them, they maintain as high a list of charges as "the traffic will bear." When we recognise locomotion as a prime social necessity, these ribbons of steel and their rolling-stock as part of the social body, and traffic and travel as social advantages rather than individual,—yes, social necessities,—then we shall encourage the widest possible use of these facilities.

We have but to recognise the vital connection between the growing social body and the growing social soul, and that the soul not only makes the body, but is made by it, to apply our immense material gain to our whole people. The results will be what our discouraged and patient minds are apt to call "too good to be true."

IX: THE NATURE OF WORK (I)

SUMMARY

Familiarity of Work confusing to true thoughts, our general attitude due to false concepts. Veblen's theory. Theory of Hebrew religion. Occasional dim perception of value of work. Effect of ego concept and pay concept. Effect of organic concept. Effect of Want Theory. Main thesis of author on Work. Physical organic action. Heart, as illustration. Social organic action. Individual consciousness no obstacle. Social circulation. Men not self-supporting. Waste, parasitism, disease. Evolution of Work. Universal transmission of energy. Appearance of consciousness. Feeling and action. Pleasure in sensation and action. Society the greatest life-form, greatest action, greatest pleasure. Social nourishment for worker, and true adjustment. Accumulation of social energy. Limitation of individual animal. Geometrical increase in social efficiency up to the sixth power. Increase of stimulus. Increase of interest. Storage and transmission of society energy. Work of art. Devotion to country. Bee and Ant. Proper human relation and action. Child's instinct to work. Resistless working instinct of great specialist. Radium. The teacher, scientific discoverer, etc. Our workers not supplied with social energy. Extinction of London labourer. Want Theory again. Our dinner. Social nutrition collective. Discharge of surplus energy not an exertion.

CHAPTER IX

THE NATURE OF WORK (I)

Work is the most prominent feature of human life. So large a majority of human beings spend most of their lives at work that the few diseased and defective members of society who do not need scarcely be considered. As usual, the prominence and constant insistence on the facts about work have prevented our thinking much about it, and, when we did think, our mistaken basic concepts made us think wrong. Our general attitude toward work varies somewhat in accordance with race, place, and time, but is traceable, easily enough, to certain general root ideas.

One line of racial feeling on this subject has been most fully and ably treated by Veblen in his "Theory of the Leisure Class." He shows how labour, being first performed by women and then by conquered opponents made slaves, was despised by the early mind, and how, further, the ability not to work, involving power to make others work for you, soon became an ingrained principle of pride; further, how the leisure class, an aborted part of the body politic, has preserved these errors of the early mind and added heavily to them by the increment of tradition and long association. This accounts satisfactorily enough for a large share of the popular feeling about work.

It is perhaps as part of this feeling that the ancient Hebrew religion, postulated by a people of pastoral ideals and Oriental temperament, takes the extreme ground that work is a curse, a punishment, visited upon man for his sins; and that Eden behind us or Heaven before us has its main attraction in ceaseless idleness.

This mischievous error, incorporated in so important a religion, and forced upon the human mind for so many centuries, has done incalculable harm. In vain have later and wiser religionists protested that "labour is prayer," a divine curse is not to be whiffled away by any such pretty phrase as that. It is not enough to receive a new truth, you must discharge the old lie, if your mind is to work straight.

Our attitude toward Work rests also, however, upon other errors than these, the most fundamental of which are the Ego concept and the Pay concept. Under the first we relate our ideas and sentiments about work to the individual, in which position no understanding is possible; we might as well try to understand mastication in relation to a tooth. Under the second, we think only of the "reward of labour"; and have carried this absurdity to its logical height in classing the industries of the world under the phrase of "getting a living," as if the maintenance of the worker were the object of the work. This again is as absurd as if we believed that chewing was done in order to maintain teeth.

When we accept the organic nature of society, the whole proposition changes, we then see all varieties of work to be social functions, performed in the interests of the whole; and that the maintenance of the individual normally depends, not on a reward for the value or amount of the work he does, but on the general health of the social body and his having proper access to its currents of nutrition. Yet even this perception will not wholly free us while we are still muddled by the pay theory, still holding that a man or a society only works in order to get something, and that, in justice, there must be a return for the effort expended.

This common assumption is accepted as basic by our political economists, and their further theories, systems, and alleged laws all rest on it. It is called the Want Theory. Fully and fairly stated the common definition of work, based on the want theory, is this: Work is an expenditure of energy by the individual in order to obtain the means to gratify a desire. This is almost universally believed. We accept it so fully that one of the steps taken by missionaries to arouse industrial energy in savages is to make them want things. As further manifestation of our belief in it we hold that if people were supplied with anything they did not work for, did not previously expend energy to get, they would, of course, cease to work. On this ground, honestly and logically held, every step toward free public provision for popular need has been opposed.

Before going further in discussion of our common errors, let us lay down the main thesis of this book, advanced as the true theory of work.

It is this: Work is an expenditure of energy by Society in the fulfilment of its organic functions. It is performed by highly specialised individuals under press of social energy, and is to them an end in itself, a condition of their existence and their highest joy and duty.

The difference between the two positions is best seen in studying organic action in lower forms. Consider, for instance, the action of the heart in our bodies. Here is a small muscular machine, which keeps up a violent and continuous activity for some seventy years. Why? and How? Why should this organ work so hard and so incessantly? My stomach gets some rest—my legs get more—but this member is always at work. What want does he gratify by it? Is he any better paid than leg or stomach?

If the heart were an individual, and were pulsating for pay, he might conceivably stop when he got what he wanted. "Why continue to beat?" he might naturally ask. "I have what I was beating for!" And if, further, you supplied this independent creature with all it wanted, free, it would quite naturally cease beating altogether.

But as an Organ, which is quite a different thing from an Individual, the heart does not act on any such basis. It has been slowly developed through long ages of physical evolution, to perform a function of *no use to itself*, but of primal use to the body to which it belongs, the body which made it, the body without which there would be no such thing as a heart. This function being so absolutely essential, the heart is fitted to beat steadily on from birth to death; when it ceases beating the body goes out of business altogether.

Now a separate animal the size of a heart could not keep up any such long-continued regular exercise, it could not furnish sufficient energy; but the large body which needs a heart can run one, it has a supply of energy on which all its organs draw. The work of a living organ is not at cost of its own energy, but of the energy of the entire organism. Society, as an organism, has a vast, a practically unlimited supply of energy, and the human being, as a member of that society, is supplied with it.

The discharge of this energy is so far from costing the individual anything that, on the contrary, any prevention of his normal work causes him acute suffering. And as in the physical body, each special organ, in order that it may devote its entire life to the physical service, is by the circulation of nutrition saved any necessity for caring for itself; so in the social body, each man, in order that he may devote his entire life to the social service, is similarly provided for by the distribution of economic products; our social nutrition.

Here we are at once met by existing beliefs, loud-voiced. "Men are not 'organs,' they are conscious individuals. Men are not—oh! palpably not—provided for by any such beneficial process of social distribution of nourishment; each man must take care of himself or starve!"

The individual consciousness of men is not denied, it is that, misconstrued, which has made these common social functions work so ill, and hurt so in the working. To that same individual consciousness this book is directed, urging reconsideration of the facts, readjustment of the industrial activities. But however conscious, men are none the less "organs," their labours serve our common ends; not their own. It is not that each man has some exact analogue in physiological type, like the heart, but that each industry holds organic relations with all other industries, and that the use and purpose of each depend on the others. The need to be supplied is a social need, the growth to be attained is a social growth, of no more value to an individual, detached, than beating would be to a heart, detached. Work is an organic function, incontrovertibly.

As to the lack of social provision of nourishment, this again is but an error. The provision is there, the whole of society contributing to it; the circulation is there, our food and other goods flowing merrily across land and sea; but there is some trouble with the final distribution of this nourishment to the workers, which will be considered later. Admitting the imperfections, it remains true that the social circulation is now in action—the shoemaker of Massachusetts eating the beef of Nebraska, and the beef-raiser of Nebraska wearing the shoes of Massachusetts.

No man could work, which is a social function, if he had at the same time to "take care of himself," which is an individual function. As a worker in society, he is taken care of, but he does not do it himself. To repeat our definition—normal human work is a discharge of social energy along lines of special development. The social organism lives in the fulfilment of its organic functions, that fulfilment is work; to work is to take part in the vital processes of Society, to be socially alive; not to work, not to take part in these vital processes, is to be one of three things:

First, mere dead matter, Waste; second, a Parasite, active as a thief, passive as a pauper; or third, a Disease, of which in time Society must die.

With the waste products of society we are painfully familiar, the great army of defectives, people who cannot work, yet whom, as part of ourself, we must support, a drag upon the Social resources. The active parasite we know in his crude form, as the little thief, and are beginning to detect in his highly developed form as the big thief. The passive parasite we know also in his crude form as the idle poor, and are beginning to suspect in the idle rich. But the disease is still beyond our diagnosis, though many Societies have died of it, those morbid processes engendered by the presence in the social body of any matter not alive and healthily active.

These features of the abnormal working of Society come later. Let us now study the evolution of Work.

The Universe as we know it is occupied in transmitting energy. The amount seems inexhaustible and indestructible. It rolls on interminably, discharging warmth and light into blank spaces; and, whenever worlds have formed, getting tangled up in a thousand shapes and sputtering mightily as it finds its complicated way out through them.

A living creature has an elaborate system of receiving and discharging energy, more elaborate as the life-form grows higher.

Force in inorganic matter has a simple channel, varying the monotony by occasional explosions. Force in the vegetable world is freer and learns new tricks—building tall trees and flaming out in blossoms. Force in the animal kingdom has wider range; these life-forms can do more things. They have more ways to express energy, and more ways to receive it. With special senses tuned to catch various vibrations, they respond to light, heat, and sound, to touch, taste, and smell; their impressions are varied and their expressions equally so.

Here enters Consciousness, with its extremes of Pleasure and Pain; the director of action, but not its cause. This complex engine, receiving so many impressions, transmitting so many expressions, must feel, because it acts; must act, because it feels. An Action is a consciously directed expression of energy. A Sensation is a consciously recorded impression of energy. Both sensation and action, if normal, are pleasurable—the conscious transmission of energy is joy.

The pleasure in sensation increases in proportion to the extent and delicacy of the sensorium. The pleasure in action increases in proportion to the extent and delicacy of the executive mechanism. Pain, of course, is proportionate to pleasure at any stage; meaning only abnormal use of the same nerves, but the higher the development of the organism the greater its ability to avoid pain.

The course of evolution has been to develop more and more complicated instruments for the transmission of energy. Society, as the highest life-form, is the most exquisitely complex of all; it has a sensorium far larger, and more subtly sensitive, and an executive apparatus commensurate; it has a degree of consciousness highest of all, and a proportional capacity for joy and ability to avoid pain.

This social transmission of energy is Work. The forces of the universe flowing through humanity come in by all our highly cultivated powers of perception, and come out in our beautiful profusion of creative activities—in work. The conscious transmission of energy reaches in us a transcendent height of pleasure by virtue of our co-ordinate action. There is larger joy in "team-work" than in the individual play. The pleasure of dancing in companies, or the rhythmic motions of a drill, is not confined to those particular activities; but, in normal conditions, inheres in all smoothly co-operate exercise. The reasons why we do not feel it in those exercises we call work are not inherent, but purely associative; or else due to accompanying conditions of a painful nature.

Normal conditions of human work require, first, that the worker shall be well nourished physically and socially, well educated to his fullest height of ability, and well-placed in the work he likes best and does best—(these two being identical). A worker, so placed, is in no way overtaxing his own energy, but is merely giving expression to the social energy, and finds in that process an exhaustless joy. We are so used to consider work as a drain upon the strength of the individual—and indeed in our artificial conditions it so often is—that we may not at first appreciate the nature of this fund of social energy.

Let us observe its development, comparing the power at the disposal of a member of society with that of an individual animal. An individual animal is a mechanism adapted to the performance of certain activities, urged thereto by certain stimuli, and governed therein by certain instincts, and, perhaps, concepts. The activities of the animal are limited, of course, by his executive machinery; he has only the tools that grow on him.

These are ingenious and reasonably effective, but their development is slow, requiring many generations of heartless "elimination of the unfit" to gradually evolve the fit. If his claws are not good enough, he dies, those having somewhat better claws survive; slowly the claws improve. He cannot in one lifetime invent and manufacture better claws, but has to be tediously and expensively "selected," the whole beast sacrificed to the defective claw.

Further, his excellence is checked by the interaction of parts,—all his tools being part of him, and modifying each other. The more things he can do, the less perfectly he does them; the more perfectly he does a thing, the fewer things he can do. The beaver, for instance, is a highly developed builder, but he cannot run well, or climb trees. Where you find the most perfect specialisation of an animal's machinery to a particular function, you find the creature practically helpless otherwise—as the ant-eater. So we find the executive capacity of an individual animal limited, first, by his body and its slow methods of adaptation.

His stimuli are also limited. This small machine is kept going by its own supply of nervous energy, replenished by food, sleep, air, and water. It will run so long, and then must rest and be "fired up." Special excitants of fear, pain, or unusual hunger may temporarily accelerate his activity, but he has then to rest the longer. His executive capacity is thus limited, second, by his small nervous energy and narrow range of stimulus.

It is further confined, thirdly, by the narrow circle of his instincts, desires, or ideas, if he has them. The governing impulse is simple race-preservation, mingled with the self-preserving instincts; egoism and familism cover his range of interests. Hope, fear, desire,—all are for self or family.

So we find in the individual animal, his efficiency is limited by (*a*) his personal mechanism, (*b*) his personal nerve force, and (*c*) his personal interests. For such an agent work—continuous expression of energy—would indeed be difficult. But now examine the position of the human being.

Man's tools do not grow on him. He has been able to evolve improved tools without sacrificing a thousand slow generations to breed them. He adds to his executive ability, (*a*) the power of numbers, and of the "relay race" (wild dogs have this), (*b*) the power of division of labour, (ants and bees have this), (*c*) the tool, detachable and exchangeable.

In this comes at once an enormous saving of energy. Where the mole has to spend not only his immediate strength in digging, but his whole racial tendency in being modified to digging, the man with a spade can do far more work in proportion to his strength, and still be able to do other things. The executive efficiency of the man is multiplied, first, by association, again by division of labour, and again by the tool. The tool being not a personal adjunct like the claw, but a separate thing, usable by many, the efficiency is again increased by the exchange of tools. It is multiplied, fourth, by the development of the tool into the machine, and fifth, by the application to the machine of extra-personal power, of the forces of nature direct. Thus where one man alone as a separate naked animal could accomplish something equal to, say 5: as a member of society his efficiency is squared by association = 25; cubed by the division of labour = 125; raised to the fourth power by the tool = 625; to the fifth, by the machine = 3125; and to the sixth, by the use of natural forces = 15,625.

In view of even this much of our human efficiency, the exertion requisite for a human creature to do his share of our human work is so slight in proportion to our wealth of power that it is exquisitely absurd for us to speak of it as an expense of energy. Where an individual animal has to pour out his full stock of strength in hunting his prey, or, if graminivorous, in wandering over great areas after grass; man, collective, can produce and distribute food for a thousand by the specialised services of ten men with machinery. The executive efficiency of humanity is raised to such an enormous height that the spectacle of human beings still spending their personal energy at long hours of exhausting labour is an incredible paradox.

As far as power goes, one human being should be easily able to "pay for his keep" for life in a year's work or less. But we are by no means done with the increase of efficiency. This five-times multiplied enginery of ours would still be comparatively futile, if the governing agent, man, had only the stimuli of the beast. The separate animal has his own supply of cerebral energy. It is something. It enables him to co-ordinate his forces, such as they are, and to undertake extreme exertion when he has to, such as it is. He maintains this energy by breathing, eating, and sleeping. Men can do these things too. Men, as separate animals, have each his own supply of cerebral energy. But Man has more.

Social energy is quite a different thing from individual energy. By as much as the dynamic force of an elephant is greater than that of the elephant's bulk in monads, so is the dynamic force of a society greater than that of the mere sum of its individual constituents,—and more. Social energy has been accumulating in humanity from its birth. It is not only that co-ordinate action allows the transmission of wider waves of force than individual action, but that society in its organic function continually stores force in material products, and so establishes an ever enlarging magazine of power. This is where the social body so aids and furthers the action of the social soul. Each material object, so that it be a normal product, embodies and continually transmits the force that made it.

We are supplied, by virtue of our social relation, with a large complex brain area; the organ of social life. That great life we partake of in using the social body, in the immediately effective tools, utensils, and machines, and necessary material conveniences of life; but even more as we have access to the great social battery, the work of art. A human brain has not only the existent sum of social energy to draw on, but the stored energy of all the past.

The Artist, highly specialised receiver and transmitter, gathers immense waves of force, concentrates and embodies them, and those around and coming after have permanent access to the power that moved him. This is perhaps clearest in the art of literature; where the thought and feeling of all time stand bottled on our shelves, always feeding, never exhausted. In music and painting and sculpture—in all arts—we have forms of the same beautiful social process.

Thus the human brain receives as stimulus such floods of force, such soundless seas of force, that it is practically unlimited. The measure of social stimulus has yet to be found. It passed the using point long ago, and has never stopped growing. The human brain, rightly supplied with social stimulus, is so fed, so fired, so thrilled and filled with energy, that it suffers agony if denied free discharge. That free discharge is social service, the splendid variety and complexity of achievement in which all may find full exercise of this tremendous power, and in that exercise find pride, peace, and joy, express love, satisfy ambition, realise human life.

Thus with our endless multiplication of executive efficiency comes a similarly endless multiplication of stimulus—yet still we hear this prehistoric claim that a man will not exert himself—unless he has to! The point is, that he does have to—by virtue of being human; that it is not so much "exertion" as it is relief. To discharge an overpressure of energy is not "exertion" exactly.

Further yet: the beast, behind his little foot-power engine, with the force furnished by gobbled rabbit or patch of grass, had no governing scheme of life wherewith to direct his small activities, save the basic animal instincts of self-preservation and reproduction—egoism and familism. Man,—Citizen, Patriot, Hero,—man has for governing plan of action, the distinctive instincts of humanity,—the social. The animal will do much for its own life, the mother will do much for her own young; but man will do more for his City, his State, his Country, and his World.

This is not a sentimental claim for what he might do, but a plain historic reference to what he has done. Athenian, Roman, Carthaginian, Frenchman, German, or Englishman—latest of all, American. True, our recognition of social duty has been narrow; consisting principally in "dying for one's country"; but that we have done with splendid heights of heroism, and no beast can do so much.

The bee and ant? Yes, of course, they too are social animals, of very high intelligence. And they, be it noted, have not this shameful fallacy that no one will exert himself "unless he has to," unless he "wants" something. With much of the same collectivism, though sharply limited as we have seen by the predominant femininity, with much of the same specialisation, with a better developed sense of common interest than we have, the ant and bee are types of contented and ceaseless industry. Yet they have to do it all "by hand," they have no extra-personal tools and machinery, they have no horse-power, wind- or water-power, steam power, or electric power. They have no great reservoir of energy in Literature and Art. And they have no wider scheme of life than a sublimated ultra-organised motherhood—everything else is subsidiary to that function.

If humanity were perfectly healthy; if our mechanical efficiency were rightly placed and fully used; if our social energy were accessible to all, and our social instincts freely developed, we should see each young human being coming eagerly forward to do his share of the world's work, not under the action of personal desire—or fear of penalty—but simply *to relieve the pressure*! So irresistible is our growth in this direction that even under all our artificial hindrances, against the combined resistance of religion, tradition, superstition, habit, custom, education, and condition, still the normal child does want to work, tries to work, and in some cases bursts through the whole cordon of opposition and does the work he is made for, though it cost him his life.

We see this conspicuously in the latest and most highly specialised forms of work, as the arts, sciences, and most developed professions. Naturally the more delicately special an organ is the more imperative is its doing its own kind of work, and no other. So we have seen again and again the people we call "great," they having more social energy at command than others, pushing forward over all obstacles to do their particular kind of work, not only without regard to the pay, which they did not get, but without regard to the punishment, which they did get. We have tried to account for this by assuming that the "desire" which actuated them was a desire for fame. We are so sure that it must be a desire of some sort! Why is it so difficult to admit the presence of radiating energy in a live creature? We can see it plainly enough in "mere matter."

Radium does not necessarily want something because it so continually does something.

To feel a lack—to see a desired supply—to exert one's energy to obtain the supply and so cease to lack, is a natural process of action, but not the only one. Organic action differs here from individual action.

The Teacher is an exquisitely developed social functionary, wholly a transmitter, using various arts and sciences to help him, but his own art involving the subtlest psychological skill. When this temperament is charged with most radical truths, when the teaching is a religion,—then we have the great souls who have appeared again and again in history, so charged with social energy that nothing, not difficulty, danger, death itself, could stop them. They would teach and they did teach, to the immense benefit of the society whose unconscious laws evolved them, whose conscious laws destroyed them. The scientific discoverer has too frequently shared the same fate; the inventor, the pioneer in any change, has a hard time. "The Push" in Society is a place of honour, but not an easy one.

Even in the more ordinary kinds of work we occasionally see the strong, clear urgency of a specialised worker toward his special work, and his pleasure in it; an urgency and a pleasure not related to honour or payment, but to the work itself. The reason we see less of the natural impulse to work in the main fields of labour is partly because we have piled our ignorant contempt most particularly on the kind of work we most needed, and partly because we have added to our contempt the heaviest practical difficulties by careful cutting off the general worker from his full share of social nutrition. The rank and file of humanity, as a result of our misconceptions about work, are so drained of nervous energy from generation to generation by being overtaxed in labour, and so defrauded of social nourishment by our system of "payment" based on those misconceptions, that it is marvellous indeed to see the work they do under these conditions, and not marvellous at all to see their steady tendency toward pauperism, criminalism, and all disease.

Of London it is stated that when the labourer from the country comes into the city to work, the second generation of his line is inferior in health, strength, and ability, the third generation much crippled and diseased, and *there is no fourth.*

Under social conditions like these it is not to be expected that we shall find much evidence of man's natural desire to work, either general or special. As well look for willing industry in a hospital. On the contrary, it is to be expected that this body of people shall be unwilling and largely unable to work, that they shall seek continually to avoid work and as continually seek to enlarge their supply of social nourishment so cruelly cut off. It will take several generations of right living to reimburse this part of our social stock and bring them up to the level of social energy required to enjoy work. But when the swift recuperative forces of physiology have rebuilt the individual animal, and the far swifter forces of Sociology have refilled them with their share of our vast resources of strength and inspiration, and their share of the social interest, pride, and love which mark the fully human creature, then we shall find our assumption, "no man will exert himself unless to gratify desire," to lack even its present justification.

There is no pain, no waste, no loss to normal work; it is a free discharge of abundant social energy, either unconscious or accompanied by sensations of keenest pleasure.

Let us consider this Want theory a little further.

A solitary animal cannot get his dinner without exerting himself. If he could, he would not exert himself. This we observe, and then, considering man as an animal like the others, we assume similarly: A man cannot get his dinner without exerting himself; if he could, he would not exert himself. Why we are so anxious to see to it that every man shall exert himself, a thing which evidently cannot concern the public if he is merely getting his own dinner, is a bit puzzling. But on perceiving that unless he exerts himself *we* do not get *our* dinner, our interest is excused.

Let us restate the proposition. Mankind cannot get its dinner without exerting itself. If it could, it would not exert itself.

Granted at once. If agriculture, manufacture, and commerce were not essential to social life, they would not have been evolved. But there is an immediate difference introduced in the "exertion" involved and its causes. Our social nutritive processes being complex and collective, require the elaborate activities of many individuals in lines which bear no relation whatever to their own dinners.

Social evolution, wiser and more practical than we, has met the necessities of the case by developing those organic tendencies in man which urge him to his social activities, and that always-increasing fund of social nutrition and social energy which enables him to do his work. The difference between an architect dreaming great buildings and eager to build them and an animal struggling for his food, is as the difference between the action of the heart and the action of a hungry fox. The fox exerts himself to supply his wants, the heart exerts itself as a functional activity it cannot help and without any reference to its wants.

Its wants are supplied, to be sure, but not in measured dole related to its activities. The exertions of the heart bear relation to the need of the organism to which it belongs, not to its own appetite. If you have to run, your heart works harder; it had no need of extra work, but *you* had, and, being an organ, it performed the work.

Man's work is called for by the social demands. Society needs Commerce, and Commerce is developed. Society needs Art, and Art is developed. But man, being a self-conscious individual, had to be convinced from without as well as urged from within, else he stoutly refused to perform his social service. "Why should I," he asks, "if it does not benefit me? A man works only to get something." Before he had got even this far in formulating his objection to work, he was forced to it, as we have seen, by the slave system and effectually coerced. To meet this later attitude of refusal he was forced to it by the wage system, and effectually coerced as before. In the first case the anti-social results of that form of labour have led to its being discarded, and in the second case we are rapidly approaching the same conclusion. Social service performed under the persuasion of self-interest is accompanied by so many deleterious and anti-social phenomena that it is high time we adopted a wiser system.

When exertion is recognised as a racial necessity and a high individual pleasure, there is no longer any weight to the first clause of the Want theory. When it is shown that our desires are gratified by the exertion of others exclusively, there is no longer any weight to the second. And when it is shown that the required "exertion" is not an exertion at all, but a relief, a mere letting off of the social steam pressure, the Want theory begins to need a historian to explain it. The only really confusing element lies in the system of exchange now in use, the wage system, and will be taken up in the chapter on Distribution.

X: THE NATURE OF WORK (II)

SUMMARY

Life a verb. Vegetable life processes, animal and social. Work is human life. A sick society. Transmission of energy, pleasure in collective sensation. Pleasure in specific function. Pain of malposition and mal-nutrition. Recapitulation. Work is making, not taking. Squaw and hunter. Maternal energy. Bee. The motherised male. Short circuit of individual action. Production of food. Common defence. The social base and ensuing variation. Attendant evils. Personal consequences and social. Social treason. Sin of common carriers. Contrast between effect of industry and war. Agriculture and peace. Commerce and honesty and justice. Work is altruistic. Steps of development. Female origin of Work. True Human Work has no sex connotation. Male belligerence in industry. The world and the home. Thief and pauper. Production collective. The Social traitor. Work is giving out, not taking in. Slavery an essential transition system, also wagery. Master, Employer, Co-operator. Shame of work based on slavery and self-interest. Social productivity has allowed disease. American attitude toward work. Conservation of energy. Work must not waste force, organic action does not. Accumulated energy must be discharged. Social energy enormous. Normal work an easy discharge. Abnormal work injurious. Social evolution in ease and happiness. Effect of false concepts. Child's delight in work. Organic action agreeable or unconscious. Conditions of normal work.

CHAPTER X

THE NATURE OF WORK (II)

Life is a verb, not a noun. Life is living, living is doing, life is that which is done by the organism.

The living of a tree consists in the action of the roots in obtaining food; of the leaves in obtaining air; of the sap in circulating, distributing these goods; and in the processes of reproduction. The life of an animal is more complex. He has a somewhat similar internal mechanism; he breathes, circulates, and reproduces; but with him the fumbling root-tip has become a paw, a mouth, a whole group of related members wherewith to meet his needs; he has more to do to find his food than just to poke in the dark. Living, for an animal, involves many interesting activities, and those activities are his life.

The life of Society is higher and wider yet. Here are the separate animal constituents whose life processes must be kept going, and here are the wholly new social life processes to be carried on. Human life involves the performance of the complex social life processes. The plant has poking, absorbing, circulating, breathing, and reproducing to do. That is plant life. The animal similarly circulates, breathes, and reproduces, but he "pokes" in a much more elaborate manner, developing also new methods of offence and defence in maintaining these essential functions. That is animal life. Man, as an animal, breathes, circulates, and reproduces in humble pursuance of previous methods, but as a social being not only has his nutritive process become of enormous organic complexity, but there have appeared also vast and subtle developments of special functions hitherto unknown: industry, trade, commerce, art, science, education, government,—all that we call Work.

In this development is human life. I do not mean that it is essential to human life, it is human life. If the gathering and circulating of nutrition, the absorption of air, the blossoming and fruition of a tree are "essential to the tree's life," pray, what remains as "the life" of the tree to which they are essential? You may truly say that breathing, circulating, and reproducing are "essential" to an animal's life; that life, as distinct from other lives, being the more special activities he has developed. So with the human creature. It is essential to his animal life that he breathe, circulate, and reproduce; it is essential to his human life also that he perform enough varied physical activity to keep him in good form; but it is his human life to be "doctor, lawyer, merchant, chief," or whatever is his department in the social economy.

Work is human life.

Thus, as health, happiness, and beauty are found in lower forms in perfect performance of their simpler life processes, so in Society we find health, happiness, and beauty in proportion to our performance of these our life processes; a greater, far greater health, happiness, and beauty in the magnificent spread and range of these processes; a far more terrible record of disease, misery, and horrid ugliness as we fail of fulfilment.

A defective, sick, or dead plant is an unpleasant sight. A defective, sick, or dead animal is a more unpleasant sight. But the depth and ramifications of misery and horror in a defective, sick, or dead society,—this is what has made us call this fair world "a vale of tears."

Such a pity, too! When it could be just as healthy as a plant or animal! It is far more fun to be an animal than a plant, more exertion and so more pleasure. And it is far more fun to be a human being than a mere individual animal, far more complicated exertion and so more pleasure. With our vastly increased capacity for happiness our misery must be accounted for by "failure to connect" with the universal energy in one or both ways. We are denied our share of stimulus, we lack social nourishment, or, worse, we are denied our right discharge, are not rightly placed in the field of social action, are not doing the work which belongs to us.

It should be noted here that the happiness of social action as beyond that of individual action increases in proportion to its collectivity. There is a larger joy in perfect "team-work" than in the best individual play. Connected as we are, the sensation that thrills through the whole audience is stronger far than what is felt by one man alone, like King Ludwig of Bavaria in the empty auditorium.

If a man is rightly placed in the world's work, doing what he is best fitted for to the height of his best powers, and if he clearly sees that by so doing he fills his place in the universal economy perfectly, then, granting of course that he is properly nourished physically and socially, he is happy. But if he is ill-nourished he is unhappy, not power enough flowing in; if he is ill-placed in social service he is unhappy, lacking right lines of discharge, his energy banking up and pushing against right doors that don't open, and moving very slack through wrong doors that do. Moreover, though well-nourished and well-placed, if he is hag-ridden by some ancient lie about work being a curse, a disgrace, or some such idiocy, then he is unhappy because his own mind, clogged and twisted, turns on cross-currents of pressure that spoil the smooth flow of energy.

To recapitulate:

Life is action.

Action is conscious discharge of energy.

Discharge of energy is pleasure in proportion to amount, complexity, and freedom of delivery.

Social action involves greatest amount and complexity, and so, with free delivery, greatest pleasure. Our free delivery is checked by wrong conditions and wrong concepts.

By altering the concepts we can alter conditions and so make social action normal.

Work is social action.

It is the expression of social energy for social use.

It is essentially collective, and we find work most highly developed among most collective creatures, as the ant, the bee, the man.

It involves a higher degree of intelligence than the preceding processes. All the efforts of animals to take food are excito-motory, and either egoistic or, at most, familistic. They are hungry, they desire something, and they go to get it, performing whatever actions have become necessary in the pursuit. But work is the process of making, not of taking. It is not excito-motory, but the result of cerebral action.

The humble squaw who drops corn in her stick-ploughed field is actuated by a concept, a knowledge of how in time there will be fruit for her children. There is no present stimulus, she pushes herself, urged by the accumulating nerve force of the larger brain. Her lord, the noble Red-man, gallantly pursuing the buffalo, is acting merely as an animal, under direct stimulus of hunger and the visible beast before him. Being hungry, he hunts. Being fed, he does nothing. He can only act in the lower circuit of excito-motory nerves. But she, not hungry, makes the corn grow. She makes the tent. She makes the moccasins and leggings and beaded belt. She makes the dish and basket. She, first on earth, works, and she works for others.

First, it was only this mother energy, producing for its young; the same power which finds its apotheosis in the sublime matriarchate of the bee. Work was primarily an extension of the maternal function; and, carried to excess, results in that ultra-perfection of specialised maternity, the ever-bearing queen-mother, the ever-toiling worker-mother, and the contemptible, well-nigh useless, barely tolerated, and soon slaughtered drone-father. But human work was saved this hopeless limitation of maternity by being forced upon the male, and by him specialised and distributed. To work and save is feminine, tending to the swollen hive, the sacrificed male. We still see this tendency among us in that long-aborted social rudiment, the home. But man, assuming the industrial function, applied to it his disseminating energy, spread, scattered, specialised, and so made possible our social life. If the bees had been led to our great economic manœuvre, the motherising of the male, they might be more than hymenoptera to-day.

Work, as an ever-elaborating discharge of energy, tends to develop under laws of inertia, like all natural processes. The "tendency to vary" in action is checked in the short circuit of individual animal activities by the immediate consequence of his own variation to the individual. This wonderful new step of ours, the production of food, gave us a new base for variation. A low grade of effort, by a few persons, kept us fed, alive. Our early specialisation in social defence kept us protected, alive. Being thus assured of life, though not on the basis of individual exertion, we acquired time to manifest new activities.

Here is one of the great keys to "the mystery of human life," no more a mystery than any of nature's laws, when you know it. A social life is assured by the basic industry, agriculture, and some degree of trade and commerce. Then the energy no longer required by each man for each day's living can be given to invention, discovery, experiment. So follows all the immensity of our growth.

The social base being absolutely firm, and requiring less and less social energy as our agricultural and commercial processes improve, we grow in arithmetical progression—or in geometrical rather—as our increase in production and distribution multiplies our ability and our increase in ability multiplies our production and distribution. This assured base and wide room for variation is necessary to society in developing its higher functions. We can afford to feed and guard for several generations the slow-maturing genius, which, when it reaches the productive point, will richly benefit us all. We can give more rest and freedom to our members than any self-fed and self-guarded beast could dream of.

A thousand delicate and beautiful specialties are allowed to grow by our broad sure social base of supplies. So far we have seen this in conscious action only where a government has encouraged certain arts or sciences, or where an established church or endowed university has bred its kind of specialty, or again where some individual has contrived to enlarge his own "social base" enormously, and "varies" as he will, but we see its converse commonly enough where the individual is not allowed any hold on the social base, but kept at the self-feeding stage in development, thus effectually checking his "tendency to vary."

Every advantage has its possible attendant evils, and Society offers a wide field for such. In the point we are treating, the evils are painfully prominent. As soon as we left the self-supplying stage, a man's sins were no longer visited immediately on his own head. An animal gains or loses by his own behaviour. A man gains or loses by his society's behaviour. In his assured position as a member of society a man can be wickeder and more foolish than is possible in any self-supported life, and he has taken advantage of his opportunities with great facility and zeal.

The peculiar treason involved in a social being's offences we have not yet grown to recognise. It is as if your own teeth turned and gnawed you. Only a beneficent society could allow the growth of these powerful beings, and with that social power they sin against society.

As conspicuous an instance as can be given of this kind of sin is in the action of our misguided common carriers. Here is a function so glaringly social that one marvels at the power of the human brain in forcibly regarding it as a private business. On public land granted by the public, with rights and franchises granted by the public, with money subscribed by the public, and with elaborately co-ordinated labour performed by the public, this form of public service is established. Then one man, or group of men, is allowed to "own" this great piece of social machinery, and proceeds to administer it, not with regard to the public advantage, but with regard to the advantage of this managing group and of that small minority of the public who furnished the money for the enterprise.

Of course this could not be done if the social body as a whole recognised the organic character of its own processes, but, owing to the prevalence of our ancient ego concept and its derivatives, the poor social body says, "Of course; why should the arteries carry blood except to feed themselves, it is their business!" Against this evil comes the growing altruism of work, founded in mother love, in the anti-selfish instinct of reproduction; work, which, as it develops, carries with it an ever-developing good will.

Watch this in history. See the two forces as they affect society. See the primitive labour of the squaw holding the village together, the village which is the tiny seed of the state, while against it push the belligerent rivalries of the male. See the instinct to fight and to take, finding larger expression in organised warfare, constantly destroying the young societies which industry was building up, both in warring with one another and in the internal effects of the same misplaced instincts.

Here is productive industry steadily adding to the wealth of the world and developing distributive industry as inevitably as an overflowing spring makes a stream. And here are these destructive tendencies, with the primitive desire to get for one's self, to get away from someone else, not only refusing to assist in industry, not only dishonourably living on its products, but so scorning and maltreating the real agents of social growth as to repeatedly destroy the societies that harboured them.

In the development of industry have grown the altruistic tendencies of mankind. Working together bred the social consciousness as surely as our physical organic relation bred our bodily consciousness. Peace, good will, mutual helpfulness are part and parcel of normal industrial growth. It is somewhat difficult to disentangle one current of social phenomena from the many crossing ones, some combining and some conflicting, but whenever any one trade can be studied in its effect on a group, certain associative psychic qualities are always found with it, and the general industrial progress of the world is accompanied by as general progress in social consciousness and the social virtues.

Agriculture brings us at least peace, an essential condition of its continuance. Trade brought the concept of justice, the market-place and its customs and its disputes evoking the early prototypes of our great courts of law, and extended peace. Commerce widened both still further.

The evils we commonly attribute to business life belong to the continued survival in it of anti-industrial instincts, not to the industrial ones at all. Where an individual enters the generous, munificent, kindly field of human industry with the equipment of a beast or savage, merely to get for himself all that he can, great evil results; but the same evil is found unbroken in preindustrial times.

Of its own nature work is altruistic. The more generally industrial a society is the more we find the higher social feelings developed. But the instincts of the pre-human beast, the powerful and ingenious self-feeder, still find expression, and the more so as society becomes more finely organised. Thief catches thief very promptly where all are thieves by profession and there is little to steal! But a large, sensitive, finely organised society offers splendid opportunities to these mischievous left-overs of ancient times.

The first step is mother labour, the next, slave labour, so up through serfdom to contract, to our present system of wage labour. The last step, one we are but just learning, most of us, though some entered upon it long ago, is man working for mankind; not under any primitive coercion, but from the action of social forces as natural as breathing. For whom should he work? What "market" is worth his highly specialised ability but this? Can he make bricks or compose dramas solely for his own family?

To associate in the complex discharge of our vast energies, and to be amply nourished by their countless products, is Social Life. It is true that work is essentially feminine in its origin, but not permanently. As it develops it frees itself wholly from sex limitations and becomes a social function in which men and women take part as members of society. "Women's work" in one stage of our life meant every kind of work. "Man's work" is now generally supposed to include the harder and rougher, the higher and more difficult. There is no real foundation for either term. Either sex can do either kind. Work, modern work, has no sex connotation whatever. Moreover, modern science has shown that the female, instead of being inferior, is, if anything, the more important of the sexes.

In no way need the association of women with work degrade either. A highly entertaining contortion of popular thought is seen in our local and temporary idea that women ought not to work! We have bred in certain classes a sort of parasitic female, most painfully aborted. It is more agonising and more ridiculous for a woman not to work than for a man, because of her initial sex-tendency and her historic habits; but we have bred this pitiful enormity and admire it as a Chinaman admires the "golden lilies" on his wife's shrunk shanks. But this absurdity is already passing.

One of the effects of sex-distinction, falsely and needlessly associated with work, is seen in the general fighting attitude of the male towards labour. In current literature and current life we continually hear man's economic activities described as a struggle—a battle—with some vague opponent called "the world." He is described as "going out" ("out" meaning elsewhere than at home, the assumption being that he would prefer to be "in" all the time!) "to battle with the world for his wife and little ones."

Katherine, the reformed shrew, makes an eloquent description of this prowess of the husband. This is held to be a noble effort on his part, and quite his place as a man, while if she, owing to loss of male provider, is obliged to go "out" to "battle" similarly, that is held to be unfeminine and a real misfortune.

The word "out" in this connection we should dismiss completely from our foggy minds. We are *in* the world once and for all. We are not planted in a lot of private holes, with the rest of the broad earth for a mere battlefield, a place to sally forth into and grab something. Can you conceive of a world of human beings contentedly staying at home all the time if their supposititious booty could be handed in at the door without "battle"? We don't go "out," we go "in" to the world for our natural and necessary activities, without which we should cease to be human.

What we do in the world is not, or should not be, fighting. Those who insist on fighting instead of working should be promptly locked up and taught better; they disturb the peace, interfere with legitimate industry, and dishonestly run off with the products of other people's labour.

An oversexed male, full of belligerence, actuated by his primitive masculine tendency to scatter and destroy instead of the later-developed, feminine-based race-tendency to construct, goes forth like a savage to hunt and fight. He finds what he wants, someone else has made it, and he seeks to get it away from that person by exercising the same traits as those used by any hunting animal, force or fraud. We have an immense number of predatory individual animals, both male and female, all included and maintained by the social organism, yet merely feeding on its tissues; we have a still greater number, indeed the vast majority of our workers, who, though in reality engaged in productive labour, imagine that their business is to get something from other people, and so strive to restrict their output and enlarge their intake as far as possible.

The plain thief and pauper we recognise as social parasites, active and passive, and seek to remove; but our frank, general attitude of parasitism and predacity we do not recognise as an evil, the evil which necessarily tends to these ultimate forms. An individual animal has no productive power and skill, he simply takes what he wants when he finds it, if he can, and cheats, fights, or kills to get it. The collective animal produces wealth by co-ordinate labour. There is no faintest element of combat involved in the economic processes of society. The only "competition" legitimate in social life is the beneficent competition between constantly improving methods of service. For any collective animal to take advantage of his safe place in the broad-based social life, and from that vantage-point to take what he can from the social product without himself producing anything, is a treason so colossal as quite to paralyse our moral judgment.

Our little egoistic scheme of ethics, while it is big enough to grasp and blame an interpersonal fraud or theft, is incapable of comprehending this great field of social injury; and, if the social traitor keeps up the personal ethical standards we are acquainted with, we do not condemn his larger sin,—we don't know how.

Here it is simply indicated that the initial error lies in looking at the world as a place to go out to and get things from by any necessary means, whereas in plain fact it is a place to go into and give things to—to labour in, to create in, to produce and distribute in, to exercise those social faculties which constitute our human life.

To work is to make something or distribute something; it has nothing to do with taking or fighting. The fighting and grabbing attitude comes from primitive animal egoism, a low rudimentary condition, and the morbid overplus of sex-energy in the male. The association of shame with work on account of the slave will pass when we see the orderly progression of human association and the place held in it by that early social functionary.

The Social organism requires a close and permanent connection between its myriad constituents. These constituents first began to combine sporadically, on lines of natural attraction, as in the family, and through the woman's industry. For men to be drawn into the social relation,—men, whose whole nature was individual and combative, whose whole idea of exertion was to fight something,—

required force. Only on pain of death, as the unkilled captive, did the slave learn to work, to apply his energy to the service of others. Most of the conscious associations of slavery were unpleasant, slavery and work were held as identical, and the slave hates work as he hates slavery. But they are not identical. Slavery is a transient, superficial relation, one of our telic processes, useful in its place, but soon outgrown. Work is a permanent, essential relation, a genetic social process increasing with our growth.

Men were first held together in exchange of labour by the force of the slave system as they are now held together in exchange of labour by the force of the contract system, an equally transient and superficial device. The real economic process going on is the gradual evolution of highly specialised and smoothly interrelated workers, with an abundant, easy circulation of their products, and the more arbitrary methods of developing this condition came first as more arbitrary political methods came first. The Owner was a primitive despot, the Employer is a constitutional monarch, and democracy is now working out a higher, subtler, freer relation—that of the true Co-operator—in economics as in politics.

The shame feeling, based on woman and slave, grew, rather than relaxed, in the period of serfdom. In fatuous ignorance of the source of their wealth and power, the fighting and governing class despised the hand that fed them, and the ancestral accumulation of this ungrateful idiocy gives us our ingrained contempt for "labour," "trade," "the working classes."

The workers themselves, equally ignorant, though more excusably, accepted this feeling as correct, and strove to escape singly from the only honourable position on earth, that of Maker, Doer, Giver, to the supposed dignity of a Social Parasite. "The Theory of the Leisure Class" has been most luminously expounded by Veblen, but there is room for much more study in "the theory of the working class," the glorious, irresistible, upward pressure of which, by its accumulating superfluity of rich product, has, besides all its good effects, made possible the morbid secretions and deleterious growths of society, the indolent ulcer of idle wealth, the waste of tissue in extreme poverty, the wide range of diseases, disgusting and terrible, with which Society is hampered in its economic processes.

This feeling of contempt for work, shame in work, once recognised as one of our evil inheritances from the black past, we should set ourselves to check and dismiss it as rapidly as possible. In the individual by consciously rebutting the old feeling and cultivating its opposite one of honour and pride, and in the race by an instant and thorough change in the education of children, through home, school, and church, book, picture, and story. It is gratifying to note that America is already far ahead of any other nation in its honour of work, and that even the woman-parasite, as well as the leisure-class parasite, is feeling it in this liveliest of societies.

Our aversion to work as being an expense of energy is quite right. Human work, as we have seen in the last chapter, should not constitute a draught on individual energy. When it does so there is something wrong. As in our constant analogy, the physical organism, we may be sure that when it is an effort to breathe something is wrong with one's lungs.

Our personal fund of energy is strictly limited, and nature's processes tend to save it—the law of conservation of energy. Very slowly and gradually has been accumulated in us our private storage battery of nerve force, with its stock of arrested energy and its power to turn it on when necessary to modify action. This supply of energy is limited. This we must not waste, it is the hoarded wealth of all organic time.

This is the precious capital which nature subtly saves by rapidly making each action into a function, passing it over from the class requiring cerebral force, volition, to the class of unconscious, habitual action, where the energy of the universe flows through the smoothly attuned organism and costs it nothing. Any new conscious action costs us an expense of our own personal and private supply of energy, and that expense is what we instinctively recognise as wrong. The organism feels that it is being robbed of its most precious store, and resents it with every conscious atom. This is what makes us hate to work, at the same time defining work as "what you don't like to do."

Against this we clearly see the passive pleasure of a long-accustomed activity, the well-nigh unconscious discharge of energy along well-worn lines; and the active pleasure, the delight of doing what one likes to do.

Detach from work the false ideas which make it distasteful to us and there remains but one thing to blind us to its joy and glory: the waste of cerebral energy with which it is but too generally accompanied.

We have already seen that the accumulation and discharge of energy is precisely what an organism is for; it is an elaborate instrument slowly developed for that purpose, as a steam engine is made to "get up" and "let off" steam. A steam engine fired up and superheated, but doing nothing, must let off steam or burst. So a human engine, fired with all our splendid fund of social energy, must either work it off, let it off in mere fizz and whistle, or burst. Our leisure class—most copiously fired and fed and stoutly refusing to work—fill all the air about them with futile sizzlings and noises. They have to, or burst.

Normal work, *i. e.*, that special social function for which the individual is specially fitted, requires but little energy to learn to do, because he likes to do it, and, once learned, runs easily for life, the pleasure steadily increasing with the power and skill. Abnormal work, for which the individual is not fitted, is a suicidal waste of energy, and we are right to hate it. It costs immense draughts on one's vitality to learn to do what one does not like, an unremitting pressure of cerebral energy, a veritable hemorrhage of what is as much life as blood is; and even when the relief of habit is attained it does not grow into joy, for the creature is crippled in the dreadful process. A man may learn to walk on his hands and feed himself with his toes, but he will not enjoy it much.

The advantage of organic life is in its specialisation. Specialisation to one thing involves lack of power to do others. We do not ask a tooth to see, or an eye to grind corn. So the whole majestic advantage of human life lies in its organic relation, in its specialised, interdependent service, each for all and all for each. This is attained by means of a subtle differentiation of individuals, developing from generation to generation a rising fund of power, of skill, of joy in execution. In this differentiation comes at once the most benefit to society through the product and the most benefit to the individual through the process of making it—the work. Without it, in any arbitrary forcing of individuals to do this or that for which they are not fitted, which, therefore, they do not like, we find the main condition of social waste and individual suffering.

The laws of social evolution, acting unconsciously through us, tend to evolve a highly specialised, intricate, organic life-form, rich, powerful, boundlessly happy. Our conscious external laws and customs, our government by "the dead hand," our insane reverence for mummies, tend to check, thwart, and pervert this orderly growth. We try to preserve the "all-around man," which is as if we tried to preserve active monads in our bodily structure.

We try to force people to do what they do not like, we boast of our palæozoic educational system that it trains the child to do what he does not like, as if to like one's work were criminal! Blinded and confused by inherited falsehoods; kept back in specialisation by our mistaken education; arbitrarily misplaced by superficial conditions; and driven, on pain of death, by our system of artificially distributed nutrition (not merely "no work, no pay," but "*This* kind of work whether you like it or not, or no pay!"), the majority of human beings are not doing normal work. What they do hurts them; they do it under pressure of necessity; and they are quite right in assuming that without that pressure they would not work—that way! But this theory falls to the ground when the false conditions are removed. A free discharge of energy—the limitless energy of the universe through our intricate machine—is pleasure, not pain. It does not overdraw on our little store, but rather augments it. We are stronger instead of weaker for right exercise of power.

Every healthy child delights in work, to watch it, imitate it, take part in it. Every healthily placed man delights in his work, the man who is doing what he is particularly built to do—what we call a "born doctor" or a "born engineer." "*Poeta nascitur, non fit*"—yes, and operator as well as *poeta*.

Social evolution is natural, and natural organic processes are easy and agreeable, unconscious if they require no cerebral attention, and, if they do, attended with sensations of pleasure. Granting, as we have done, that waste of energy is an evil, and any overdraught on our reserve fund of cerebral energy is naturally resented by the organism, it is still maintained that normal human work does not involve any waste of energy or any draught on the cerebral reserve more than is pleasant to expend, and results in increase rather than diminishing of that store.

The conditions of normal work are these: First, the individual should be well stocked. A sick man cannot enjoy work, a crippled, deformed person is not fitted to work, and a congenital pauper, one born without that inheritance of nervous energy which should increase with each generation, is unable to work with pleasure. But given, first, a normal individual, he should, second, work at what he likes best. This means social specialisation, and requires for its right development such education and opportunity as shall bring out all possible differentiation of faculty. So widely lacking are these conditions, so hampered is our choice of work, and so undeveloped our power of choosing, that we look with honest envy at the man who does love his work and can do the work he loves, like Agassiz or Lord Kelvin.

In normal social conditions every man would do the work he loved and love the work he did, so life and happiness would become synonymous.

XI: SPECIALISATION

SUMMARY

Organisation means specialisation. Military organisation, trades-unions, and trusts. Guerilla bands in industrial organisation. Unspecialised primitive life, the higher the life-form the more specialisation. The "all-around" savage. Injury of our present specialisation under false conditions. Waste of energy. Man of thirty who died of old age. Canoe and steamer. Effect of errors. Normal conditions of specialisation: shorter hours, variety of work, wide education. Ownership in collective production. Specialisation should increase product and decrease effort; it does, but the advantage is misplaced. Hours of labour in proportion to interest. Especial cruelty in our conditions of specialisation. Specialisation proves collectivity. Absurdity of "self-support" idea. Our progress due to such social distribution as we have, not to "self-support." Society feeding on itself. The Social sacrifice. "Unskilled labour" a product of high social development. Our mistaken attitude toward it. The real nature of it. Serf and noble. Savage's exciting monologue. Unskilled labour does not require inferior men. Line of social growth. Highly specialised work involves extremely simple details. Our misuse of above fact owing to false concepts. Unskilled labour is high social service. We punish instead of paying, or promoting. Height of ingratitude.

CHAPTER XI

SPECIALISATION

Human work being an organic process, it must of course specialise. Those who cry out against specialisation and seek to uphold a mythical "all-around man" are ignorant of the nature of social functions. The very first condition of organic life is division of labour, and as the organism develops the complexity of that division develops with it. The strength and efficiency of any organism depends not so much on its bulk and weight as on the prompt and perfect co-ordination of its parts.

This is a truism in military organisation, which is an old game with us, but we do not seem to understand it in industrial organisation, which is a new one. In the military body we have long ago learned to consider the whole before the part and the purpose of that whole as a measure of action for each part, but in the economic body we are yet a mob of savages. The ego concept is perforce set aside in military life; in economic life it still rules. In military ethics one never hears that "self-preservation is the first law of nature"; no soldier thinks of justifying rank cowardice and insubordination with the plea that "a man must live!" Neither is there any objection to the widest specialisation, to careful grading of officers, to the complete separation of surgeon and chaplain, engineer and commissary. No one seeks to maintain the "all-around man" in the army.

Military organisation is our oldest and so best developed form. Its purpose is crude and easy of perception; its impulses are inherent in the masculine nature; its methods, like those of old-established churches, appeal to the primitive instincts. The gorgeous ritual of military form has much to do with our allegiance to it. But in the now far more important co-ordination of industrial forces no such progress is made. In place of splendid uniforms we have the soiled and soul-depressing garments of our miscellaneous workers. Instead of *"esprit du corps"* we have the beautiful spirit of "every man for himself, and the devil take the hindmost."

Instead of "glory" we have before us only "booty"; instead of "honour" we have the incessant struggle of the civil law to check the ceaseless manœuvring of dishonesty. And in place of one resistless organisation we have at best the progress of the trades-unions and at worst those guerilla bands, the small, fierce hordes of warring trusts, fighting each other and preying on all of us.

The inevitable increase of specialisation has gone on, but under the disadvantage of this crude position it has carried with it a wholly unnecessary burden of evil. Specialisation in labour starts at the very beginning of our growth, at first being only an arrangement of whole men, each man making a whole thing.

To this stage of social evolution some are now wishing to revert—a sad waste of wishing! We might as well wish to be invertebrates again as to sigh for past periods of social development.

The lower the creature the less its organic specialisation. There are some so indeterminate and undivided that they do not know their heads from their tails; cut them in two and they promptly produce a new head and a new tail and go about their business as before. This beast is a fine example for the "all-around man."

The higher the creature the more specialised. The more worthily a part fulfils one function the less worthily it can fulfil others. When the paw becomes a hand it ceases to be a paw. The more fit the hand for a hand's use the less fit for a foot's use. It would in no way benefit the body to have a set of loose, interchangeable organs capable of doing a little of everything and nothing very well. An "all-around" organ would not be as valuable as any single-hearted servant that gives its one regular contribution to the body's good.

So in the social organism, our line of progress has been from the "all-around" savage to the absolutely one-sided activity of the specialised workman who contributes his best efforts to one line of service. "To learn to do one thing and do it well" is what makes the great artist, the great scientist, the great preacher, the great mechanic, the great electrician. Social service requires the steadily increasing specialisation of its constituents.

When you want a dentist you want to find him in his office, with the accumulated skill of long study and constant practice; you do not want to wait for him to come in from the plough and wash his hands. All this we know well enough, and yet we recognise the injurious effects *to the individual* of the kind of specialisation we see about us, and have not yet been able to reconcile the two.

If the individual is injured there must be evil somewhere, that is quite true. No society can prosper at the expense of its constituents. If the individual is reduced in physical strength and health, in personal happiness, or in the best social usefulness by his work, the process he is engaged in must be abnormal. Now let us see whether the evils so conspicuous in the lives of our highly specialised workers to-day are inherent in their degree of specialisation, or whether they are coincident rather than consequent and due to quite other causes.

What is it that injures the man who turns a crank all day? It is an evil both of omission and commission, involving a waste of cerebral energy in compelling the attention of the human brain to a point of execution so narrow and uninteresting, and also the lack of development involved in doing nothing else. To forcibly focus the attention on a detail for a long time is a ruinous expense of nerve force, and it is this which makes the employment of children in such work so doubly damnable. To concentrate and hold attention is not natural to childhood; that is why they fail to do it and are so frequently killed and injured by their machines. Accidents to working children happen mostly toward the end of the day's work, as they grow more unequal to the unnatural strain.

And when the child does prematurely muster all his powers and display as a child the concentration of a man, he is thereby ruined for life, prematurely aged, a wasted and broken thing before he is grown. In the work of the Chicago Settlements a case was found where an honest, industrious man of thirty broke down and died, and the doctor's verdict was that *he died of old age*; every part of him was used up by excessive labour from early childhood. It is bad enough for the adult. The paralysing effects of twelve hours' repetition of some one small mechanical effort is painfully clear to any observer.

Does it follow, therefore, that we must discontinue the machine and go back to the period where "one man makes one thing," the ideal of our well-meaning reversionists? Is it so much more noble for one man to make one canoe than for a thousand men to make an ocean steamer? Must we go without the ocean steamer and go back to the canoe period of civilisation because it is better to be an all-around savage than a man who makes rivets by machinery? Is there no way of saving the individual life of the rivet-maker without "giving up the ship"?

Assuredly there is. The evil effects of this complex, modern work do not lie in its complexity, or its delicate mechanical accuracy, but may be traced straight to the door of our existing economic fallacies and errors; to the overwork and underpay and general evil conditions based on those errors.

Approach the blissful savage making his own canoe and hire him at a minimum wage to make canoes for you all day and every day for the weary years of a short, worn-out life; the fact that he made a whole thing would not suffice to make him happy or develop that so desirable globularity. If the riveter took the same interest in his steamer that the savage did in his canoe, and worked no longer at his riveting than the savage at his cutting and sewing, his fractional production of an enormous common engine for common good would give him more pleasure than the savage's unitary production of a tiny private engine for private good.

The natural conditions of social specialisation are these: In proportion to the degree of specialisation the time of work should be shortened and the interest of the worker extended.

It does not hurt the human mind—a strong, healthy, well-developed mind—to make rivets for a little while.

"Ah, but," you will reply, "if the riveter only worked a little while he could not earn enough to live on."

Here is where our economic fallacies come in. The man with the machine can turn out as many rivets in an hour as the man working by hand could in a day. Therefore his hour's work is equal to what was a day's work. That is the value of machinery. It gives more wealth for less effort, the maximum product with the minimum expense of nerve force and of time. Every step of our elaborate mechanical specialisation should have relieved the worker of more and more hours of labour and set that much time and strength free for other use.

The infinite multiplication of wealth by machinery meets its own problem of overspecialisation. Here are a hundred men, making cloth alone on a hundred hand looms, and earning thereby a dollar a day each—one hundred dollars. Here are these hundred men organised, specialised; ten of them run machine looms, turning out cloth tenfold, equal to a thousand dollars a day. Other ten, specialised, run the mill and its business; twenty of them with machines earning ten times what the hundred did, or forty of them working half a day each, or eighty of them working quarter of a day.

The earning power of the man plus the machine is so enormously multiplied that he is richly able to take the needed rest and variety of exercise which will enable him to do his wearing work without injury, and at the same time give society the benefit of the extreme specialisation.

"But—but," cries the offended reader, "the man does not own the machine! he did own the loom. It takes capital to run a mill, and capital has to be paid!"

The question of property rights comes in later, in Chapter XV. This is all a question of men, of human beings, and how they best work together, doing the most for Society with the least injury to themselves. This chapter is not taking up the question of capital nor of property, but simply seeking to show that specialisation, as such, need not injure the worker, because the very nature of specialisation is to reduce man's work. Why we have also made it reduce man's pay is not so easily explained. That the greatest multiplier of wealth should impoverish the producer surely indicates some defect in our methods.

Specialisation perfects and multiplies production, and reduces effort. This inevitably increases wealth and leisure. If the wealth and leisure are monopolised in one quarter and the contributory specialist is sacrificed in the process, it does not prove the specialisation to be wrong, but the distribution of result; and that we will take up in the chapter on Distribution. Meanwhile the law of specialisation goes on and gives us social servants more and more exquisitely adapted to some one function. With normal economic conditions they would take full share in the resultant social gain, and be quite free to combat the possible ill effects of their position.

The shortening of hours allows of another quite simple and natural effect. Where work is so broad and general as to require a whole man's whole working time, as of the teacher, artist, or large manager in any industry, it is thereby so interesting that a man can give his whole time to it without belittling effects. ("Whole working time" need not be more than four to six hours, even at our stage of mechanical evolution.)

Where work is so narrow and fractional as not to interest a man for his whole time, it is therefore so specialised that he need not give his whole time to it.

The simple turning of a crank for an hour wearies the brain equal to larger effort, but does not forbid that brain some other labour. If the specialty is one of exquisite subtlety of particular skill, as with those girls in the Treasury who test banknotes by touch, no other labour should be entered upon which would tend to blur or weaken that skill, only rest and recreation.

A properly educated human creature, in full touch with the whole great working world, can support his or her own concentrated effort by virtue of conscious connection with the whole, can see the ship in the rivet. Well nourished socially, keenly alive to our gain, our progress, and to the relative value of his own department of service and his own share in it, not looking at the work as his, done for his pay, but as ours and done for our benefit, the normal human being can not only sustain extreme specialisation, but glory in it.

Our especial cruelty in this regard is that we condemn to exhausting hours of extreme specialisation the very people least fitted to bear it, the ill-nourished physically and socially, the uneducated, the dull and dark of mind. Or, conversely, we deprive our extremely specialised social servants of exactly those things by which alone they can sustain the demands of that service.

A man with widespread, active social consciousness, in full contact and exchange with all parts of the great body to which he belongs, will not suffer from its concentrated and exclusive service, but will take glad part in forming an "all-round" Society.

One would think that specialisation in labour ought to have forced upon every observer long ages since the fact that human work is something done for others. The shepherd and fisherman, first stage above savagery, may live upon the fruit of their labours; and so, in part, may the farmer, first stage of really civilised growth. They exchange the surplus, but they do directly consume part of what passes through their hands.

But the specialised workman, whether he carry a spade or a hod, swing an axe or hold a lever, is so obviously doing it for thousands of unknown other people that his position under the ego concept becomes miraculously difficult. He holds it, though, and, what is perhaps even more miraculous, so do we! So does the general consumer, whose life is maintained by the service of thousands of fellow beings,—who is housed by them, clothed by them, carried by them, guarded by them, taught by them,—still have the incredible face to maintain that these people who keep him alive are working for themselves!

Harder than steel must be the cell walls of the brain that can live in such complex social relation as ours to-day and maintain that he or anyone else "takes care of himself." The error dates back in essence to the ego concept; but it becomes a thousand-fold more erroneous when first the machine, and then the use of "natural forces" applied to machinery, made possible our vast increase in specialisation.

That one man must give his life to the art of weaving did not so narrow his mental area, or so cut him off from appreciation of other branches of human work, as this later development where a man wears out two sets of oak planks in one spot, standing still all his life, making nails! It seems "a far cry" from the fractional construction of nails to the social consciousness, and yet, in the true order of industrial development, it brings it nearer. The more extreme the specialisation the more extreme the interdependence, and that universal interdependence is the condition which calls for, and which develops, social consciousness.

In the true order—but that order has been grievously interfered with by our own mistakes. Acting under the ego concept, and the system of competition which rests upon it, the increasing specialisation which is so normal a condition of social growth has been made to carry increasing evil consequences to the specialised worker. A just and rational position on the part of Society! As fast as its members specialise in compliance with the demands of social benefit, so fast does the benefited society stunt and degrade its benefactors!

That there has been improvement in the rank and file of society is not denied, but it is due to our partial and grudging distribution of the social good along normal lines of public provision, such as free schools and libraries, and not to our idiotic ideas of individual work and pay.

Where there is no such public provision our economic concepts act to crush and degrade the worker. That increasing specialisation with its mechanical adjuncts, which should make it possible for a man to discharge his social obligations in an hour and then be free to contribute to progress by larger growth, we have taken advantage of to compel an amount and grade of labour alike ruinous to the individual in his immediate sacrifice and to the society composed of such sacrificed individuals. Men dying of thirst have been known to bite madly into their own flesh and suck the blood, but for a prosperous, growing society, rich, powerful, safe, intelligent, to make a steady diet of its own meat, is unreasonable.

"The social sacrifice" is a very real and noble thing. It sometimes requires the lives of some of its members to preserve the life of the whole body. This sacrifice is always cheerfully made in war. It also requires the surrender of individual freedom of action to that complex interaction and unswerving duty which makes up the social service. But this sacrifice is more than compensated by the advantages given the individual in the life of the whole. A member of a big, complex society has not only a far better and happier personal life than his freely individual savage ancestor, but he has also share in the large, glorious, common life of that society.

That is, he should have these things. As it is—owing to our antediluvian errors—he has to make the sacrifice, and in return he is reduced to an individual life far less gratifying than that of a healthy savage, yet knows no more of the splendid social consciousness belonging to his position than if he were that savage still.

There is one feature in social specialisation so prominent and so important as to call for more detailed explanation. This is the relation of what we call "unskilled labour" to social evolution. Our ideas of justice in payment, of the necessary "cheapness" of certain low grades of work, our patient tenderness or impatient contempt for this immense class of humanity, rest on the assumption that human beings are widely unequal in ability; that most of them are of this low and cheap order, and that social progress lies in the advance of superior individuals, assisted in a humble way by the inferior.

For these we must "furnish employment" of a simple character suited to their powers, and pay them with a modesty equal to their other limitations. Because there are so many of them, their competition for the humble tasks allotted keeps the price of unskilled labour very low indeed. Through organisation they have forced the price up a little, but most of us consider this as unjustifiable in strict economic law.

If it is shown that low wages for low labour keeps that labour always low, and indeed makes it lower; that out of the impoverished environment we inevitably breed defectives and degenerates, diseases and crimes; and that farther, because a hard and unfavourable environment promotes fecundity, therefore this low rate of wages tends to increase the birth rate of the lowest people, thus making a vicious circle of social stagnation and deterioration—if these things are proved to us, we say it cannot be helped—it is a condition of human nature. These inferior people are the bulk of humanity; they cannot do high-grade labour; it would not be fair to pay the plentiful "cheap labour" as much as the scarce and therefore more expensive kind, so there you are! As a way of escape from this position "the brotherhood of man" tries to uplift the lowly, but the majority do not accept this brotherhood theory. Or they say, "Brother or not, these are such hopelessly inferior brothers that we will not consent to any levelling which would reduce us to their grade, and they cannot be raised to ours."

Now here is the true position. "Unskilled labour" is a product of social evolution. Among savages there is no unskilled labour. Each man must be skilled in several lines to keep himself alive. In his pre-social condition of individualism, his life depending immediately upon his own exertions, he necessarily develops skill in his essential activities. No heavy-eyed, slow-witted, hod-carrying grade of efficiency could maintain itself in a status of individual savagery. The "man with the hoe" comes later—much later. He is produced, developed, maintained, by a highly differentiated society. The nobleman evolves the serf—they are parts of one fighting organisation. The mill-owner and his "hands" are part of one working organisation.

The individual savage is swift, alert, vigorous, sentinelled by the keenest of senses, served by prompt and varied abilities of many sorts. But his action, though more perfect, is on a lower grade in industrial evolution. He would not be capable, though under never so dreaded penalties, of working, his life long, in one fractional line of social service.

The more society develops the more widely differentiated become its labours. In its differentiation there comes to be an immense proportion of very simple things to do; simple because they are tiny parts of something extremely complex. The savage's life is anything but "simple." His elaborate and exciting monologue requires of him the whole gamut of individual capacity in constant shock and change. But in the peace and power of a great civilisation, in the organic spread of social functions, there are more and more kinds of labour which are so infinitely simplified that a dolt can do them.

It does not follow that a dolt must do them! It does not follow that we should hunt out all our inferior persons to do these unelevating things, and so remain inferior. It does not follow that we should keep the inferior person so long at his unelevating task as to further lower his inferiority; that we should pay him so little as to prevent any development from outside advantages; or that, worst of all, we should so condemn his children to their subminimum share of his "minimum wage" as to make them lower yet.

In our ignorance of the nature of society, and the nature of work; in our cheerful blindness to the lessons of history; with our poor choked and twisted brains, so crammed with the follies of our ancestors, and so weakened by what we have called education that they cannot *think*; we have taken for granted that society had to have about so much "unskilled labour" to provide for, and could only provide for it by "furnishing employment" suited to its powers.

If we can once recognise the facts in the case, we will change our behaviour fast enough. Observe the line of social growth. Here is a nascent society of a vague group of savages, feebly held together by the pressure of a common danger; feebly drawn together by the attraction of a common need. So held and drawn the same forces which grouped the cells and started the growth of physical organisms worked upon them, and they began to differentiate in function.

Follow one line of work, such as the clothing of society. The individual savage took a skin off another animal and put it on himself; that was the beginning. It required in him, and in his squaw, the highly exciting and agreeable exercise of the rudiments of many trades. He hunted, fought, killed, and skinned the beast. She tanned and dressed, cut and sewed, with elaborate decoration. All very interesting.

Now comes the evolution of that industry on inevitable lines. First, the division of trades; one hunted, another tanned, another sewed, and so on. Then, as society increased, as skill increased, as productivity increased, as commerce increased, we find these trades increasing in importance, in bulk, and in complexity; until now we have one garment going through a thousand hands between the wool or cotton fibre, and the wearer of the dress.

In this process, a perfectly healthy social process, the fractional details of the work become extremely small and simple, and our mechanical ingenuity has made them smaller and simpler yet; till no more skill or judgment is required than a factory child or poor dull sweated "garment worker" can apply.

In these familiar facts see the real principle involved. Social progress has so differentiated labour as to make infinitely short, easy, and simple to a thousand co-workers what was once long, difficult, and complicated for one. These beneficently simple processes make possible the use of "unskilled labour"; make it possible for society to maintain in its service individual working capacity lower than that of a savage, lower almost than the beast.

But here is our great error. Unskilled labour does *not* require the unskilled labourer. Unskilled labour can be performed equally well by skilled labourers of the highest sort, as mere play, as rest from these more exacting functions. In proportion to its simplicity and ease, its extreme mechanical perfection of adjustment, is, or should be, the saving of time involved.

Here is a world, all shod, at the expense of a large amount of individual labour, every man making his own shoes. Here is a world, all shod, at far less expense of labour, when the shoemaker gives his specialised skill to the business. Here is the world, all shod, at infinitely less expense of labour; when the shoe manufactory, with specialised labour and machinery, produces a thousand-fold more swiftly and easily; and a developed commerce distributes around the world. Now, if the shoes of the world are made socially, with a thousandth part the time and labour required to make them individually, how does it happen that the makers of shoes are working harder and longer than ever? Save indeed as the trades-union, in ceaseless and costly combat, has in some degree shortened the time and raised the wages.

It is because of our familiar group of delusions in economics. It is because we so wholly fail to see the organic nature of the process, and what is really the line of social advantage in it. We see the heavy, awkward, dirty, ignorant men digging in our streets, and say, "Poor fellows! Such as they can do no other work! Stern nature has made them inferior, and it is fortunate for them that there is this plain, simple work, which they are able to do."

What we do not see is that the plain, simple work is part of a highly complex social process. Your nimble savage has no ditch to dig; no road to build; no sewer to clean. This is social service; not of the lowest, but of the highest. The more advanced the society, the more simplified the minute subdivisions of its great and complex processes. Your nimble savage does not have to do one thing, one fraction of a fraction of a thing, for twelve hours a day—or ten—or even eight. If he did—if we did—we who look over the fence at the rude gnomes who labour in the trenches in our vivisected city to-day—we should become as they.

Unskilled labour is high social service, and social sacrifice. It is not so interesting and developing to the individual as the activities of savagery, but it is more essential to the country's good, to the power and peace of the world. This noble service could be rendered without its present awful penalty. I do not speak of its low wages, but of its heavy punishment.

Here is work done for the service of humanity; not for any low and primitive service either, but to maintain our highest social grade of development. This work, subtle, elaborate, important, only simple in its extreme subdivision, we have chosen in our ignorance to consider "low." The people who do it we first compelled by force; we now compel on pain of starvation; they are "low" too, and cannot help themselves.

When we understand the real grades of labour, we shall see this to be of the highest, and as such, to have its limits and dangers. Such highly specialised work cannot be followed for long hours, that is a cruel injury; and never needs to be followed for long hours, because the very law of its development is the saving of time and energy. Society, as a whole, loses the major part of the advantage of its specialised development, by ruthlessly degrading and defrauding the very functionary through whom that development is attained.

XII: PRODUCTION

SUMMARY

Work is production and distribution. Joy of production. Transmission again. Pleasure in expression more than impression. Social stimulus. Arrested distribution. Increase in production. Shoes. Collective pride. "Owned" machinery. Effect of false concepts. George Eliot's "Stradivarius." Art recognised as world-service. The "Pot-boiler." "Saving" and "serving" one's country. Traitor and coward. Line of evolution in a productive industry. Effect of errors. "Duty to employer," etc. Payment not the right incentive. Reactive effect of production. "Greeking." Effect of great work on society. Physical heredity, social heredity and transmission. Bicycle. Benefit of making, of using. We "exhaust the soil" of humanity by denying it right use of its product. Want theory. Degraded press. Object of production. False production. Individual is society—feels and represents it. Social consciousness mistaken for self-consciousness. "Self-expression" and social service. "The songs of a people." Position of the artist. Expression is also transmission. "Poor Jones!" Art a social function. Depravity in highly specialised function. The presumptuous eye. Art for humanity's sake.

CHAPTER XII

PRODUCTION

Work is in two main lines, Production and Distribution; to make something, or to hand it about, is human industry.

To create is an intense satisfaction; to combine elements and produce new results, whether it be a bridge, a basket, or a loaf of bread—to make is in itself a joy. But so is it a joy to give something to somebody, whether at first-hand, or in a combination with many; to spread, to disseminate, to feel the current of human good flow through you; both functions are happy.

The universe is an everlasting production, force taking form, energy embodied, disembodied, re-embodied—this is the game of living. Our little mid-station of consciousness feels the pressure of natural forces on both sides, pushing in through the sensory nerves; pushing out through the motor nerves. Owing to our early mistake about the superior pleasure of impression, and our perverse insistence that expression is only a guarded outlay of limited force, by which to secure desired impressions, we have never understood the nature of human production.

The pleasure of right impression is not to be denied. Every sensory nerve should have its proper stimulus. And man, with his immense collective sensorium, with his highly developed personal sensations, due to social evolution, and his power of feeling with and for other people, has enormous capacity for the reception of pleasure. But what is all this pleasurable stimulus for? The brain is not merely a reservoir for stored sensation. A sensation is a certain amount of energy going into the human battery. Once in, it must be discharged in commensurate activity.

Most interesting experiments in psychology are being made to-day, proving this, even in some immediate result of a strong mental impression in unconscious bodily motion; as shown in studies among school children. As the brain develops it has increasing capacity to receive impressions, to retain and to arrange impressions; but nevertheless sometime that mass of impressions must come out in commensurate action, else disease ensues. The human brain, socially developed, and socially stimulated, has great power of expression; that expression is in work, and work is in Production and Distribution. The productivity of the human race, even with its past and present checks and perversions, is the wonder of the ages. Guaranteed the swift and easy satisfaction of those "wants" our economists build so much on, the steady increase of impressed energy has resulted in as steady an increase of expressed energy, necessarily.

Man receives stimulus from a thousand sources. Since we made mental impressions permanent and exchangeable "in book form," knowledge and emotion bottled, preserved, and distributed broadcast; there is practically no limit to human stimuli; and, since with this increasing stimulus we have steadily reduced the difficulties of execution, our real problem is, how to provide right outlets for the productive energy of humanity. This normal increase of power and execution we have managed to check, however, quite materially. We have gravely interfered with the natural distribution of stimulus up to the present time; but now our rapid multiplication of free school and free library, with similar tendencies in other educational and recreative lines, is producing its natural result in increased energy.

Even with what stimulus was open to us, our production should have been very great; but we have interfered with that also, in more ways than one. The principal obstacle here is the basic error of the Want theory. Holding that man works only to satisfy desire,—*i. e.*, produces merely to consume,—we prostitute our share of the social energy to a factitious personal advantage; and try to govern the productive processes of society by the dictates of self-interest. Here you have a factory in which a hundred men turn out ten hundred pairs of shoes a day. What for? Why, for the feet of ten hundred people, of course—to shoe the world. "Not so," they protest. "We are making these shoes for ourselves." "But you cannot wear ten pairs of shoes a day, my man!" "No, but I only do this work for the pay—and I can easily consume the pay for ten pair of shoes a day."

This poor man never understands his position as a social functionary with all its honour and pleasure. The Ego concept and the Want theory becloud his mind. Even his personal pride in his personal work has lowered since the machine made his work collective, and his mind failed to keep pace with the machine, and make his joy and pride collective too. His pleasure is only in what he gets back from society in return for his labours, and he gets very little. As part of this same ancient misconception of what work is, we find the incredibly multiplied machinery of production "owned" by individuals; and manipulated by them under the same befogging ideas that lead the workman to "limit his output."

Never were any of the gross and childish superstitions of remotest savagery more injurious—or more ridiculous—than these rudimentary errors under which our economic development so blindly labours. We have our alleged "overproduction" on the one hand—though a full supply of the good things of life is obtained by scarce one-tenth of the population of the world; and we have the ensuing and even more colossal absurdity of the restricted output—whether of the man who stints his day's labour, or the group of financiers who "corner" some social product, and say how much the world shall have.

These muddy follies of our common mind—for if we did not all, or nearly all, believe in these principles of action, we would not for a moment allow such economic treason and misrule—together with allied fallacies of a similar nature, most seriously interfere with production. Nevertheless, as the laws of nature are somewhat stronger than our evanescent misconceptions, we do see the tremendous increase in our productivity; and, in favoured instances, its grandeur and delight. As good an expression of this feeling as I know in literature is in George

Eliot's poem of "Stradivarius."

Here is a man, developing an extremely specialised line of production, and clear of brain enough to see the joy and dignity of it.

"Antonio Stradivari has an eye
That winces at false work and loves the true,
With hand and arm that play upon the tool,
As willingly as any singing bird
Sets him to sing his morning roundelay
Because he likes to sing and likes the song."

Our best known instances of normal or nearly normal production are found in art and science. Here you have a product which the world recognises as its own—not that of the individual maker. "He has given to the world" such and such a picture, or statue; discovery in science or composition in music; to this world-service we give some, though an imperfect, honour; and we pity and even blame the man who "prostitutes his art" to the level of "the pot-boiler." Art is world-service, truly, but so is manufacture or commerce. A man should no more prostitute his "trade" than his "art." It is as base to make a "pot-boiler" of your day's work as of a book or a picture. No soldier is more actually "serving his country" in his occasional fighting, than is the workman in his continual working. One's country sometimes has to be "saved" in sudden emergency, at considerable cost of immediate exertion and sacrifice; but one's country has to be kept alive all the time, at considerable cost of unceasing labour and some sacrifice too. Our patriotism, which rushes madly forward to "save the country" when it is in visible danger, and, having saved it, proceeds to exploit it for personal advantage all the rest of the time, is on a par with love for one's family, which would risk life to "save" it, from flood, or fire, or injurious attack, and then mercilessly cheat it, starve it, keep it cold and dirty and ignorant and sick and vicious—when not "in danger." The danger to our country from our general neglect and misuse, and our frequent positive injury, is far greater than that of occasional war. We need a patriotism that will operate all the time.

The human worker, whether a captain of industry or in the ranks, who puts his personal safety and advantage before that of his country is exactly the same traitor and coward that the officer or private in the army would be who did the same thing. He does not know it, we do not know it, therefore no odium attaches to these public offenders. But the mischief they do is apparent in every branch of our economic processes.

We have seen that human production is checked in amount by our lack of knowledge. It is injured in kind from the same cause. Normal production has an evolution of its own. Follow the development of any one trade, and you will see as natural a growth as in a physical organ, marred of course by our errors, but there under all. Take the building trades as an example. At the beginning we find primitive man enlarging a cave somewhat, or, lacking that retreat, putting up some shelter of boughs to screen him from the wind and rain, or spreading a hide for the same purpose. The act, repeated, develops skill, and the mind, dwelling over and over on the same problem, develops too, and sees better ways of accomplishment. The shelter of hide becomes the teepee or wigwam, and, cloth superseding leather, the tent in all its forms; but its growth is limited by mechanical conditions. The shelter of boughs is more open to improvement; and evolves slowly into hut, cabin, house. The materials used depending on the environment, the Eskimo builds of ice, the Chaldean of clay, and, slowly, by proof of superiority, stone was used wherever found. The principle of specialisation acting steadily upon this widening current of functional ability, we have now that group of allied trades required to construct for modern man the material form in which he lives and works—without which he cannot live and work.

A genealogical tree could be made, showing just where each branch diverged, the workers in wood, clay, and stone dividing early; the gradual appearance of the system of pipes and conduits which vitalise a house; the development of windows in all forms, of doors and their particular line of improvement, of interior finish, from daubed mud to artistic decoration; and so on and so on, until we have now the house which stands knit to the city by waste pipe, water pipe, gas pipe, and electric wire; a house which represents the slow fruition of a thousand centuries, the contributed intelligence and skill of a million men. The evolution of this "social form" is as natural and orderly as the evolution of any physical form. To the men through whom it grew the whole course should have been a pleasure and a pride, and in large measure it has been, in spite of all our misbeliefs.

To feel within one's self the tendency toward a certain line of production, to "learn the trade," *i. e.*, submit the brain to the accumulated stimulus of that line of production—to feel the racial skill begin to flow through one's fingers—to do the thing well—better—best!—and then, still unsatisfied, to relieve the pressure by new invention of ways even better than the best—that is the *natural* sensation of the producer. Against this have operated at every step the weight and darkness of our leaden lies. The child is not so watched and trained as to develop the fine sense of special "calling" which shows the best path in life. Only the extreme case, the boy who *would* be a sailor, or a mechanic, or whatever he was meant to be, has the advantage of being where he belongs in the world's work. But the average boy, with no special aptitude or pleasure in his trade, is put to work under the dominant idea, drilled in from infancy, that he is to work only because he has to—he has to in order to get the pay. The whole outlook of his position is lost. He has his head in a bag. All he sees is the week's wage, and the work is merely to be gotten through in order to get the wage.

We have known all along that this was a wrong attitude, and have tried to inculcate upon the worker a sense of "the nobility of labour," of "duty to his employer," of the "common interest of capital and labour."

It does not ennoble the labourer to enlarge his selfishness to the size of his employer's. The employer is in exactly the same boat. He has no more sense of what his work is for than the "hand" has. He too is looking only at his wages,—salary, income, profits, rent,—looking only at what he is *to get* from society, instead of what he is to do for it. The common interest of employer and employee, which is merely an interest in their common income, does not lift the cloud from labour.

No interest is large enough to satisfy the human mind, except the social interest; the thrilling glory of working with and for the whole world at the trade you love best, and can do best.

The workman should have such education as shall give him for a background the full knowledge of social evolution; and the special place of his own trade in that evolution. He should know just where it first appeared, how it grew, and why, the importance of its place to-day—and here there would, no doubt, be warm differences of opinion, debates and competition. The payment for his service should no more be the point of ambition with the workman, than with the pen-man, paint-man, or rifleman. The producer is entitled to feel the full power and pride of production; and, in spite of our errors, this power and pride is felt by the well-placed workman, whose life is better than his belief—as human life always is.

One of the most important features of this great social function is the reactive effect on the functionary. The maker is inexorably modified by the thing made. If the thing made develops along normal lines, the maker develops with it. If it does not—if it is checked or perverted in its growth, so is the worker. Working is humanity's growing. In the act of working the individual is modified, and by the work accomplished humanity is modified. Also the accomplished work remains, like coral, the record of the height of those who did it.

In the case of those who do not work, who consume copiously, and produce nothing, they have no chance of normal development, add no step to human progress. See in conspicuous instance the Grecian marbles and literature. Those who gave the work were themselves developed by doing it; the society which received the work was developed by using it; and by the work as it remains to us, we know and judge Greece. But the possession of these works does not make us Greeks. To be able to do them was to be Greek. Many causes combined to make the Greek; and the Greek blossomed into that kind of work—he was, so to speak, merely Greeking in the doing of it. We have the result as we have fossil bones. From it we may learn what the Greek was, but not how to make him.

A person, or a race, is something, owing to antecedent conditions. Then they *do* something by virtue of being what they are, as an apple tree bears apples. ("By their fruits ye shall know them.")

The thing done does have some reactive effect, however—else we should have no power to modify each other, and this is one of humanity's chief advantages. The modifying effect of the work accomplished is indeed large, it is no wonder we so long to create the things whereby we can thus progressively serve each other. See, for instance, the endless effect upon society of such work as Plato's, Angelo's, Stevenson's, Edison's; all work counts in both ways; in the doing it affects the doer; when done it affects the user.

But it is more blessed to give than to receive. In animals the modification of species is effected only in the direct line of heredity. A change of condition modifies his action—the change in action modifies him—and the modification is transmitted in his single line. But there is no means of widening the effect—it has to be filtered down through direct heredity. With man, in his organic connection, there is a race modification through our transmission of energy in work, which multiplies his progress million-fold. Some local change of condition modifies the action of one person, the change in action modifies him, and the modification is transmitted in his single line. Thus far we are even with the animals. Then we pass them; man's action is work; it is not mere putting something in his mouth; it is making something. And the thing made holds and transmits his energy, passing it on forever to all who use it, making the growth of one the growth of all.

One man, or some few men, make a steam engine. They personally are by so much developed as makers, and their children after them. That is so much gain. But if we had waited for our inventors to modify the race through physical heredity, we should be still in the Bronze Age. The engine, being made, becomes part of the social structure, and proceeds to modify the society it serves.

The bicycle is perhaps a better instance. The effect of the making is not materially different from the effect of making watches. But the thing made has modified society by the reactive effects of its use. It has modified the dress, the activity, and so the physique and character of women, to their great improvement. It has modified roads—to the great material benefit of the regions affected. It has modified inn-keeping, livery-stabling, tailoring, the relative distance of residence—the effects of the bicycle on society are great, even upon the most superficial survey. But this is no reason why the maker of bicycles should be a better man than the maker of chronometers, or that either of them should be paid more than the maker of pianos, or less than the maker of poems.

The first effect of work, its result, return, or payment, is to the maker in the quality and quantity of his effort. No one can measure his pay or deny it. The second is to the user in the fulness of his use. This, alas! can be measured and denied, and has been, to our racial injury. No tyranny was ever able to prevent the steady development of man through the work he did. If he laboured faithfully and generously, he grew in the outputting of his strength, and his growth ultimately overthrew the tyranny. But tyranny of various sorts has withheld from the workers the reactive benefits of using the product of their work; and so hindered race development.

The builders of beautiful houses, working well, are necessarily benefited by their own working; but if they are forced to live in poor, ugly, unhealthy houses, they are not benefited by the results of the work. This is a grave limitation of a man's income; and if his income is checked, his output is checked also. As an unwise farmer exhausts his soil in greedy harvesting without due fertilisation, so we have drawn upon the creative energies of humanity and denied the rich replenishment which would have made the product so much more prolific.

Here the mischievous effect of our Want theory comes in plainly. The man who is working merely for pay must *cater to the purchaser*. He must please existing tastes. Looking at his product, not as an end, to benefit society, but as a means to benefit himself, he must so produce as to secure a buyer. This is the "pot-boiler" again. The artist who paints to suit his patrons and get their money is not the true artist, and through him art does not grow. The maker of coats or hats or houses or dishes submits to this degrading pressure, and the result is seen in our debased and vulgar forms of manufacture everywhere.

The evil effects to the consumer are more manifest in some trades than in others, as, for instance, in the liquor trade. Here we have human beings producing what they know people will buy; and then, not content with the existing demand, using all possible means to excite and maintain a further demand—simply that they may make money.

Again, in our degraded press, we have a most conspicuous instance of this prostitution of a great social function to private ends. Under the mistaken idea that the distribution of news is a process for feeding owners of papers, and thus being led to arrange their news so as to please the most buyers, they rapidly descend along lines of least resistance to a wholesale catering to the worst tastes of the most people; and supplement that by elaborate efforts to foment and spread the low appetites they so obsequiously serve.

Naturally there is no growth and grandeur in a trade like this. To spread knowledge, sympathy, instant information of the world's movements good and bad, is to take part in one of society's chief functions; in the general nervous system of the world. But to ascertain that society enjoys certain sensations, and to force the general presentation of news into a special arrangement to give those desired sensations, is to turn healthy action into a loathsome disease. In any form of human production, the object is to serve the consumer by the best development of the product, *not* to use the consumer as a means of profit for the producer. The producer must, of course, be provided for; as must the soldier, artist, physician; but self-interest is not the object of the work.

In the production of shoes, again, the object should be a constant improvement in material, shape, wearing quality, and general utility and beauty. Deliberately to change the shape and size, the proportion and make of human footwear, merely to cater to low tastes, is the degrading "pot-boiler"; the prostituting of a social function to a private end.

All forms of cheap and dishonest production, of adulteration, of an artificially forced market, are directly traceable to our Want theory; to our persistent superstition which still crudely imagines this vast and intricate world of interservice to be a primeval forest, where beast and savage hunt for prey. The mistake in object degrades the product, and the degraded product degrades the man. Thus our immense field of production is not only checked in output and arrested in distribution, but weakened through and through by adulteration and bad workmanship; with evils in result, unending. The natural trend toward a wider, fuller, easier, and ever better production, accompanied at every step by growing pride and power and pleasure in the producer, is hindered and perverted to large degree by our prevalent economic fallacies.

Another conspicuous point where our errors touch production is seen in the arts especially; the particular mistake here being in the persistence of the ego concept; our confusion of self-expression with social service. The social consciousness, unrecognised, presents itself to our minds as a huger self-consciousness.

We have often wondered at the inordinate selfishness of man, compared to which the innocent egoism of the beasts is angelic. This tremendous range and depth of selfishness is because of that essential enlargement of self which comes with socialisation—the individual of a given society is that society—feels it as a "self." The Roman, to the limits of his capacity, is Rome. The socialised individual carries in him the enlargement of his society. He has a wider soul, perforce, that is our human quality. This larger self, a thing frankly essential to social existence, enabling the individual to so think, feel, and act with and for his society, comes into action long before it is recognised by the "local office"—the mind of the individual. The mind has to learn its own contents as well as its outside environment. Our traditional labelling of those contents is no more correct than our primitive misconceptions of geography or physics.

What we personally call a quality does not affect its nature, but does affect our own conscious behaviour. The ability we display to mistake and miscall our own qualities and those of other people, is apparently immeasurable. So we feel this social soul, this larger aliveness; a power of caring for millions, of wanting for millions, and of doing for millions; and, since we ourselves feel it in ourselves, we call it self-consciousness.

A man, joining a regiment of old and splendid fame, comes to feel and act strongly from the regimental consciousness. He feels it with his own mental machinery; but it is not an enlargement of his personal self-consciousness—that is forever limited to his personality. This larger self—society, and its accompanying social consciousness—we calmly appropriate as a personal quality, and proceed to act on it. Having the capacity to think, feel, act for a thousand, we proceed to think, feel, and act a thousand times more for ourselves. Therefore we are naturally appalled at the limitlessness of "human selfishness."

The whole mistake is natural enough—the conscious mind always lagging behind our unconscious growth; but to-day the social consciousness is finally forcing itself on the perception of the individual; and that which we have called selfishness, and which is really socialness misused, will be lifted from vice to virtue as we re-name it. Once properly recognised, we have quite ability enough to measure the man who uses a public power for a private end; to measure and condemn. But while this misconception still exists we have a minor confusion as to "self-expression" and "social service."

The artist feels this more perhaps than other workers. He feels it because his feelings are more prominent, and more often handled, than those of the workman in the more mechanical trades. A man may make tremendous engines or run them; and never "feel himself work" so much as the maker of very inconsiderable poems. This is because the poet is so highly socialised a product. His power to be a poet is a social power. What he feels is the heart of his people, and he, poor man! thinks it is his own. He thinks his heart is far more exquisitely sensitive than theirs, whereas it is their hearts he is feeling! His capacity for pain and for pleasure is their capacity; it is greater because he is *more people,* or at least is the specialised point of sensation and expression for more people.

"Let me write the songs of a people and let who will make their laws."

The songs *of a people*—not his songs forced down upon them, but their songs forced up through him. "The proof of a poet shall be sternly deferred until his country absorbs him as affectionately as he has absorbed it."

Artists, of all men, are most exquisitely specialised to the social service. Their work, of all men's, is least valuable to themselves, most valuable to others. They are absolutely *for* other people to so extreme a degree as nearly always to warp and injure their personal relations, even under the fairest conditions. They must do the work for which they are built, cost what it may, and this compelling power, this insistent force from within which will out through whatever medium is at hand, this they call "self-expression"! An artist, they say, must not consider social service in the least; he must express himself.

It is a true recognition of the kind of work he must do; he must indeed express that which is good in him quite regardless of whether the people around him want it or not; will pay him for it or not; will kill him for it or not. But that unfaltering expression *is* his social service, his true function, what he was built for. And it is not "himself" that he is expressing, it is "themself." He is, of that people and that time, a voice, an eye, an ear, a hand to do. Holland made the Dutch painters, not they Holland. They in return in their accomplished work made Holland Hollander, so to speak, but the lives of many generations of Dutchmen and Dutchwomen went to form those painters first.

There is no necessary conflict between the two conceptions of the artist's duty—to express himself, or to serve society—as far as the special performance goes: but the misconception carries wide error and evil with it none the less. It makes the artist morbid in what he fancies a vast self-consciousness, whereas he might remain as free and unassuming personally as any child, once he recognised that it was not *he* who was doing all this, but they. It would save him too from the common mistake of applying his splendid range of social sensitiveness to his own personal affairs as he too commonly does. Had Carlyle, for instance, seen truly what was the nature of his place and power, he would have been less haughty and less irritable—also less lonely.

The individual must needs suffer under the isolation of his strange overdevelopment, unless he is able to detach himself from it, and be a person among other persons freely. The power to separate the man from the office, to come down from the throne and play ball, is a healthy one. On the other hand, much true artistic service is lost to the world through this misconception about "self-expression" when the power is not overwhelmingly great, and the individuals are strong in their sense of duty as they see it. This is especially true among women. To such, the inner impulse demanding expression is considered "selfish," and a thing to resist; and their energies are forced into other lines because thereby they imagine they are best serving. If they recognised this inward propulsion as the call for social expression—not self's—it would stand differently in their scale of duty.

A question rises here of large importance, and not easy of answer. Suppose the social expression actuating the individual be a bad one—visibly a bad one—resultant from wrong conditions and tending to promote others as wrong—should such a tendency be followed? Is that the social service? How far may the individual judgment give check to such social tendency?

As, for instance, certain wrong economic conditions, say in France, before the Revolution, tended to produce many social phenomena, including a tendency to debased literature and art. Should the artist, in such case, say to himself, "Why, dear me! This is a vicious and reactionary social impulse. I am out-Heroding Herod—this stuff shows how bad we have been, and doesn't help us to be any better. Now I will not indulge my inclination to paint these torture-chamber scenes, or these subtle indecencies. I like to—but what of that? It is a social tendency, but society is not always right, she goes backward and sideways by spells; it will not do her any good to let out this stuff. No, I'll choke it off, and, if I can't paint better things, I'll take to pottery or weaving."

Whether this is best, or whether it is the artist's duty humbly to voice that which is in him—saying, "Well, this is the way you feel, is it? Better let it out then. Perhaps you'll change quicker if you *see* your badness," this is a very large question.

Perhaps the truly morbid and vicious tendencies, thus recognised by the artist, would cause him as much shame as if he had unfortunately inherited some scrofulous disease, and he would be unable to proceed. This, at least, should be held steadily in mind, that human work is not mere *expression*, of self or of society, but is *transmission*, and therefore to be watched.

If speech were merely a relief to one's own feelings, poured forth into empty air and earless waste places, then foulness and profanity would be merely indications of how the speaker felt, and hurt no one. But where speech goes to other ears, it must be measured, not merely by the speaker's emotions, but by theirs. So the artist is not merely an unconscious spring bubbling over with fair water, or foul, according to its hidden sources, but is a conduit, taking the water *to* something as well as from something. And as a conscious intelligence bound to act "up to his lights," if he judges the water to be bad in its effects, he has no right to convey it to others. This would leave an easy alternative to the artist. Let him, if he *must*, write his decadent literature, paint his decadent pictures; and then, having so relieved himself of these foul secretions, let him decently destroy the product, lest it prove contagious. Some friend, having seen, would say compassionately—"Poor Jones! He has to write about so much of it in a year—he cannot help it, it is better to come out, I suppose. But don't look as if you knew—he is very sensitive about it."

In a more advanced civilisation we may have Public Health ordinances as to these expressions, like the signs in our street cars. The assumption of the artist that his form of production is beyond all social responsibility or control, that "there is no ethics in art," is a very interesting instance of the ego concept at its most insane height.

If ever there was a "social function," it is art. As a civilisation advances, there is more and more development of art; as we look back along the path of social progress, there is less and less of it. In its inception it was more or less common to all workers, a little of it; as it grew, it demanded more wholly the work of a whole life. No ultra-specialised social servant is more removed from self-support than the artist, whose work is of no faintest possible use to him as an individual. He must absolutely depend on the advanced society which made him, which feeds, clothes, shelters, and defends him, and whose highest needs it is his duty to serve.

Higher than kings or captains, higher even than the giant producers and distributers of wealth, comes this delicate, sensitive, exquisitely specialised organ of society. For true service he deserves all the love and honour society can give, as well as the support due all of us—nothing can overestimate his value. For true service,—but what service does he give?

The more highly developed the organ, the more open to disease. No feature in human production is marked with worse depravity than is found in art. Because of the extreme pleasure found in the transmission of his peculiar power, because of the special sensitiveness involved in his form of service, we too often find the artist sunken in a sublimated selfishness and arrogant to a degree beyond comparison. It is as though an eye should plume itself loftily on its power of sight. "You poor, blind body! You cannot see, but I can! I only can see, and I like to see. It gives me pleasure. I will see only what gives me pleasure. It is my pleasure to see things pink—all things pink. And round—all things are round." The poor blind body cannot deny that things are pink—if the eyes say so; but it has hands at least, to tell it that some things are flat and others sharp; so it works on, sadly misled by its servant.

And if we reason with the servant, saying: "Are you so sure that things are pink? It does not seem reasonable—it does not seem right,"—the servant loftily and unapproachably replies: "The Eye does not reason! There is no right or wrong to the Eye! I am an Eye, and I see as I like. If you differ with me, go blind!"

When we recognise production as a social process, for the social good, all work will change its standard of measurement. The worker, artist or scientist, inventor or teacher, must often differ with the purchasing public; must modify his work by his own reason and conscience, not by that of the other people; but the purpose to which he modifies it is social service. It may cost him his life at the time; he may have to set himself and his views against those of the past and present; but he should do so with unfaltering devotion to what he believes the social good; not in this lunatic position that he and his work are unique in the universe—that he owes no responsibility to anything—that "art is for art's sake."

When we are alive to the nature of our social processes, when we see that production is both duty and pleasure, personal good and social advantage, we shall bend our tremendous powers to develop and educate the productive energy in all our children, and provide the best conditions for its free exercise.

XIII: DISTRIBUTION

SUMMARY

Distribution the field of most social disorders. Advantages of Distribution. Physical Avenues of Distribution. Mechanical means of Distribution. Social nourishment flowing around the world. Evils of local production and consumption. Social instincts developed by common interests. Love rests on service. International dependence means international peace. Long circuit, wide base, gives room for larger development. Present system of Distribution does not properly supply the world. Mysterious coagulations. False concepts again. Ego concept. Want theory. Working and eating, which comes first? Parent not competent to provide for child in society. Social parentage. Public education. Making and taking. How to supply social energy. Pay concept. Patent failure in application. Selling kerosene as a social service. No true relation between work and pay. Pay idea wrong. Nourishment first, work after. Heirlooms in our heads. The Bear. Competition and survival not useful among our vital organs. Our improvement mutual, collective, organic. How to raise the productive value of society. No ratio between want and work. Reductio ad absurdum of Want theory. Not "pay," but investment. A man's work is his payment to society for value received. Slave labour could not conceive of wage labour; wage labour fails to conceive of free labour. The normal "incentive" is pressure of social energy. See effect of false concepts on distribution of wheat. How it should be. Real "business sense" for society.

CHAPTER XIII

DISTRIBUTION

When we come to the subject of Distribution, we are facing what may be called the main field of our social disorders. Under this head, and that of the next chapter, Consumption, come all questions of property rights, with the vast structures of the civil law ensuing; the whole money question—laboriously complex; the demands of the labour movement; the protests of the "leisure class"—we are on the great battlefield of modern thought.

Let us approach it simply and naturally along the lines laid down in preceding chapters.

Distribution is a natural corollary of production. Society produces through its individual members in ever-growing surplus, and must distribute that surplus among its members to the best social advantage. What that advantage is needs no abstruse exposition; it is simply to have all the members of society supplied with what they need in order that they may so continue to serve society.

As social functions develop, the rate of production increases, as well as the relative distance of the consumers; and with them increases the necessity for an ever wider, swifter, and easier distribution of product. The circulation of our social supplies is as essential to social growth as the circulation of blood is to the growth of the body. This is seen plainly in the course of history. In the earliest times the young civilisations depend on great waterways for their life and prosperity as the easiest means of transportation; and water transportation remains one of our most important avenues of distribution. But seacoast and river bank were not enough for us, land transportation must develop too, and it has done so, wonderfully.

At first the mother-of-all-industries, the savage woman, was the only beast of burden. Then stronger animals were pressed into the service, and reached their height of usefulness in the age of caravan traffic. The drag, the sled, and final triumph—the wheel, were invented, and the world rolled on more and more swiftly. With the wheel grew the road, and civilisation leaped forward. The road became a railroad, tireless mechanical forces superseded the quadruped, and the distribution of social products to-day is truly marvellous.

The goods of the round world are gathered into local distributing centres, carried across continent and ocean, and scattered in tiny parcels to the millions upon millions of remote consumers. Each section contributes its particular wealth. The ice goes south, the oranges go north, the coffee goes west, the tobacco goes east, the manufactures go everywhere.

If we could watch a little globe in action and see the coal pouring slowly up out of little holes, and flowing off in black streaks across land and sea; the oil going with it, but farther and faster; the wheat yellowing whole provinces, heaped up in golden mountains, carried off in thick yellow streams in train-loads and ship-loads; the gloves of France on the hands of Americans, the tools of Americans in the hands of Russians; the whole flux and swing of our social circulation wherein one man's life is fed and strengthened by the fruit of thousands of far-born foreigners,—if we could get this clearly in mind, the organic relation of society would be plainer.

On what line of race-advantage has this tremendous evolution come to pass? Why distribute so widely? Why is it not better to produce and consume locally, each man for himself, as Tolstoi would have us?

The advantage is easily demonstrated if we accept the working plan of organic evolution. If the development of Society is in the universal line of march; if it is, if not an "object," at least an observed tendency, for the loose scarce-human proto-social stuff to move on steadily toward an always-increasing degree of common intelligence, common activity, common enjoyment, common peace, and power, and love,—then every process which promotes this movement is advantageous.

Since the development of a society requires common service, and that common service requires for its wise direction a common consciousness, therefore every modification of human activity which develops common consciousness is advantageous. Since the line of advance in socialisation is from a state of self-supporting individualism toward a state of collectively supporting socialism, therefore every extension of our economic processes along that line is advantageous. Self-support develops only egoism. Mutual support develops mutualism. The more general the base of our maintenance, the more general our advance toward omniism—toward that degree of common consciousness which shall best protect, supply, and develop everyone.

When each man took care of himself, he had no interest in, or love for his neighbour; when their small "spheres of influence" touched, there was a combat. In such conditions no Society was possible. When small communities or large are self-supporting, they have no interest in, or love for each other; this stage of development is the stage of war. Their "spheres of influence" touch, and there is combat. When the economic processes of the world are in common—and they are already beginning to be so—we have the sure basis for common consciousness, for international peace, and all high development; only hindered by the preserved ghosts of previous national, local, and personal "states of mind."

That mutual love which Tolstoi and his kind would see established depends primarily on the widest extension of our common interest, the widest distribution of our specialised production. The law of organic advantage in such relation is clear. Self-support is a very short range of life. Any trifling accident may break the circuit, and the individual is lost. The wider the circuit of distribution the safer the component individual. With the universal insurance of Society's whole working base, there is the largest wealth possible; the largest safety, the smallest risk from any source. There is also, still more importantly, a gain in development.

In a large well-running organism there is room for rest, for the accumulating of energy to apply to special needs. Too prolonged disuse will ultimately eliminate the neglected part, to be sure; but for the time being, a well-organised society can support in idleness those whose service is no less valuable for being intermittent and irregular. The basic "vital organs" work all the time. The later "special organs" not only may but must rest. Our "special senses," our delicate nervous system, the dominating brain, are easily injured by use which is perfectly normal to heart or lung. By wide distribution society is enabled to support all its parts, whether active or passive, and so preserve a greater sum of usefulness. We approximate the same idea in any mutual benefit or insurance society.

It is to broaden the base of supplies and extend the time of payment—a sort of physical credit system. A society where the widest possible range of productivity is maintained, with the largest margin for emergencies, is richer and stronger than one which has "all its eggs in one basket." So the underlying laws of social advantage have worked upon the human race, developing transportation facilities, physical, mechanical, and psychical (meaning here those purely mental agreements and hypotheses by which we facilitate commerce), until we have a system of distribution which would seem, at first sight, quite equal to the needs of the world.

But well we know that it is not! Bitterly and deeply we know that it is not. Some malign force is working at cross-purposes to clog and check and divert this social circulation, and produce the morbid conditions we know so well—the congestion of supplies in some quarters, with the ensuing train of social diseases, and the lack of supplies in other quarters, with another train of diseases consequent.

If there is one conspicuous fact in social economics, it is this peculiar perversion of our distribution system. Those streams of coal and wheat and oil are mysteriously checked at various points, they accumulate where they are not wanted, they filter, slow and scant, in insufficient driblets where there is most need. They are violently pumped out in sudden jerks, they sullenly retreat and coagulate for long, slow periods. What is it that ails our all-important processes of distribution? Merely the human mind. Only our superstitions. Simply the action of false concepts upon conduct again, our old enemies, the Ego concept and the Want theory, gaining headway in these vast currents of modern industry, and doing in large conspicuous ways the same evil they always did, less visibly. From the very beginning, the men through whom these great processes must needs be carried on, have been labouring under a delusion. They supposed that all this commerce and exchange was due to their individual exertions, and that the purpose of it all was to *pay them*. Better proof of the elastic capacity of the human brain could hardly be asked.

That a man carrying a pack on his back should say, "I do it," is natural; that he should still say, "I do it," when he puts the pack upon a mule and drives the beast unwillingly along, is still natural. But that this "I" should swell and swell from mule train to train of cars, from canoe to *Kaiser Wilhelm der Grosse*, is marvellous.

Now that such a myriad "we" do all this work for such a myriad "us," it would seem as if the various component "I's" might have been lost in the shuffle before now. Not a bit.

Acting under the Ego concept, with a sense of justice and of ownership dating from the Ego period, we have arduously bent our minds to the development of a system of laws more elaborately ramified than the twigs of a tree; to follow and preserve the individual rights along every broadening branch of social growth. Governed by the Want theory and its derivatives, we have planted an arbitrary system of inter-individual exchange, like a set of interlocking toll-gates, along every inch of these great roads of progress.

Let us analyse again this group of allied errors, the Want theory. "Work is an expenditure of energy by an individual man whereby to obtain something for the gratification of his wants." This rests on the assumption that what the man needs to gratify his wants is to be had only by his working. As we know that he does not himself manufacture the articles needed to gratify his wants, but that these articles all and several are made by other people; we assume further that each man owns what he makes, and will not give it up to another without value received—"If a man will not work, neither shall he eat." And as the supplies of the world are assumed to belong to the existing inhabitants in private ownership, each newcomer, unless inheriting a share in the privately owned world, is expected to "work" before he receives anything.

Confronted by the glaring fact that a new human creature cannot work before he receives anything, but must be supplied with many social products for many years before he can produce in return, we then fall back on the parent and say, "the new human being shall receive nothing from Society except so much as his father is able to earn," *i. e.*, pay for in work. That system of supplying the young by the unaided activities of the parent, which we find among animals, we assume to be the best for the human race, and so the final distribution of social products is filtered through, not the consuming capacity, but the "earning" capacity of individuals.

If the man with ten children is but a low-grade workman, his earning capacity being but $1.50 a day at our rating, his children receive from Society less than fifteen cents' worth of supplies each. Their consuming capacity is naturally much greater, but under our assumption that the father represents the family as an economic unit, and that the family shall be restricted in consumption within his power of production, the children are thus supplied with the equivalent of one-tenth an individual's output.

In some ways we have recognised the mischievous results of this method of distribution, and have begun to supply some of the necessities of life on a wiser plan, as in our system of public education, where we frankly reverse the position. We therein say: "Children are members of Society. The maintenance and progress of Society require that its members be educated to some degree. This degree of common education the individual earning power of the parent cannot provide, but the collective funds of the community can." So we publicly distribute education, and even enforce it—or try to—on the clear ground that the output of the future citizen depends on his income in youth, and that Society cannot afford to leave that income to be measured by a fraction of a low-grade worker's output.

Some strictly logical and scientific-minded thinkers do indeed object to this free public education, maintaining that since effort is only made to satisfy wants, therefore, if you satisfy any of man's wants, you decrease by so much his efforts, you lower the output of Society.

The advocates of free public education, though still clinging to their idols in other departments of life, maintain that education is a different matter, and point with honest pride to the results, showing that a publicly educated community does produce more and behave better than one wherein each man must provide as he can for his children. But in spite of this patent proof they still refuse to fairly admit the new principle involved, and to fairly give up their fallacious old one.

The Want theory assumes that a man has a supply of energy which he may or may not discharge, but that he will not discharge it unless forced to by necessity. If you supply his needs he will discharge no energy whatever, he will not work. This does apply, fairly enough, to an animal's effort to take things, but does not apply to man's effort to make things. The fact is that a man has energy according to (*a*) his physical well-being, and (*b*) his access to social stimulus; and that, having it, he must discharge it or suffer in the forced retention. The practical question before existing Society is how to supply the most energy to its members and direct it to the most use.

In free education we do supply the young social factor with both energy and direction, so that he grows up better able to work and to work rightly than if left to the degrading influence of this pitiful theory, that the way to make a man work is not to give him anything until he does.

The real process of distribution is to circulate our stores of social nourishment as widely and freely as possible, that we may be always more and more able to work. We are quite consistent in this Pay theory of ours. We carry it out even in regulating the amount of our payment. We hold that not only shall a man have nothing unless he works, but that he shall in no case have more than the equivalent of his work, that no person shall receive anything unless he has "earned" it, given a full equivalent. We are forced to admit that in the life about us this principle is a conspicuous failure; we see those who work the most getting the least; we see those who have the most working the least; and we seek to explain this anomaly by a modification of the Pay concept to this effect: that a man should be paid not only in regard to the amount, but to the value of his work.

With this idea we thought we had reached the height of justice, yet we are forced to admit that this does not serve, either: that the men who do the most valuable work for Society are precisely those least paid, sometimes most punished, and that the men receiving the largest rewards are often the most ordinary functionaries and sometimes rascals. Does anyone presume to claim that selling kerosene oil is so precious a service to Society that the head pedlar should have more money than anybody on earth? Is the maker of steel rails or huge cannon a nobler servant than the maker of bread or the teacher of children? All these are forms of social service truly, but are they fairly paid? The facts do not bear out our theory at all, and we only attribute it to other malign influences, never dreaming that our basic idea is wrong. In sociological law there is no relation whatever, either in amount or quality, between normal human work and any possible "pay," any more than there is between the work of an eye and a leg and the amount of blood they get. Normal human work is organic action. It is a result of previous good received, not an effort to obtain goods withheld.

That under the system of slave labour a man will work under fear of pain is true. That under the system of wage labour a man will work under hope of a reward is true. But both these systems are transient, superficial, soon outgrown by any live society; neither of them affects in the least the underlying organic law of human work. Our conscious minds have not kept pace with social growth. We are trying to administer the processes of an advanced society on lines of pre-social theories. If anyone seeks to point out these great sociological facts, we cry, "These are Utopian dreams, millennial visions; you are a thousand years ahead of your times!"

Whereas it is we—we, the general public, with all these hereditary heirlooms in our heads in place of facts—that are ten thousand years behind them! We try to explain and assist the highly developed and absolutely interdependent social processes by arguments from a long-outgrown era of individualism. Theories of individual effort, incentive, reward, competition, and "survival of the fittest," we apply to our own organic functions. If they do not fit, so much the worse for the functions!

If we *were* individuals, like the beasts, it would all hang together well enough, thus: Here is a Bear. His business is the same old series, maintenance, reproduction, and improvement; to be, to re-be, and to be better. All of these ends he serves by the exercise of his own personal abilities. These abilities, being *purely personal,* are only called into exercise by personal wants or impulses. If the Bear found his food on a plate before his cave every day he would indeed suffer from fatty degeneration; his powers would decay, he would become less and less Bear because he did less and less Bear-ing.

And conversely, if suitable difficulties (not too great) intervene between him and his food, he develops the faculties to meet the difficulties, and improves. If he is not a smart or strong Bear, and cannot get much for himself and the little Bears, why, let them die; better Bears will survive them, and the race improve by their absence. If too much survival of the fittest left too much food for the survivors, so that they became less fit, why up would pop others less fit also to compete for the food, and thus a beautiful level of Bearishness is maintained. This method of evolution we see plainly and admire, perhaps unduly, as a "natural law." All laws are natural. If not natural—they are not laws; we only thought they were.

The essential difference between us and the Bears is in our *organic relation.* The Bears have no common interests, common functions, common good; we have. A perfect balance of highly superior Humans, muscular and ferocious, with just food supply enough to keep up the fighting, and just fighting enough to keep down the food supply, is scarcely a social ideal. The social organism alters the matter completely. The human race improves through production and exchange of products—Work. The work of the human race improves under laws of organic evolution, of increasing specialisation and interdependence. As society advances a man profits less and less by what he does for himself, more and more by what others do for him.

The improvement of a human being is not in his own hands, but in the hands of other human beings. Our line of racial advance is in serving one another, like any other group of organs. This common profit in a common product leads us to wish to improve that product. The product of human beings is improved by supplying the needed energy, stimulus, direction; by *putting into the individual* in order that we may get out of him the pay first, the work afterwards.

This reverses the whole proposition. It is no longer a matter of the individual workman seeking to satisfy his wants *à la* Bear. It is Society seeking to raise the productive value of its integers by carefully supplying those forces which produce more and better work. Quite without knowing it Society does this to a considerable extent, hence the working value of a member of an advanced society is greater than that of a member of a low society; but because we have not known the real laws of human production, we have continued to interpret the whole field of social activity in terms of individual competition.

The supply of a man's needs we have tried to limit strictly to his earning power, refusing to observe that there was no ratio whatever between what a man needs and what he can do—unless, indeed, an inverse one. The fact that a man, well started in lines of work suited to him, will produce continuously long after all his needs are supplied we have tried to account for by assuming new needs as the necessary incentives. Nothing could be clearer—to our view. If a man works only in order to supply his needs, then a given man who does work worth a thousand times as much as another man's must of course need a thousand times as much. He *must*, because there is no other reason for his working. And if the working power of the average man shows large and general increase, it is only to be accounted for by shining ranks of hitherto undreamed-of needs, which were evolved to lead him on!

So the missionary, acting on this theory, tries to rouse the contented savage to want things, holding that attitude to be a productive one; and the economist, satisfied with his theory, never looks to see if there is any observable connection between want and work, in race, class, or individual. In *reductio ad absurdum* the Want theory comes to this. Man works to supply wants. As the act of working does not supply wants, this involves another clause; man works to get wealth to supply wants. And this, if a real law of nature, involves some inevitable connection between the clauses: work must produce wealth and wealth must supply want. Also, if a real law, there must be some proportion between these clauses, the less the want the less the work, the greater the want the greater the work, with the same proportion in the "wealth" which is the intermediate factor understood.

This would make the proposition: A given amount of want urges to an equal amount of work which secures the desired wealth; or, Want equals Work and Work equals Wealth.

If this be so we shall find in society those who want the most do the most work, and those who do the most work have the most wealth. Poverty would be a healthy state, inevitably developing into wealth. Is this the fact? Hardly. What is the fact? This: that man does the most work who is best able to do it, and likes it most.

The way to make people work is to make them able and willing, strong, skilful, ambitious, enthusiastic. When we wish to develop horses to work more and better than previous horses, we do not seek to attain that end by cutting off their oats. The power to work comes from the energy already supplied, not the hypothetic energy of a future reward.

The "pay" comes first; not as payment, but as investment. A man's work is his payment to Society for value received, and he has to receive it before he can return it. The conscious attitude of the worker should be that of gratitude, of a proud and lavish return for the rich supply received from infancy; his unconscious attitude one of irresistible pressure, discharge of energy. Each of us owes the world our best, because to it we are indebted for all we are and have. In personal intercourse we all know the difference between services done for love, or from a sense of honourable obligation, and services done merely for pay. We know the dignity and honour of the first attitude, the meanness of the second. And yet we prefer to have the whole world's vital processes degraded and minimised to the level of that hireling service, rather than elevated and multiplied as the limitless outpouring of richly developed members of society.

To which the Want theorist replies: "It is not what we prefer, but what is," to which again I answer—It is not. The facts of sociology do not bear out the Want theory. The true place of that theory is in the stage next to primitive slavery. The first compulsion to co-ordinate effort was force and fear and pain. Only the slave in danger of death could be made to work. The next compulsion to the still unsocialised ego was that of hireling self-restraint, of withheld food. Observe that this is a purely arbitrary and social condition, involving the ownership of that food by someone else. Primitive man ate without working for many thousands of years, and does yet in many a favoured isle.

He simply picks his food off trees, or hunts and fishes for it, even fights for it. But he does not work for it at that stage of social evolution, much preferring starvation. Later on, being no longer a free agent, the food being forcibly detained until he worked, why, work he did, under the action of such pressure as he could then feel. In that period of evolution when only cruel slavery made men work, the thought that they would ever work in the comparative freedom of the contract system would have been scouted as wildly visionary and Utopian. We can see something of this among our own freedmen, members of a much earlier social status, forcibly incorporated with our advanced body and failing to respond at once to the same stimuli.

Under compulsion they worked. Free, and under no compulsion save self-interest, they do not work as industriously as further advanced races. This does not prove that self-interest is less powerful than compulsion, or that slave labour is better than wage labour, but merely that the negro race is less socialised than the Anglo-Saxon. And we, in order to aid in his social development, are learning to supply him with the social stimuli he needs. Wage labour was a useful stage in economic evolution, just as slave labour was, but the incentive of self-interest is no more final than that of compulsion.

A man will work if you make him, but also, being further developed, he will work if you do not make him, but merely pay him. A man will work if you pay him, but also, being further developed, he will work if you do not pay him; that is, if he is not "paid" individually, through personal advantage, but collectively, through social advantage. We must remember that in the way of relating effort to result collective man must "work for his living" as actually as individual. But it is *their* living which they work for; the effort and the result are in common, and to the individual is supplied the great organic energy to work with. The normal goal to labour for, in a highly socialised race, is the common interest, a far stronger attraction than the personal interest.

See how our misbeliefs affect the course of a single industrial process. Here is the wheat crop, for instance, one of the world's most important products. The human race, collectively, produces an enormous amount of wheat. The same number of workers, without the support of a large organised society, could not produce that crop, or in any way distribute it. This amount of wheat, produced collectively, is for our collective consumption. The individual producer raises a large surplus beyond his own needs for the social needs. The line of economic advantage is plain: To produce the most wheat with the least expense of social energy, and to distribute the most wheat with the least expense of social energy to the largest number of consumers. The social advantage lies in the food-value of the wheat, in the ensuing increase in the productivity of the race.

Now see how our wrong ideas work against this advantage. The individual producer, shutting his eyes to the collectivity of the process, considers that he "owns" the wheat, and that he "raised it himself." Therefore, instead of facilitating its distribution with the least expense of social energy, he seeks to obstruct it by demanding as much social energy as he can get,—*i. e.,* the price,—the first step in the exchange. Of course, being largely isolated, he does not succeed in getting much, and, equally of course, he is at present not supplied with his fair share of social energy beforehand; but admitting these facts, it remains true that his mental attitude is the same as that of the larger dealer: he looks on the world's wheat as a source of profit to him to any extent that he can reach.

Then come the great army of transporters. Thanks to the high organisation of this social function, the distribution of the wheat goes on with great facility and dispatch as far as mechanical convenience is concerned, and, by the concentration of the business in a few hands, much of the dribbling man-to-man subtraction is saved; but alas—the little subtractions of many small private carriers are only exchanged for the enormous subtractions of the few great public carriers.

Even at this extremely developed stage of evolution in the social process, even in a business so public as to require public grants of land and privilege, and designated as "a common carrier," in the very face of these flaring facts, this weird survival of a remote past, this prehistoric Ego, with its Want theory, sits gobbling in the stream of social distribution, like some dinotherium mysteriously preserved to do mischief. This Common Carrier, managed by a few men, seriously believes the distribution of the world's wheat to be intended for the private aggrandisement of the Carrier, and sucks from that life-giving stream as large a supply of racial nourishment as "the traffic will bear"—sometimes more! Of course the Carrier must be provided with his share of social nutrition in order that he may carry, but why he should claim this vastly disproportionate amount is not so clear. It is not clear, that is, in the light of social laws to-day, but it is clear enough as a logical deduction from the antique premisses so devoutly believed in.

The stream of wheat, robbed of much of its value, pours on and reaches the final stationary points of distribution, and there again the dealers, wholesale and retail, imagine that this mass of food was brought across the world for *their* benefit, and proceed to extract from it as much as they are able. Thus the food reaches fewer people in smaller quantities, and those who get it are obliged to give back a large proportion of its nourishing power in payment. The circulation of the world is very seriously interfered with by this morbid action.

Conceive now for a moment of wheat as a means of promoting the social good. Of a Bureau of Agriculture carefully posting from year to year the amount needed in different localities. Of a Bureau of Transportation carefully arranging from year to year for the most prompt and easy transfer to those localities. And of a Bureau of Local Distribution seeing to it that the wheat was as promptly and easily spread among the consumers.

That would mean the greatest gain and the least waste and expense. That would be business sense on the part of the world. To reduce the outlay of effort and increase the income of nourishment, with a commensurate increase in social productivity,—that is the line of economic advantage for the Society of our time, as it was in the physical economy of the Individual of the Palæolithic Past.

But this Palæolithic Individual with his pre-Palæolithic ideas is a great nuisance to-day.

XIV: CONSUMPTION (I)

SUMMARY

Previous propositions. Alleged selfishness. Social instincts as natural as individual. Root error on Consumption shown in Heaven, Utopia, etc. Honour in acting. Contentment theory. Limit of happiness in getting, limited; in doing, unlimited. Pleasure in eating, result of idea. Effect of this concept on Society. Impression merely incentive to expression. Transmitters, not vats. Collecting mania. Nature of ownership. Right of property. Social relations psychic. Movable rights. Law of property rights. Consumption means to production. Consumption must precede production. Natural limits of Consumption. Cause of excesses. Ill effect of morbid Consumption on producer. Must produce more than consume. Ten houses. List of propositions. Existing economic concepts. Influence of position of women. Women natural producers. Men natural destroyers. Men have monopolised production. Women made purely consumers. Women's powers, confined to family, breed selfishness. Generosity bred outside home. Feminine consumption become morbid. Vampire. Parasite. Hired matrimony. Woman as excessive consumer cause of "Society." A disease not a "function." "Society columns," medical bulletins. Effect on consumption.

CHAPTER XIV

CONSUMPTION (I)

We have laid down certain propositions in the preceding chapters, namely, that men are part of a great Social Organism; that as parts of it they are continually supplied with its stimulus and nourishment; that as parts of it so nourished and so stimulated, they must discharge the swelling current of social energy in social action, which is Work; and that the business of a conscious and intelligent Society is so to produce and distribute social wealth as to maintain and increase this flood of energy, the discharge of which in our highly specialised industries is supreme delight. Against these propositions will be at once erected that common bulwark of ancient superstition, man's selfishness. We generally believe, and as generally act on the belief, that the individual selfishness of man is such that nothing would induce him to act for the good of society, even though that good plainly included himself.

This theory of our selfishness is not borne out either by the scientific facts of our sociological position or the everyday facts of life about us.

The theory dates from a time when men were still mainly individual animals, when it was true. Being imbedded in that heavy, slow-going, ancient brain, and hammered in by each subsequent generation, it has remained with us until to-day. What we need to realise is that social development has brought with it other feelings, quite the opposite of selfishness, but equally natural, which are found in us all in varying degree; which we see at work about us, and yet which we refuse to admit into our "minds" as facts. On the contrary, we sturdily maintain in our minds the false ideas and act upon them, working much evil thereby.

The organic connection of human beings develops among them those social instincts which are necessary to promote their common good, a class which we, seeing their pre-eminent value, have classed as "virtues," calling the disproportionate action of more primitive individual instincts "vices." Neither term is true. Egoism was a virtue in the individual status; altruism, or rather, omniism, is a virtue in the social status; both are natural. Our misinterpretation and false naming have prevented our easy assumption of the new qualities, that is all, the past concept being more potent to our minds than the present fact.

Among the group of root errors still retarding our development, none is more mischievous than that wherein we assume pleasure to lie mainly in impression rather than expression. We believe that what we get makes us happy rather than what we do, and therefore consider our doing as a means of getting. Perhaps this idea antedates even the Want theory; but it is needless to grope too critically among the errors of the remote past, they are all old enough.

The utmost extreme of this early error of ours is found in our general scheme of Heaven or even of an earthly Utopia. When we give free rein to fancy in seeking to portray happiness we arrange that an individual may have everything he wants, and be provided with some eternal miracle in the way of appetite, it is to be hoped, that he may keep on wanting it!

The Happy Hunting Grounds of our American savages and the old Norse Walhalla had some action in them, probably because the savage believers knew of no other way to procure food save by hunting for it. With the red man and the brawny slayer of Scandinavia, action was so intimately connected with gratification and with honour that their future state had something doing as well as eternal banqueting. But observe the more sophisticated Mohammedan Paradise, with its ecstatic debauchery, and our own Hebrew Heaven, with its music and jewelry and the chorused adoration of an oriental court,—no action is predicated of these, save that necessary to get there. We postulate rest, peace, plenty, rich and beautiful surroundings, things to have for eternal joy, not things to do.

Some of our seers and philosophers have often perceived the fallacy of this belief, and have preached in various voices to the effect that man should "Act well his part—there all the honour lies."

Moreover, most of us practically find that there is more pleasure in doing what we are best fitted for than in having anything whatever; but still the dominant governing theory of humanity holds that a man's real business is to get such and such good and that "he won't be happy till he gets it"! I heard this theory well expressed in passing by two men in the street recently; well-dressed, important-looking, elderly men:

"Yes," said one of them, shaking a handsome cane, "they get their money all over the world and come here to spend it, to live!"

A better expression of this dominant belief it would be hard to find. The immense world-wide activities of the business men alluded to were defined merely as "getting money," and the spending of that money, the obtaining all manner of materials for consumption, was defined as "living." Acting under this belief we see the majority of mankind using continual effort to get things for themselves and their families, and, when the things they desired are attained, yet no resultant satisfaction follows, they merely transfer the ideal and seek to get more, other, and different things. Against this tendency a minor line of philosophy has been levelled, preaching contentment, but this philosophy is still on the wrong basis, for it is still *the things* we are told to be contented with—those we have instead of those we have not, that's all.

In practical truth the happiness of man in what he gets is limited, extremely limited, but the happiness of man in what he does is unlimited. The receiving capacity of our nervous system is soon exhausted, but the discharging capacity has no limit but that of natural periods of rest. The pleasure in expression increases with use, the pleasure in impression decreases with use.

It is interesting, pathetic, and absurd, to see the spasmodic contortion of nature under the effort to enjoy having things. We enjoy food, naturally. The use of food is, plainly, to enable us to do things, and if we do enough we always enjoy food. But the foolish person ignores doing things and seeks to enjoy food as an end in itself. The enjoyment soon palling, and even decreasing as the natural appetite decreases, the foolish person then pushes on in a line of artificial enhancements of this natural function, bringing in an elaborate convocation of other senses, with various luxuries and arts, so as to prolong and increase his enjoyment. The enjoyment receding vaguely before him, he adds eccentricities to his luxuries, runs the gamut of elaborate changes, and plays Hob with his internal organs, all in the persistent endeavour to hold on to the enjoyment of eating.

In this particular field of enjoyment no animal alive has attained such subtle, exquisite, and long-drawn pain as we have achieved withal. Our array of alimentary diseases is really instructive, yet does not seem really to instruct us. We still persist in putting the cart before the horse and looking for pleasure in what we get. In the field of economic action, this fallacy exerts a constant evil influence not only by checking the output, but by degrading and distorting that output to suit the growing vitiation of taste which always results from this belief.

The governing concepts of any society at any period tend inevitably to such and such results, but their effect is modified by interaction and by many external circumstances. As the society grows and circumstances change we may see one and another root-thought working to its special result; checked by this, modified by that, but always tending to its own end. So this one thought, acting with all our others, right and wrong, may be followed in the ever-present social tendency to luxury and excess.

If you believe that happiness lies in the impressions you receive, you naturally modify your action to the purpose of securing the desired impression. Seeing the impressions fail to produce the expected happiness, but still believing in the theory, you simply strive to secure further impressions. Finding, as jaded emperors have found, that to have everything in the world you want does not make you happy, you still hold on to the theory and merely sigh for new worlds to conquer; or, if your religion is also built on this theory, look forward to an eternity of having things to make you happy.

The demand for happiness is perfectly healthy and right, but we are mistaken as to the means. Every possible impression receivable by the human sensorium is merely an incentive to *expression*. We are transmitters of energy, not vats for storage. Our capacity for storage is merely to give us wider and longer range in our discharge. The living force of the Universe is pushing through man, and as that force is greater than he, so is the joy of doing greater than the joy of having. "It is more blessed to give than to receive." Of *course*!

Let us study some of the practical results of this false concept of ours. One of the most exquisitely sublimated extremes of its action is seen in our distinctively human practice of what is called "collecting." It is bewildering at first. That a squirrel should collect nuts, and, on the same line, that Pharaoh should collect wheat, or that the housewife should collect food in advance, is all "natural." That anyone should collect that "greatest common denominator," money, is the same tendency as above. But that a human creature should collect a vast supply of objects which he does not use, never intends to use, and could not use if he wanted to, is truly remarkable.

The objects may be of use to other people—if they had them—as in innumerable pieces of china, but of no use to him; or they may be of no use to anybody, like defaced postage-stamps—but that does not affect the collecting instinct. This depraved appetite, seeking to acquire for personal "ownership" without even the excuse of consumption, frankly waiving the pleasure of using the things and affixing that pleasure solely to the getting and having of them, is as morbid a process as could well be imagined. It is "the mania for owning things" in full delirium.

What is the normal law of ownership? It is simple, like all natural laws.

Social processes are served through the social body, through a great number of detached mechanical structures. The social functionaries, in order to carry on their functions, must have a certain extra-physical environment. The family and the individuals therein must have homes, the body must have its clothes, the worker of all sorts must have his tools, his shop, all that is necessary for his work. Society requires of the individual the performance of certain functions. That performance requires the continuous use of certain mechanical adjuncts. Society must guarantee to the individual the continuous possession of those adjuncts, of the things necessary for him to do his work. That is the social "right of property."

All property is a social product, evolved in the course of social development, needed by society for the social service. Any social factor, a carpenter, for instance, is a working agent consisting of a human animal specially skilled and specially tooled. Without the skill and the tools he is not a carpenter. Society having evolved the skill and the tools, certain members of Society then become carpenters. Since their skill is essential to the social service, Society must educate them; since their tools are essential to the social service, Society must *secure the tools to the man*. This is ownership, a social right, quite just, and perfectly natural.

Social relations are psychic. Property rights are psychic relations. We agree that such men shall own such things, and they do. We deny that such men own such things, and they don't! Men once owned slaves—everywhere. This "right" was gradually withdrawn by the givers, until it now only exists in certain localities of low social development. Parents once "owned" their children, could kill or sell them. This right has been withdrawn.

There is no ultimate basis for human rights but the best interests of Society, and our conscious recognition of human right depends on our knowledge of those interests. Thus our rights change from age to age, as Society changes, and our laws and customs slowly follow the new developments in social consciousness. In our time we are in the active throes of change on two great subjects, the rights of women and the rights of property.

On the latter head this formula is advanced as a safe one: The individual has a right to those things necessary for him to best serve Society. That is, the carpenter has a right to his tools, and the musician to his instrument, both to their special education, and they and all men to the food, shelter, clothing, and other things necessary to their *best social service*.

Not a return *equivalent* to, as we try to arrange our system of payment, but a supply *necessary* to, in advance. If a man is to write books for humanity he has a right to his pen, ink, and paper; and to such other conditions as are essential to his best productivity; but because one man's books are worth ten times as much as another's, is no reason why he should have ten times as much pen, ink, and paper.

Consumption is a *means to production*—impression is of value as it conduces to expression. The pleasure and the duty are in Doing. Having is merely contributory.

Our mistake about consumption is what our payment system rests on; we work merely to obtain something; and that something is rigorously measured according to our previous labour. In changing the ground of our thought, we shall recognise that production is the main issue of life; that consumption is essential to it; that each social factor has a right to such supplies as shall best promote his productivity, and that they shall be provided him in advance.

"The mill will never grind with the water that"—hasn't come!

If this position be reluctantly admitted, there follows the alarmed demand: "But if the consumption of the individual is not measured by his previous output, how shall we measure it—how shall we prevent him from an inordinate, a disproportionate, socially wasteful consumption?"

How do you measure the dinner for your family and friends? What prevents them from eating a bushel apiece? The natural limit of consumption is capacity, the natural measure is necessity and appetite. A constant and sufficient supply of anything does not provoke inordinate consumption—quite the contrary. A refined and moderate selection is the result of full and adequate provision. Inordinate consumption is the result of a deranged supply. People who customarily do not have certain things cannot develop taste and judgment in selecting them.

People who generally have too little, are quite apt to take too much when occasion offers. Knowing that the supply is uncertain leads to taking more than is wanted, so as to store for future use; and the "pecuniary canons of taste," so ably described by Veblen ("Theory of the Leisure Class"), lead to that meretricious display and cultivated wastefulness which form another phase of our abnormal consumption.

Natural production tends to fill the world with constantly improving supplies. Natural distribution tends to place those supplies where they will do the most good. Natural consumption tends to appropriate all that is good and beneficial, and thereby promotes production—a spiral of social progress.

We have seen how production and distribution are injuriously affected by our misbeliefs, notably by the attitude of the obsequious caterer to the desires of the purchaser. The reason these desires are so deteriorating to the world's production is in our false attitude toward consumption. The combined effect of our popular economic superstitions reaches a considerable height of injury to society.

Here is the producer limiting his output, as far as possible, to something well within his income, each man striving to get out of the world more than he puts in: whereas all our wealth and progress is conditioned upon our putting in more than we take out—and thanks to the marvellous productivity of the race, we do, we must, so put in, in spite of our ego-centric struggles. Here is the producer, again, guiding the kind and quality of his output, not by real human needs, or by the laws of improvement inherent in the product, but by the weaknesses and artificially fomented tastes, as well as by the purchasing power of "the market."

If "the market" has a small purchasing power, that means, under our economic system, that the human beings composing it are low-grade stock, cannot produce much themselves. Under sociological law it would follow that they be supplied with the best things, in order to improve their productive power, in order, again, so to add to the social wealth. But in our method, measuring what a man shall have by what he can do, we give the least to those who need the most! Surely anyone can see how stupid this is—to limit consumption to the value of previous output, and so steadily to maintain a low output. Conversely, by seeking to increase consumption in proportion to output, we again do evil; for consumption has its own inexorable limits, bearing no relation whatever to output, *after the needs of the producer are really supplied.*

Surely, this too, is plain.

So much fertiliser to the acre will increase the crop—but not indefinitely. So much fuel to the fire will increase the steam pressure—but not indefinitely. So much oats to the horse will increase his speed—but not indefinitely. And so much of our great stock of social goods will increase a man's social value, his health, happiness, and working power—but *not* indefinitely. Because I am the better worker for a house suited to my needs, I am not therefore ten times the better worker for ten houses suited to my needs.

Food, clothing, education, painting, literature, music, entertainment,—a certain amount is good for a man, improves a man, belongs to a man; but the indefinite multiplication of that amount merely injures the man.

Now suppose we change our minds about consumption. Suppose we do fairly recognise these plain, natural facts:

(*a*) Man lives by virtue of social relation.

(*b*) Social relation consists in specialised interservice.

(*c*) That interservice consists in the production and distribution of all our human goods—from potatoes to poetry.

(*d*) The advantage to Society lies in the constant development of its processes, a better and easier production and distribution.

(*e*) The duty of the individual lies in his best service to Society in these vital processes; and the duty of Society lies in supplying to the child the best conditions for full growth and genuine education, and in continuing to provide to the adult those conditions essential to his full, free, and most efficient service.

(*f*) All that we produce is intended for the maintenance and development of Society.

(*g*) All that we consume is intended to promote our productivity and general social value.

(*h*) The advantage of the individual lying absolutely in the hands of Society, it is the obvious business of the individual to see to it that Society performs its duty to him—to all of him—and, as obviously, to perform his full duty to it—which is merely all of him.

With this economic creed we should see each individual doing his best work, and Society eagerly hastening to supply to each individual all that he needed to do his best work. As against this consummation devoutly to be wished stand our existing economic concepts:

(*a*) Men live by virtue of their own work.

(*b*) Men have to work in order to satisfy wants.

(*c*) The satisfaction of wants is the purpose of life.

(*d*) The advantage to the individual lies in his getting as much as he can, and doing as little as he can—in "buying cheap and selling dear."

(*e*) The improvement of the individual lies in Society's not giving him anything till he has shown that he has it already—or its equivalent in labour. Thus the less ability he has, the less of anything he gets—which improves him.

(*f*) All that a man produces is his own, and he has a right to consume it all himself, or destroy it—in any case, to withhold it from those who want it till they give him as much as he can get for it.

(*g*) All that a man consumes is pure advantage—the advantage of life. To have everything we want, to accumulate more than we want, to invent new wants with infinite pains and supply and oversupply them—this is happiness. And since we find practically that the few who do it are not happy, and that the many who cannot do it are not happy either, we assume an eternal appetite, and an eternal gratification in another world!

(Singular thing—the unsatisfied desires of Man! Trying to put a quart measure in a pint cup through an india-rubber eternity!)

(*h*) The advantage of the individual lying absolutely in his own hands, it is his obvious business to take care of himself; and since the pressure of social relation cannot be ignored, we assume that the business of society is simply to preserve "a fair field and no favour" for individuals to struggle in!

"That government is best which governs least."

"Give us natural opportunities and freedom."

"A man has a right to do anything he pleases that does not interfere with the rights of others."

Fortunately for us the working of natural law is that of the first creed; and our personally misguided conduct of affairs cannot wholly crush back the social growth belonging to our time.

In this connection it is important to note the influence of women, in their artificially restricted position, upon the world's consumption, not only in economic fact, but in our inherited feeling and education on that subject.

Women, as we have repeatedly seen, were the first producers. Creative industry is theirs by the deepest laws of nature. The female is the original reproductive stream of life; and in the higher stages of her development she still manifests the larger range of race-activities. In the human species for by far the longest period of our life, the proto-social, she was the main—almost the sole—producer, men being mostly destroyers. But for the most of our historic period, all the time that is best known to us, women have been prevented from taking part in progressive human production and restricted to the duties of a house servant.

What tendency to specialised social service they might manifest was promptly banned as "unwomanly," belonging only to men. The man elected himself to be sole producer, in the large social sense; and the woman was to be only a consumer, to depend on him for her maintenance and take what he gave her.

The position is acutely abnormal—quite opposite to the inherent nature of the female. It is her instinct to *give*—not to take; ably to do, not feebly to be done for.

This unnatural attitude was forced upon her, however, with two results, inevitable results, as regards consumption.

One is that all her flood of power and patience and infinite service being confined to her one master and their children, she has developed in them inordinate appetites and morbid tastes. The productive force that should flow broad and smooth in Society at large, being bottled up at home, with no consumer but the family, necessarily accustomed the family to receiving more than was good for it; thus maintaining in the world the ancient selfishness of the primitive individual, which real social life tends steadily to reduce. The social instincts, those large and outflowing feelings we call generosity, justice, altruism, are bred in the mutual service of specialised social industry; but the individual instincts, once virtues, now become vices if too prominent, are nursed and fed continually in that hotbed of all personal indulgence, the wife-served home.

Thus the position of woman promotes the tendency to inordinate and morbid consumption in man and child.

But it has also a direct influence on her. She is born and reared in this same atmosphere; she inherits from father as well as mother; the habits of many generations have a gradual effect upon her, and all old civilisations show one monstrous sight, the bottomless greed of the artificially bred women.

As Cleopatra outdid Antony in "conspicuous consumption"—swallowing a dissolved pearl worth more than all his gobbled delicacies; as Nana destroyed expensive furnishings just to amuse herself; so have these horse-leech's daughters outdone any sons that estimable sucker may have had, in the cry of Give! Give!

Burne-Jones' picture of "The Vampire" typifies well man's opinion of this horror which he has so carefully made. Our instinctive dislike of greed in a woman is based on its unnaturalness, it is essentially foreign to her sex. But the fact remains that women, in their false position, have become greedy beyond description. The bountiful producer, aborted, has become a destructive parasite.

The boundless pouring love, compressed to primitive limits, becomes morbid and works evil; and the habit of always taking, and never doing, has produced its unavoidable result, and given us the woman we all know, who takes, greedily, from a childhood of wheedling, through a youth of coquetry, and a lifetime of hired matrimony. When it is not matrimony, language fails to express our horror; but when it is, the commercial basis discolours the relation; and the plump and beautiful creature in the costly surroundings she never thought of giving a return for, is in the same category as a consumer with her less respectable but no less plump and expensively surrounded sister.

To find the pleasure of life in getting and having, to feel no honourable impulse to *do*, to *give*, to *work*, to return to labouring humanity your quota of service,—this is the degraded position into which we have forced our women, and which expresses itself not only in them, but in their children, who are all the world.

Such women play the game we call "Society," whose trivial performances are celebrated so respectfully in our newspapers in their record of dinners and dresses and dances, as if where these people ate, or what they wore, or how they hopped about, was of any earthly importance. The seriousness with which this class of people who have cut themselves off from human life by refusing to take part in its active processes, who neither produce nor distribute, but consume in ever-increasing ratio, take upon themselves the distinctive name of "Society" is one of the most paralysing jokes of history. They even designate their pitiful amusements as "social functions," a misnomer as consummately absurd as "Christian Science."

For a lot of richly caparisoned human animals to get together and eat, or embrace one another and caper about to the sound of music, has no more relation to a social function than St. Vitus's dance has to chopping wood. A disease is not a function. This fatty degeneration of the social tissues is a sad and important fact, deserving careful study; but its importance lies in its danger to the rest of the body politic, not in any inherent dignity.

If we take our "Society Columns" as medical bulletins, they have some value perhaps; but vulgarly to enlarge on our forms of disease is at least bad taste. What we commonly call "Society" is a morbid growth in the real social structure, developed to meet the artificial needs of these misplaced women; and such a society, influencing as it does, through widening ranks of imitators, the markets of the world, has a most evil effect on our habits of consumption.

If we saw clearly on these lines, recognising production as a law of Human, *i. e.*, Social Nature, then our women, as our men, would take part in the healthy processes of real social life. If we saw that this constantly increasing expression of a constantly increasing fund of social energy was limitless happiness, we should turn our competition another way, cease this painful effort to show who can get the most, and begin to run races to show who shall do the most, with the result that there will be more for everyone to have.

Meanwhile, under the action of this special delusion about consumption, we continue to fill the world with false products, and to spend strenuous lives trying to get them away from one another. Can we not recognise this one thing, that consumption is but a means to an end; that production, Work, is the end to which a legitimate consumption is a necessary means, and that the only natural and practical measure of consumption is the need of the consumer.

XV: CONSUMPTION (II)

SUMMARY

Resistance of false concepts to true. Spread of literature. Use of imagination. Hypothesis as to natural laws in consumption—free clothing—Veblen. An unnatural market. Commodity money a check to distribution and production. Real conditions. Enormous producing power of civilised man. Legitimate consumption. Truffles. Free transportation. Free provision reduces demand and increases productivity. Property rights and personal ownership. Evolution of ownership, ownership a psychic relation, a social condition, based on social needs. True law of ownership: "Society must insure to the individual those things which are essential to his social service." Decrease of self-interest. Success of our surviving savages. "Making money." Normal wealth must circulate. Belief in polygamy. Natural relation not Communism. Legitimate personal property is in goods consumed—not in goods produced. Normal ownership inheres in normal consumption. Production belongs to Society. Man does not consume his own product, but that of Society. Human rights social—essential conditions of true social relation. Previous position, based on Ego concept and Want theory, does not work well. Compulsory production not normal. Owner and Employer. "Iron law of wages." Want not a productive force,—tends only to consumption. Organic action of Society. America's productivity does not show commensurate greed, but fuller supply of social nourishment and stimulus. Parent's relation to child, and Society's. Social duty.

CHAPTER XV

CONSUMPTION (II)

Our minds are so thoroughly accustomed to thinking along false lines in economics that true and natural social processes, when described to them, seem but fantastic dreams.

This is only according to the brain's working habits; it takes time to change it, and we need much patience with ourselves and one another while changing. Fortunately for the age we live in, there has been so much change in so many lines that further progress is easy, compared to what it was a few centuries ago. Fortunately in especial for the country we live in, its national attitude is that of welcome to the new, suspicion of the old.

In the wonderful spread of the great art, Literature, and particularly the branch art, Fiction, as distributed so universally among us by our libraries, our periodicals, and the daily press, we have far more general use of the imagination-our brains will stretch. This faculty of imagination is no mere factor in telling fairy-tales; it is that power of seeing over and under and around and through, of foreseeing, of constructing hypotheses, by which science and invention profit as much as art. Distance, perspective, proportion, these are obtained, in our consideration of facts, by use of the imagination. The rocks and stars confronted the savage as they did the beast, and with little more result; they were visible facts, that is all. He could not imagine any further content in his observation. We observe, similarly unmoved, the facts in economics.

Now let us use this common faculty of imagination; and, judging by man's behaviour in conditions we do know, try to measure what it would be in other conditions. Let us take one concrete instance in this process of consumption, a perfectly conceivable hypothesis, and see for ourselves how it would work out.

We will now assume that clothing was free to all. This does not mean that it was dropped from the sky; we are still to produce and distribute it; but the final absorption by the individual is unchecked. What would be the consequence? At first there would be a rushing seizure by the people who have never been satisfied in clothing—they would take and take again—greedily—inordinately—sacking the shops and stuffing their houses. But suppose the supply is maintained, steadily. They would soon find it was inconvenient to stuff their houses, if the stores remained always to draw from. The hoarding instinct does not spring from continued plenty, and becomes foolish in the face of it.

Then, though not carrying off so much, they would perhaps choose the most beautiful and expensive fabrics. Finding that all wore the same, these distinctions would cease to distinguish; if everybody was wearing velvet at will, the result would be that those who did not really like it would leave it off. If everybody was wearing lace, they would find it was too frail for outing costumes. If there was no artificial glamour on one stuff more than another; if the supply was steady and free; then, slowly, gradually, timidly, would appear for the first time among us true personal choice! People would at least know what they personally preferred and have it; clothing would be adapted to genuine need and genuine taste.

Our habits of consumption are so complicated by long deprivation on the one hand, and by "the pecuniary canons of taste" (Veblen) on the other, that most of us live and die without ever knowing what we really want. "The Market" for which our producers competitively cater is an unnatural one. What we call "the demand" is not a healthy, legitimate demand; it is uncertain, capricious, subject to strange fluctuations and reactions; and in endeavouring to "supply" it, the most experienced and far-sighted producer often fails.

What is legitimate consumption? Is there any measure by which the world's market could be regulated? No measure is needed. Our mistake here is due to continually seeking to govern production by an arbitrary system of payment. On the theory that a man will not work except for pay, it follows that his work will be strictly adjusted to the pay; and thus the tendency to a constantly increased productivity is held rigidly in check by our existing means of payment. Commodity money adds the last straw to this heap of folly.

Men will work only for pay.

Pay must be money.

Money must be gold.

So the amount of human productivity must be measured not by the muscular power, brain power, and machine power of society; nor even by the amount of corn and wool, wine and oil, wood and stone, and other necessaries; but by the amount of one particular metal. It is fortunate we have not elected to measure human production by radium!

It was bad enough to try to check our vast output by an arbitrary equivalent in goods; but it is so much worse to squeeze and strain it through this tiny gauge that it does seem as if we might have seen our foolishness long since. But that is where the power of a concept is so much greater than that of a fact. As a matter of fact, the bulk of the world's business is done on credit; and its material vehicle is paper-a mere matter of record of transaction; but in our minds we still deal only in gold; and every once in a while we must interrupt the course of production and distribution to see if all accounts can be balanced in gold. As the business is necessarily in advance of the gold—always and always—we have to exert ourselves to get more gold—even if we must go to war for it.

Try the imagination again—see the consequence, if gold suddenly grew common as dirt—and lost its supposed "purchasing power." Talk of "fiat money"—never was any fiat more purely arbitrary than this solemn assumption of ours that a hungry world cannot eat—a strong world cannot work—a vast and intricate organism in full swing of vigorous life cannot perform its functions—without every act of mutual service being measured in gold. The vital facts in the case have no more connection with gold than with wampum. Production and consumption go on as conditions of our organic life; distribution facilitates both; and we, governed by this Punch and Judy troupe of primitive ideas, check and pervert all these great functions.

What are the facts in true social economics as concerning this question? They are these. The earth furnishes us with the raw materials for living. Civilised man is able to combine those materials in consumable form, and to distribute them to all, with increasing facility. Even under all our obstructions, the rate of production and distribution increases with rapid strides; if free—it is impossible to estimate the gain.

Put it something like this:

A primitive man can obtain the necessities of life by giving all his time to it. A civilised man of our day can produce his share of all the necessities of life, in say one-tenth of his time. In the other nine-tenths he can produce comforts, luxuries, all the higher products of human life. Under right conditions, civilised man could produce the necessities in a hundredth part of his time, and could so grow and improve as to lift all the higher products to a far more advanced stage. Fully supplied with all he needs of this social wealth, the producing power of civilised man is far beyond his needs. "His needs" brings us again to the question, "What is legitimate consumption?"

We assume that, unless rigidly kept down by arbitrary forces, man would riotously consume in unending profusion; that he could not possibly supply enough for general consumption; and that since the supply is limited, it should be rigidly confined to those who can pay for it. This is an unwarranted claim. Normal consumption does not increase in any such wild way.

The normal demands of the whole human race for food can be met by the materials at hand. Observe that they are in some measure met now; our millions do live, do eat, even under present conditions. They might live better, have a more improving diet, under better conditions. But if, like Mr. Bounderby, we assume that everyone will wish "to be fed on turtle soup with a gold spoon"—we are wrong. "Have some truffles!" urges Mr. Newrich. "I don't care for any," answers Mr. Bornrich. "Not care for truffles?" cries Mr. Newrich; "why, they cost five dollars!" "What of that?" says Mr. Bornrich; "I don't like 'em!" "Conspicuous consumption" is a feature of leisure-class culture, of illegitimate wealth founded on illegitimate poverty. With consumption on a natural basis, there would be no great demand for nightingales' tongues.

Observe the existing facts in any department of social supply we have made free to all. Our highroads are free—but we do not therefore run continually up and down on them, just because we can. We travel as we have need of it, that is all. Free roads facilitate normal traffic and promote civilisation. Yet, when it is urged that free railroad travel is a necessity to-day, there is a horrified dissent. "What? let people travel on the railroad without paying for it? Why, they would travel all the time!" You see we do use our imaginations a good deal. These objectors imagine that mankind would desert both business and pleasure, forego the joys of home and the attractions of both city and country, to spend their days in the discomforts of a railroad train, and their nights in those culture tubes of all bacilli, the sleeping cars,—just because travel was free!

Have we never seen the plain and common fact that free provision of anything reduces the demand to the normal at once? Things "common" are not wanted, unless they are *really* wanted. All artificial demand drops off. There is no pride, no element of "conspicuous waste" in having what everyone can have, in doing what everyone can do. But the normal demand goes on, and the world is enriched, all progress is promoted, by the gratification of that need.

Sometimes people do things merely because they cost money,—to show financial superiority,—but they do not do things merely because they do not cost money. Free consumption would not increase any legitimate human demand, but it would increase our power, and skill, and so our wealth. Recognising that human production is conditioned upon previous supply, upon right inheritance, right education, right environment of all sorts, it follows that the more fully and freely we supply that environment, the more we produce.

Against this clear sequence stand, like a range of mountains, our theories of property rights—of personal ownership. Personal ownership, private property; we believe in these things as we believe in God,—and a good deal more so. These we hold to be basic principles, they underlie all else, nothing can shake them. Whoso questions or criticises them "strikes at the foundations of Society."

It is not the first time that Society has been challenged in what it held to be foundation principles, has been led to change those principles—and has still survived. Cautiously, and gently, not to jar or strain our unused brain areas too much, let us draw near this mighty pile and see on what it rests. Bear steadily in mind the history of human life—and of all life behind it. See all the ages of pre-human evolution going on in their majestic work without any dream of such a thing as property, or ownership. See humanity in its slow beginning, developing the extra-personal medium of life, the garment, shelter, tool. See how these things, detached, yet essential, exchangeable because human, yet had to be connected with the holder for his personal good and social efficiency.

Here, as we have shown in the preceding chapter, arises the true law of ownership, and ownership as natural as that of the beast of his teeth and claws, a true social law. It has no individual basis. Individuals carry their property on their bodies, it grows there. Society evolves detachable material adjuncts, the made things, the social medium. So far as this social medium is usable by all, it should be free to all. So far as it is peculiar to the specialised social functionary, it must be guaranteed to him. Society must guarantee to the individual those things which are essential to his social service. The civilised man has given up his power of caring for himself in order the better to serve Society. Society, to profit by this service, must insure right provision for the individual. In a clumsy, unjust, ill-managed way, it already does so, has always done so, it could not live else. But it has not done so fairly, or well, and, therefore, it is ill served, it suffers and sickens, and in repeated instances has died.

Again and again in history we may see the process: the nascent society developing, growing more and more specialised and interdependent, that development reducing the power of individual constituents to take care of themselves, self-interest weakening in the mass as social interest became increasingly necessary; and then the most primitive members of Society, those still most actuated by pre-social instincts, the surviving savages in civilisation, taking advantage of the immense social productivity, and claiming for themselves the social wealth.

They are not the world's best servants. Their power is not the power of highly specialised talent or genius. It is a truism that the more ability a man has to serve Society in its advanced needs, as in the arts and sciences, the less ability he has to "make money," as we call the process of individual absorption.

The gold miners and the mint "make money," all productive labour makes wealth; but those who secure the most of it for themselves are of quite another class. The verb "to make" and the verb "to take" have not the same root.

This illegitimate development of ownership is injurious to Society. Wealth, in normal circulation, is productive, is a social advantage. Wealth, in abnormal secretion, is not only unproductive of good, but absolutely evil in its influence. Yet, the whole process, with all its mischievous results, is conditioned upon our false concept as to personal property and the right of ownership. Its glaring heights of evil are most conspicuous; but the mischief lies not in the special extreme instance, but in the general condition.

See the effect of a belief in unchecked polygamy. Under economic pressure, the mass of the people have but one wife, and so are saved the worst effects. But the crowded harems of the great show most shameful results—sensuality, cruelty, idleness, physical deterioration, conspiracy, murder. Are we then to blame the polygamist in proportion to the number of his wives; or merely to recognise the principle as wrong,—and the one-wived believer as much in error as Solomon? It is our common concept of ownership that is to blame, not Carnegie and Rockefeller.

See how the true principle would work out. Society is a unit, we are but parts. Social life develops the power to make things—the things which are essential to social life. Increase in these things is increase in social wealth and social power—a ceaseless line of development. The good of Society requires the best development of all its parts—that they may so produce more. The best development of all the parts requires the full supply of social goods.

The social goods belong to Society, are made by Society, for Society; and should be distributed to Society as widely, swiftly, and freely as possible; so adding to the social good. Now this line of talk, to the general mind, means a wallowing sea of communism. We see visions of a flat and uniform world, of no ambition, no distinction, no privacy, no private property, and therefore no life worth having. This is because we do not know what private property really is.

Legitimate private property includes all that the individual needs to consume. All the food he needs, all the clothes he needs, all the education he needs, all the tools he needs; to each person what he separately needs, and to each group what they separately need of the great fund of social advantages. Is not that property enough? All that a man can legitimately consume is his own, but not what he produces. That is his return to Society. What he produces is of no use to him, his dentistry, or surgery, or masonry, his teaching or acting, his manufacturing or transporting,—this belongs to Society.

We have erred in attaching the claim of ownership to the goods produced. It belongs only to the goods consumed. The property rights of the individual to his own food, his own shelter, his own clothing, his own tools of production,—be they paint brushes, books, or chisels,—need never be questioned. So fast as production becomes collective, the means of production become collective. Where a separate weaver had a right to own the separate loom with which he produced cloth, now the group of operators, from "hand" to "head," have a right to own the mill with which they produce cloth, but not the cloth.

To whom then does the cloth belong, if not the maker? To the wearer, of course. Cloth, as we have shown before, is a social tissue, it is evolved for social advantage. It has to be worn by members of Society. We recognise this so clearly as to have laws commanding people to wear clothes, punishing them if they do not. Such laws might be justly applied to silkworms, but hardly to human beings, unless their clothes are also provided. No doubt a position like this seems impossible to our minds, so used are we to the other, to the present belief that a man owns what he produces, and no one has a right to it; but that he has no right whatever to the necessities of life—to the means of production.

Let us think fairly and courageously about it. Here is a man born. This product of his is yet potential, he cannot produce until he is grown. What he produces when he is grown, in kind and quantity, depends on what he consumes as a baby, boy, and youth. Now since Society needs his product,—not *he*, mind you, he has no use for the bricks or the books he will make,—since Society needs his product, and since that product is conditioned upon his previous consumption of previous product, Society, in its own interests, must see that he is supplied with all proper provision,—he has a right to it.

"A right" means an essential condition. Human rights are all social, conferred by social consent, and resting upon the social good. The right to individual liberty, the right to justice, any right of any time rests on the general acceptance of social benefit involved in those rights. We have seen long ago that the good of Society rested on the best human productivity; but because we believed that productivity to be conditioned upon subsequent reward, instead of previous supply, we defined our rights accordingly.

Our position was like this: Society needs our best product. Man will not produce, except to gratify his own wants. What he produces is his own, because it is essential to the gratification of his wants. Therefore, Society must guarantee to each man the product of his own labour.

The effect of the position is this: Conceiving ourselves to be independent units, conceiving our end to be the gratification of our wants, conceiving our product to be a personal possession, and only produced in order to gratify wants—we necessarily seek to limit the output of our work to the measure of our wants. The consuming capacity of the man is made the measure of his production, and under such a standard we see no way to increase production, except by increasing the consuming capacity, the wants. This is held by our existing economists to work well, but they overlook certain essential elements in the position.

The free production of the world is obviously not that of the persons who want the most or who get the most. No one can show that a man's social value depends on his greediness. To want all things, to want them intensely, to want them continually, to want them to be of the best,—this does not add to a man's industry, or intelligence, to his skill, ability, talent, or genius. The best and most work comes from those who have the most ability and inclination to work, though they may be, and often are, the most modest of consumers. But—and here is the neglected element in the case—if production is not free—if productive labour is under any compulsion, then truly those who want the most will, if they have the power, *compel other men to work the most.* That is, if you do not make things, but merely take them, it is obvious that the more you want the more you will take.

To recur to the status of slave labour. In this system productivity is under direct compulsion. It is proportioned to punishment. The owner of the slave labour, if he wanted things, took from the slaves the product of their labour, and the more he wanted the more he took. In this case the greediness of the owner is productive, his slaves produce more because he wants more. But if their labour were really free, his wants would not affect their productivity.

Again, in wage labour, we have the employer and the employee. What is an employer? He is one who "owns" what other men want. They cannot get what they want unless he gives it to them. Since these things which they want are the necessities of life, they must work for pay, they are not free.

The employer, if he wants things, takes from the employee the product of his labour; and, as before, the more he wants the more he takes. Since he must, in order to gratify his wants, keep these men alive and productive, he must return them something; but the action of his wants upon their labour tends to keep their share at a minimum. This we call the "iron law of wages." We hold that it stands to reason that a man will give as little as he can to get what he wants. This is quite true, want does not promote productivity.

But these employees are not free. If they were independent of the employer, he could not make them work to gratify his wants. Personal desire does not add to personal power, neither does it add to other people's power. Desire, want, hunger, may direct action; but it is not a productive force, it is a tendency to segregate and consume, not to produce and distribute.

Now see the effect of the position here laid down.

Consumption is but a means to production. Production is a natural function of Society—organic, interdependent, instinctive. Production is promoted by increasing social energy and social consciousness, besides the self-evident condition of maintenance.

The organic action of Society necessarily involves a common nourishment, as it is even now seen to involve a common defence, and beyond that it requires a progressive increase in social stimulus. Our increased consumption is an accompanying condition of our increased activity, as the hard worker should eat more than the idle; but it is the well-distributed nourishment that promotes the activity, activity does not nourish. Now since the life and progress of Society depend on our best production, it is the natural duty of Society to so distribute nourishment and stimulus as to promote that production. A rich, strong, free, intelligent, thoroughly educated society will produce far more than a poor, weak, foolish, uneducated society.

The tremendous productivity of America does not result from our wanting more than other people, as is popularly supposed, but from our having more. Not only the great natural advantages of the country, not only the independence which left men more free to work, but our public institutions for wide distribution of social advantages, such as free education,—these have combined to make the American not a greedier, but an abler man. Note in small instance the difference between our custom of free service of ice-water in the theatres, of programmes and the like, of toilet conveniences in the great stores, and all such matters, as compared with the twopence or fivepence you have to pay extra for so much as a napkin in an eating house in England.

"But," says the Englishman, "you have to pay in the end." We are willing to pay in the end. Any decent man is willing to pay for what he has had. It is the difference between the "European plan" and the "American plan." So soon as a more enlightened society provides more and more fully and freely for the needs of its citizens, so much the more cheerfully will they be willing to pay for it.

Our personal work in the specialised service of the great social body which maintains us is our payment for goods received. The slave works to avoid the whip. His labour might be termed whip-dodging. The employee works to obtain bread withheld. His labour is called "bread-winning." The free and socially conscious human being works because he likes to, because he can't help it, because it is his honourable return in small degree for the immeasurable benefits he has received from infancy from his supporting society. We have established a very binding sense of "duty to parents" because we believed that the father by his unaided arm supported the child; the mother by hers reared and trained it. The parents unquestionably give the child its physical and mental endowment. But if we proportioned our duty to parents to the value of our inherited constitutions and temperaments, some parents would get short shrift.

Beyond the gifts of birth, the mother's breast, and the tendency to benefit of parental love, what else the child receives is from Society. Parents were parents and did what they could in savage and pre-savage eras. That parents are wiser and tenderer is due to our progress in Socialisation. That they are richer and more powerful is not due to parenthood, but to Society. The heaped-up increment of all the years, the highly developed products of our industry and skill, the discoveries in science, the masterpieces of art,—these are all social products not parental.

The child needs to be supplied with all that he can healthfully consume of this his social inheritance, his birthright as a human being. Some children have more of the social products than others because their parents have an arbitrary and unnatural "ownership" of these products; but as a normal condition of sociology, all children have this claim upon their great social entail, with no "right of primogeniture" or other usurpation to interfere. So supplied, and so taught to recognise the true supplier, it will be as easy to rear our children in a sense of duty to Society as it is now to duty to parents, and more so, because this later, larger claim is so indisputably true. With the full productive power of the race finally set free and pouring out on normal lines, there will be no lack of social benefit for all.

We have seen the economic advantage of wage labour over slave labour; can we not see the even greater economic advantage of free labour over wage labour?

XVI: OUR POSITION TO-DAY

SUMMARY

Fact and delusion. American advantages and possibilities. Possible consciousness. Perverted Press. Falsely maintained position. Grade A and grade G. Soul paradoxes. Old Adam. Arbitrarily opposed "Leisure Class" and "Working Class." Parasitism actual and potential. Dead matter in live body. Sour grapes. Charity an evil. Helplessness of rich man trying to establish right relation. Furnishing employment, i. e., furnishing payment. Unhealthy secretions resultant from over-consumption. Law of private servants. Doctor with a herald. Degraded art. Human value in work. Painful result of social disconnection in leisure class. Working Class suffers differently. Higher social position of Working Class. All human labour collective. False classification. Economic relation of sexes, result. Effect on child. What he should be taught. The round man in the square hole. Extended ill effect of malposition in social organism. Waste of energy, inferior workmanship, deterioration of social tissue. Progressive mal-nutrition. Genius.

CHAPTER XVI

OUR POSITION TO-DAY

The difference between our real position in social development, and that maintained in our minds, is very great. It is as if a strong, capable, rich man suffered from mania, had a delusion that he was a puny, feeble, evil-minded wretch, and acted like one. Could the delusion be removed, he would act like what he really was and be happy.

Taking our own country as a type of social progress, what do we find to be its real conditions? In the first place, it has every material requisite for health and growth. It occupies a piece of the earth's surface big enough and varied enough to supply all the physical elements of triumphant advance. It has, second, not only a base of the best human stock, but a large and steady influx of all human stocks; it represents the blended blood of all races, a world-people truly, prototype of that cosmopolitan race which will ultimately cover the globe. This gives a chance for all possible development in stock and manifests it. It allows also all religions to contribute their best, all arts, all sciences; every line of special usefulness known to man is known to us.

There is already sufficient intelligence to administer world-interests competently, as shown in clear-headed captains of industry. There is already sufficient "social instinct"—*i. e.*, human love—to make elaborate and costly provision for our defectives and degenerates, to push earnestly for reforms and improvements in every direction. Yes, there are quite enough ardent "homophiles," warm lovers of the kind, already in the field to do all of that sort of work we really need. The reason they do not accomplish it all is partly the lack of intelligent recognition on the part of the rest of us, and partly limitations and errors of their own minds. They care enough, but do not know enough. So here we are, in plain fact, rich, strong, intelligent, loving, quite able to live in magnificent wealth, peace, and happiness.

In equally plain fact we are living quite otherwise.

We should manifest perfect physical health and beauty. We are, on the contrary, nearly all sub-well, very many sick, and very few beautiful. When we look at the possibilities of the human body, as shown in ancient Greece, and then at the kind of cattle we are content to be now, it does no credit to our intelligence. We should manifest a common grade of education which would give to each mind an area of thought including the earth and sky, plants, animals, and minerals, the wonders of science, the powers of manufacture, the whole history of the human race. This would be possible to practically all of us with right use of our educational advantages. We do manifest, on the contrary, a universal ignorance, even in this comparatively well-educated country, a feeble, purblind, sticky little brain stiff with prejudice, shackled with habits, blinded with superstitions, and narrow, narrow to the paltry limits of one human animal's own family!

Of course most of us know in a vague way that there are other peoples, that there were other times; but these knowledges hang in the background of our minds like faded wall-paper, lie far from us, disused and unfamiliar. The occupied area of the brain, the part we think in and feel in all the time, is the tiny spot of ego-consciousness. It is as though a man owned the Waldorf-Astoria and was content to live in a bushel-basket. It is quite possible for the average mind, properly educated, to waken each morning to a consciousness as wide as the world, full of light and air, with the facts of life seen in true distance and proportion. This does not necessitate accurate, special knowledge of all branches of human achievement, but a general knowledge that there are branches, and how they branch. A rightly spent youth should easily give this to every normal child.

But we, on the contrary, waken each morning to the cramped, overtrodden field of our immediate personal consciousness only. The affairs of the world, our world, loom vague and distorted about us, while our own, forced upon us by night and day, are so absurdly magnified by being held too near that they easily shut out the world. Our press, which should give to each mind each day its world-view of current progress, is so perverted in its function by the cramped minds of its egoistic functionaries, that it gives instead a weird kinetoscope of what it thinks will interest us! As if a general, waiting for dispatches from the field, should be entertained by competing orderlies with funny anecdotes! As if those anxiously waiting for bulletins from the sick room should be provided with impressionist pictures of the patient's relatives!

We do not occupy a hundredth part of our mind-space, no, nor a thousandth. And in this darkness, this cramping limitation, with but a partial and restricted education and the false world-views of our misguided press to relieve it, we blunderingly creep about in the great world-functions we *must* serve, each of us imagining that he is taking care of himself. The difference between our real position and our false and artificially maintained one is like this: If, for instance, certain marked improvements in telegraphy have been invented, raising our social efficiency in that line of distribution to grade G, that is our legitimate condition; but if these improvements are destroyed by misguided workmen, bought up and suppressed by misguided property-owners, keeping our telegraphic efficiency back in grade A, that is an illegitimate social condition. We are *really* in grade G, but artificially in grade A.

If, again, the machinery of democratic government is open to all, our legitimate condition is that of full democracy; if a large proportion of persons fail to exercise their political functions, preferring to remain in a lower grade, or if an entire sex is forcibly prevented from exercising them, that is an illegitimate condition.

The economic conditions of society to-day are confessedly paradoxical. The gain in facility and speed of execution is million-fold, and yet men are required to work almost as many hours as before their improvement. The expressed wealth of the world is enormous, and the power to multiply it not nearly used, yet a vast proportion of our members are not fully supplied with the necessaries of life. In ways too commonly known to need enumeration here we may observe this strange difference between our *real* period of social evolution, with its beneficent results, and the existing state of Society.

The persistent survival of lower social forms, becoming more injurious with each advancing age, is one conspicuous feature in the case. That we, the foremost industrial nation, should have preserved that early status of labour, chattel slavery, past the middle of the nineteenth century is a historic anomaly; that we still preserve the yet lower status of female domestic labour is a worse one. That we should maintain side by side, in the same age, a democracy for men and a patriarchate for women is a brain-splitting anachronism.

Taken generally, the confusion and irregularity of social progress furnish some ground, at least apparently, to those who assume it to be extra-natural, and who postulate direct interference by Spirits of Good and Evil to account for the peculiar facts. We need no such childish hypothesis, the facts in the case are quite sufficient. Our painful and irregular social development is due merely to the presence in a highly organised body of the artificially maintained egoism of a previous unorganised condition. The "old Adam" in us is simply the individualistic animal, still protesting that he is an individual in the face of centuries upon centuries of socialisation.

Perhaps the most conspicuous feature of our position to-day is that of the strangely distinguished "Leisure Class" and "Working Class." Here is a social body whose existence requires mutual service. Here is that service performed by that majority of mankind known as the "Working Class." The Working Class is the world. However he prospers, the man who works is he who keeps the world going. His labours are the social processes, he is Society. The Leisure Class deliberately cuts itself off from Society, refuses to take part in its processes, yet continues to live on its products.

This is parasitism, pure and simple. That it is not so pure nor so simple as would render it easy to handle, or as would warrant us in ruthless excision of a diseased mass, is due to the resistless law of social relation which holds us still connected even when we think ourselves separate. Your wealthy social traitor, refusing social duty and absorbing social gain, is no more to blame than the workman, *who would do the same thing if he had the chance,* because he believes in the same false principles of economics. But as they stand the leisure class is doing incomparably more harm.

The mere extra drain on our material wealth as rich a social body as ours could easily stand. The mere malingering, the refusal to work, we could stand; the social energy is so abundant, there are so many to serve the world. But the position of the overconsuming non-producing class is not merely negative and cannot be. Withdrawing from normal social processes, the leisure class forthwith becomes the seat of abnormal social processes, which affect the whole body most injuriously. Every recognised folly and vice of these conspicuous ex-members of society spreads its corrupting influence around in the healthy structure which supports them. A live body cannot maintain dead material in its substance without injury.

Much deeper than the recognised follies and vices, though they alone have blackened history, lies the influence of the falsehoods on which the leisure class rests its position. Let no live member of the body politic make the mistake of *blaming a disease*. If any part of Society works wrong, it should be studied, not hated; cured, not punished. In our great organic union any common error works out its natural result, varying in accordance with the part affected. The callosities and deformities of our social body, its sudden illnesses and slow, wasting diseases, call for our utmost wisdom and for a change of conduct, but they do not call for childish rage.

This mischievous by-product called the leisure class can be eliminated by healthy action on the part of the real social body. It has no existence except as we make and uphold it. Like the criminal class and the pauper class it is an inevitable result of our imperfect social action, and that imperfect social action springs from errors in all our minds, not merely in the minds of the diseased portion. The attitude of the non-productive consumer is the legitimate result of our general economic fallacies; logically, if conditions allowed, we would all cheerfully join their ranks. As it is, we all, or nearly all, try to, and the successful, knowing this full well, are naturally not much moved by the criticisms of unsuccessful competitors. The flavour of sour grapes is clearly perceptible in most of our animadversion against the rich.

Moreover, when a human being of our day, coming into some share of the social consciousness proper to the time, feels that he has no right to this mass of other men's labour in money form, he can find no way out of his position on any basis of strict political economy.

Charity we know to be evil, though we still fool ourselves by organising it and putting great numbers of intermediaries between giver and givee.

The currents of human production, as forcibly modified by our laws resting on false economics, do accumulate masses of capital; given individuals find themselves on top of the heaps, and they cannot get off! If they flatly abdicate it is only to let some other eager aspirant mount after them. There is something genuinely pathetic in a modern rich man or woman, striving to readjust what he recognises as a disproportionate provision and absolutely unable to do so. Every step he would take is cut off by some traditional error.

"I too will go to work!" cries the uneasy Crœsus. "I will not sit here and live on the wealth made by others!" But all cry out against him. "Stop! Go back! You 'do not have to work'! Work is only to get money, and you have got it; be satisfied and leave the field to us! If you work for nothing you lower the scale of wages! If you work at 'union rates' you rob some poor man of the job!"

Hemmed in by these theories there is nothing for the rich man to do but to keep on working for even more money, which is commonly allowed to be excusable if not commendable, or to go and play. The true "Leisure Class" only plays.

Their playthings cost much money, but as this money goes back to those who make the plaything they justify themselves by the "furnishing employment" theory. This is a very old fallacy, and impossible to refute while we believe that work is a thing done to get wealth, and that wealth may be legitimately "owned" to an indefinite amount by individuals.

As Society increases in productivity wealth increases, and by our arbitrary apportionment it increases in the hands of individuals—it has to. These individuals holding all the goods and other people needing the goods, yet the Pay theory—no goods except for previous work—acting sharply here, the only legitimate method of distributing these individual congestions of wealth is by "employing" as many as possible. And as we do not consider *the work* as the important part of the exchange, but the pay, so we do not care at what the beneficiary is employed, so long as he is paid.

What we call "furnishing employment" we really esteem as "furnishing Payment,"—looking at the good, the real good in question, to be the holder of many things, making it possible for the worker to also get things,—the "Pleasure-in-Impression" theory acting with the Want theory and the Pay theory.

So every developing society raises its specially rich individuals who do not produce. They, in the increase of their inordinate consumption, demand more and more service from their fellows, till, instead of one healthy human creature easily producing more wealth than he can consume, we have this spot of local disease consuming more and more of the labour of other people, thus depraving more and more of the substance of Society. All these caterers to abnormal appetites cease to be producers in a healthy sense; they do not add to the well-being of Society by legitimate products for social distribution, but add to the ill-being of Society by unhealthy secretions centered in one spot.

If the production of this mass of workers abnormally localised is in itself legitimate; that is, if the "employer," *i. e.*, the consumer, consumes only useful and beautiful things, even so the effect is injurious if he consumes too much; it is still local congestion, though of healthy blood; but that position is intrinsically untenable. No leisure class ever contented itself with really useful and beautiful things. You do not make a Vitellius on wholesome food. Consumption, pursued as an end, naturally develops into morbid excess, and the caterers to it must produce unhealthfully. This is the hole in the "furnishing employment" theory.

It is not being employed that benefits a man. If I pay a man a hundred dollars a day to sit in one spot and twirl his thumbs, or to climb up and down one post continually, I am not benefiting him, I am injuring him. If I subtract a human being from social service and add him to my private service I degrade him, unless I do more work by virtue of his service. Here is the law of private service:

A human being is entitled to as many servants as he can do the work of better.

That is, if two men, working separately, can produce to a certain amount each, but if the two, combining, one serving the other, can then produce through the one served more than the previous amount of the product of both, that is a legitimate social relation. For the doctor to have a helper to take care of and drive his horse enables him to do more and better doctoring; he can justify his having a servant. But for the doctor to "employ" a driver, a footman, a page, two outriders, and a herald, would not add to his efficiency as a doctor; that would be an illegitimate relation.

The overconsuming rich do mischief first in withholding from the social circulation an undue amount of social products, as a mere miser—social congestion; second, by withdrawing from the social service an undue amount of labour for their own aggrandisement—a social excrescence; and third, by *perverting the product* of their private commando of workers, generating unhealthy secretions in the body politic—a social disease.

The miser merely robs society to a certain degree, the employer of much labour for his own gratification robs it by so much more, and beyond that comes the steady deterioration of an illegitimately directed product, a true poison, with the progressive breakdown of the tissues ensuing.

This effect on Art is quite plain in history. The artist doing great work for the public grows and serves the world. The artist catering to an employer does not grow, but deteriorates. The work is not only withheld from Society, to which it belongs, but is lowered in kind. Art is always corrupted and lowered by the patronage of luxurious wealth. So is manufacture. No plea of "furnishing employment" to the artist can cover this injury to the world.

The artist should be working for the world which made him instead of putting his social product in one man's hands, and the work he does should be noble and should improve, as it cannot in that position of personal dependence. The value of an artist to the world is that he shall do as good work as he can for as many people as he can reach; it is of no use to the world that he be "employed" on other lines, nor is it good for him.

Every worker stands in this same social relation. The value of a workman to the world is that he do the best work for the most people, not that he be "employed" to make clothes for dogs, or to wear an ostentatious livery behind a mutilated horse. Every human being is to be measured by his value to society, and the value is in his work, not in his being "employed"—or paid.

Our non-productive consumer, therefore, is unable to return to a healthy place in the world. He cannot work because he "does not have to," and his efforts to re-distribute the wealth for his own gratification form merely a "vicious circle" of futile and injurious activity.

Now see the pitiful results. Cut off from normal connection with the living world by failure to produce, and only generating disease in his efforts to consume, the unfortunate ex-human begins to die. He may, if sufficiently wise and self-restrained, keep his body alive; members of the leisure class frequently live to a great age; but this well-preserved animal existence only allows more time to suffer from the unnatural exile. He is not part of the living world, and so falls victim to various hideous abnormalities. He dwindles and shrivels in social usefulness till, instead of a vigorous, valuable man or woman, you have the futile, inadequate creature which cannot even wait upon its own wants; or, keeping up animal health by caring for the body, he shows the deformity of his position in furious and senseless activities.

The most conspicuous feature of our leisure class is the elaborate round of purely arbitrary and unnatural activities in which they ceaselessly whirl. The only natural activities open to them, the physical, become abused and perverted in vicious excesses, and their other activities are a series of arduous games and sports, changing from age to age and year to year, the purposeless and hopeless spasms of social energy misused.

The working class, on the other hand, suffer differently. That they are underpaid is plain, that they are overworked is plain; we hear much of this of late years; what we do not hear so much of is that they suffer most from the same misunderstanding of what work is. Looking always at the Pay as the end, the Work only as a means, they labour drearily on like a blind horse in a treadmill, never seeing their real position in Society, their real duties, nor their real power. That the unproductive consumer should believe the absurdities on which his absurd position rests is comprehensible; but that the producer, not properly supplied with social nourishment, and overtaxed in the production of the very supplies he does not get enough of, should accept the basic fallacies which hold him in his even more absurd position,—this is not so comprehensible.

Perhaps what does account for it is this: that with all his labour and suffering the worker after all *is* Society; he is in the main performing great service; he has a right to be more contented than the ex-man who does not work. He is in the more normal position, though he does not know it; and the sociological laws are always stronger in their action than our notions. As a matter of fact the working class, which does not mean merely the "labouring class" of our present terminology, but which includes all workers with hand and brain, is the world. They are the acting factors in those processes which constitute social life.

Through all these centuries of unbelief and misbelief they have done the things which kept the world alive. They have clothed the world, fed the world, housed the world, taught the world, beautified and improved the world; yes, and have lifted it from savagery to its present level. To-day in our democracy they need only enlightenment to see a further duty to the world in a better organisation of its economic processes. Thrilled as they are by the swiftly growing current of social consciousness, conscious as they are that things are wrong, anxious as they are to set things right, they are still hindered by these economic errors of us all.

Under the Ego concept they speak of "every man's right to the product of his own labour," a sociological absurdity. In the first place no member of Society has any "own" labour, our labour is all collective and co-ordinate. In the second place it is not the product of his fraction of our labour that a man wants, but the product of the labour of many other persons, of all times and places. In the third place it is not even "the equivalent" of his fraction of our labour that a man wants, it is a previous supply of the social product bearing no relation to his subsequent output except that of nourishment and stimulus.

In short, there is no true class-distinction in acceptance of those deep-seated errors which together modify the conduct of mankind so injuriously. The false classification we are treating is *the product of those errors*. With right economic belief and action there would be no division of Producer and Consumer, no Leisure Class, no Working Class, no serried ranks of Capital and Labour. All would produce, all would consume; all would work and all would have leisure; all would share in the social capital and the social labour,—both elements of social advantage.

The economic relation of the sexes is of enormous importance in our present-day problems, as I have endeavored to point out in my previous book, "Women and Economics." The economic dependence of the female on the male, her food being obtained, not in industrial relation with society, but in the sex relation with the individual male, affects the race not only through the ensuing overdevelopment of sex, but through an artificial maintenance of primitive ideas and feelings in economics. The woman's artless attitude of taking all that is given her and frequently asking for more, without ever entertaining the idea of return in kind, of paying for her keep, maintains in the race, as we have previously shown, the tendency to inordinate consumption, the quenchless appetite of a parasite. This parasitic appetite is the invariable result of economic dependence. We need not wonder at the evolution of a parasitic class when we maintain, or seek to maintain, a parasitic sex.

As we have seen in an earlier chapter, another effect of this condition is, by its resultant exaggeration of the sex nature of the male, to maintain in him the belligerent and destructive tendencies which belong to a remote period of race improvement through sex competition, a period of animal individualism, and which work much evil in a period of constructive and co-ordinate industry. Where wealth and progress depend on the cordial intelligent interdependence of the group, it is most deteriorating to have maintained this primitive attitude of sex combat. Again, the male, being obliged to provide goods for several persons besides himself, and yet being limited in goods to the amount he can himself produce, the natural desires of the individual are augmented by the accumulated desires of the whole family, yet gratified only through him; and each man faces the world, with the output of one, yet requiring the income to support six—or whatever number he represents! According to the Want theory this is a beautiful provision of nature for augmenting the man's output. In the light of fact it does nothing of the kind. It simply augments his desire to get—in no way adding to his power to give. That moving mirror of life, our literature, is one long picture of the effects of this incarnate appetite at home, dragging ever at the man's purse strings, and pushing hard against social honour, social duty, all the high traits of citizenship.

The child, most important of all, reared in this atmosphere of continual demand, seeing his father looking on the world as a place to hunt for prey for his mate and young, seeing his mother do nothing whatever but minister to the family needs, inevitably grows up to look at life in the same way. To his growing soul, the world appears to be a number of houses with families in them. The business of life appears to be to keep house for these families. The mother does this in a life of personal service. The father does it in mulcting "the world" as far as he is able.

If, on the contrary, a young human being grew up to see his father regarding his work for humanity as the chief duty in life, his mother with the same attitude, both regarding the consumption of goods as but a means to further and better work, and those goods always explained to him to come, not from the individual exertions of his father "wrestling with the world," but from the combined exertions of that world—that great, rich, kind, ever-fruitful, and generous world of willing workers which feeds all its children so well,—but I stray into consideration of future conditions instead of present.

At present we have for the common lot of humanity that painful exhibition known as "the round man in the square hole." Of all human troubles, none is so universal as this—a man's work does not fit him. His income is insufficient, his output is insufficient, and he does not healthfully enjoy the process of living. A general condition of misadaptation, with necessary results of mal-nutrition and mal-production,—that is the prominent and visible symptom of our deep-lying psychological errors.

Consider the life of a typical average man.

He is misborn, misfed, mistaught, mis-clothed, misgoverned, to a varying degree. Instead of having a clear view of the social life and his place in it, he has a false and distorted view of his personal life, and only sees the social action as it infringes on him. He is surrounded from infancy with poor workmanship, the grudging product of those unhappy, misplaced men in square holes. The education which should be his introduction to the great and beautiful facts and laws of life, is too often a "bread-winning" process, practised by celibate women, as being more respectable than other work, and introducing him merely to a mass of unrelated facts and old ideas. The higher the field of social service, the less does "whip-dodging" or "bread-winning" help, and none is higher than teaching.

Thus mishandled, the boy grows up without the aid of that subtle discernment and delicately applied special training which would have brought out his best faculties. He is a blurred, indeterminate, self-contradicting group of faculties, he has no unerring organic preference to lead him to his work. He is the nearest approach we can make to that "all-round man" we hear so much of; but the intricate duties of social service do not furnish us with one-sized cylindrical holes for our machine-made pegs. Into some hole he must go, we will not feed him else; so in he pops, and "settles down for life."

That is our common phrase for a permanent establishment in the active service of Society, otherwise known as "self-support," "earning one's living," "maintaining a family." Our average man is not expected to love his work, to enjoy it, to grow continually through it. He does all this sometimes, but too rarely. Our methods of education have been specially esteemed, not because they taught the child to like what he did, but taught him to do what he did not like. We take it for granted that he will not like his life work, and so seek to fit him for continued application to distasteful service.

In such work as this, there is a continuous waste of nerve force. Compelled attention, and action that is not led by interest and fed by the natural discharge of energy along preferred lines, are suicidally wasteful. In Nature's effort to reduce this steady leakage of life force, she transfers the action to the domain of habit as rapidly as possible; and the sufferer experiences that much relief. Dislike, the exhausting effort of enforced attention and the plunging and kicking of more normal impulses toward other activities, give way at length to a dull contentment, a patient submission to monotonous routine, and some pale pleasure in its monotony.

There are three large distinct evils to Society in such an artificial misplacement of its members. First, the work done is not as good nor as plentiful as if it were done on lines of true organic relation, by the men specialised in power and preference for that work. In the second place, the man is weakened and worn out prematurely by the unnatural effort to do what he does not like, what he is not fitted for, what is not his own special work; thus further reducing the output. And in the third place, the overtaxed and unhappy worker requires all manner of extra inducements and palliations to keep him at his unsuitable task. He has to have rest, more and more vacations and changes, or breaks down sooner. He has to have various fictitious excitements in his work—making it a game, a race, or a fight; to make up for its lack of normal interest.

And he has to have "amusement" and "recreation" also of an unnatural, morbid kind—heavy doses of social stimulus coarsened and concentrated to suit his exhausted nerves. All this beyond the prominent well-known evil of the resort to physical stimulant and solace, such as alcohol and tobacco. These last rapidly deteriorate the physical stock of the race; again injuring Society in the stuff it is made of; but the degraded and excessive amusements injure the very soul of Society; lowering every kind of art which caters to them, and so demoralising the highest lines of advancement.

A thousand minor lines of injury may be traced, such as the increase in defective children, owing to exhausted parents, and its accompanying tax upon Society's resources; but these main lines stand forth clearly: The limitation and degradation of the social output, and the deterioration of tissue in the constituent members of Society.

The deterioration of human stock is twofold; partly due to the strained, unnatural position of the worker; and partly due to the effect of inferior supplies furnished by his degraded product. In the more directly useful human products there is less injury than in the higher forms. In food and clothing and carpenter work it is easier to detect fault and falsehood, and there is less of it; though even in these departments our adulterated food, shoddy clothing, and jerry-built houses do harm enough; but in the more advanced professions, the evil is enormous. The faults and falsehoods in product, in literature, art, religion, government, and education, that spring, first, from their being done by the round man in the square hole, and second, from their being done for the unhealthy demands of the other round men in square holes,—these work incalculable harm.

Here is the girl who is trained to be a teacher because it is reputable, and who accepts her square hole and does her unsatisfying work as patiently and dutifully as she can. It is excellence we want in work, not a patient and dutiful inferiority. This inferior quality of teaching is further lowered by the unwise demands of the misplaced people who pay the teacher, and so a continuous morbid action is generated. It would be a hard task to show one human grief, one human sin, that does not find part of its cause and maintenance in this so general condition of our life to-day. See the comparative result in our physical organism if we set fingers to serving as toes, eyes as ears, lungs as livers. If any such misplacement were conceivable, it would involve so low a degree of development in the various parts that it was possible to exchange services, and none of them could do good service.

In the social organism such high specialism and efficiency as we have is due to the progressive force of our economic development, calling forth such positive preference in some men that they will do the work they like best. All the world's great servants and helpers have been thus driven from within, by the rising flood of social energy, specialised to one burning focal point of expression. Such men work without reward, and regardless of opposition; work their lives long, often live and die poor and unhonoured, simply because they were true to their fundamental duty as human beings—to serve Society in the function for which they were evolved. In spite of their neglect, abuse, and injury, they are not to be pitied; for, on the one hand, they had the enormous joy of serving humanity; and on the other—even if they were not aware of that high pleasure—they had the intense functional satisfaction of doing the work they were made for.

We are so used to "the dull level of mediocrity," and the labour whose noblest height is conscientious effort, that when we do find a strongly specialised individual so highly fitted to perform one service that he can do no other—we call him a genius. So great is the power of working in these "geniuses"—the happy lavish outpour of social energy through a natural channel—that we have put the cart before the horse as usual, and defined genius as "the capacity for hard work." There are a thousand hard workers for one genius, but a fact like that does not worry our shallow generalisers. Unfortunately, owing to our lack of true education and the crushing weight of the false, only the exceptional genius now and then succeeds in forcing his way to his true place, and he does it by breaking through the poor, blundering, reward-and-penalty system with which we obstruct social development, and by letting out what is in him, producing his natural fruitage of work, quite irrespective of pay or punishment.

Thanks to this quenchless functional vigour of Society we are never without some natural work; and thanks to our vast facility of transmission we all share in the products of genius to a greater or less extent. Yet it is but a painful and niggard harvest compared to the universal crop we might enjoy if we would let it grow. Happiness to the individual is in fulfilment of function, it is as much in farming as in fiddling, if you like it—"every man to his taste." And the benefit to society lies in every man's working "to his taste"; as beautiful and desirable a combination as need be imagined.

This does not mean that all would manifest transcendent genius, but that each, in his place and degree, would have that strong instinctive tendency, that vivid delight in fulfilment of function which should accompany human work in every department.

XVII: THE TRUE POSITION

SUMMARY

Duty of improvement for individual and race. Effect of Ego concept. Collective nature of Christianity—"'our' daily bread." Unity of man. "Kingdom of Heaven." First human duty to assume right functional relation to Society. Right social relation tends to develop all virtues, to eliminate all sins. Want Theory and theft corollary. Normal distribution prevents abnormal acquisition. Sins against property and person. Thieving produced by clot of wealth. Right organic relation. End of "the wolf," of "our" sins, of unnecessary diseases. Twofold duty—to change concepts and conditions. Public school and library. Social debt to the worker. Malthusian doctrine. True law of increase in population. Natural selection among individuals. Difference in organic development. Artificial selection. Stirpiculture. Superior methods of social improvement. Poverty increases number of births, but decreases quality. "Individuation is in inverse proportion to reproduction." Splendid opportunities. Two roads to health. Right condition—right action. General cause of local evil. The home, effect on social consciousness. Better housing. Way to growth. Human nature. Happiness.

CHAPTER XVII

THE TRUE POSITION

To be—to re-be—and to be better, none can deny this order of duties; and the last is the highest.

To become better as individuals has long been preached to us; to become better as a race is no unnatural proposition. Heretofore, the Ego concept ruling, we have supposed that this was only to be done by improving as many individuals as possible. And as individual conduct, ego-guided, consisted in each doing things for his own benefit, here and hereafter; our improvement has been somewhat hesitant and tortuous, both in person and in race. It is really singular to see how the Ego concept has held us from understanding what was best in our religion. The one great advantage of Christianity over Buddhism, or Mohammedanism, is in its radical *collectivity*. As far as a pure monotheism goes—the constant worship and service of God, the Mohammedan is beyond us. As far as a pure morality goes—an exalted sinlessness, the Buddhist is beyond us.

But none of them prays: "Give us each day our daily bread." Now is it not, truly, a strange thing that we should have been taught that prayer for two thousand years, and yet every man Jack of us goes forth stoutly, to get his own private and personal daily bread as rapidly as possible?

The strongly enthroned Ego concept of more ancient times; buttressed hugely by the dark savagery and sordid barter of as ancient religions, has successfully evaded the recognition of Christianity's great central truth, that man is one. Not only that God is one—Jew and Mohammedan know that; but that *man* is one—that we are inextricably interconnected, and cannot be considered separately. "No man liveth to himself, nor dieth to himself." "He that seeketh his life shall lose it, and he that loseth his life for my sake [man's] shall find it." "Inasmuch as ye have done it unto one of the least of these, ye have done it unto me."

Resting on the firm basis of natural law, and affirmed insistently by our prevailing religion, is the fact of human solidarity.

The improvement of human life does not consist in withdrawing as many individual souls as possible for a "reward" (that everlasting payment theory!) in Heaven; but in a diligent bringing about of what that same principal prayer of ours sets clearly before us—the Kingdom come, and the will done, right here. This, too, we have intellectually admitted to be desirable; but have united in transferring the occasion to a remote and uncertain period, known as the millennium.

Now, what, in the light of truth as at present open to us, is the best way to improve the human race, and therefore our highest duty? Recognising the organic relation of Society; that our very life, to say nothing of our improvement, rests on our becoming properly related to each other in the specialised service which constitutes a human life; and to perform that service ever better—the first duty of a human being stands prominently forth. It is this:

To assume right functional relation to Society, to one another. Not charity, not philanthropy, not benevolence, not self-immolation or self-sacrifice or self anything; but simply to find and hold our proper place in the Work in which and by which we all live.

To do one's right work involves all the virtues.

Our virtues are always matters of interrelation; they concern our attitude toward each other, our treatment of each other. An individual man, alone, can manifest no virtues beyond those of a clean beast. Human life is interrelative, and all its virtues, *i. e.*, distinctive qualities, are interrelative. Once accept this basic duty in fulfilment of specialised service, and all those virtues, we, as individuals, have been so fatuously striving for, appear in us, as natural corollary of that right relation. Conversely our "sins," namely, our various forms of social disease, manifest in the bewildered individual, will of themselves go out as naturally as the virtues come in.

Classify our sins. One enormous mass we call sins against property; all forms of theft, robbery, and the larger and subtler kind of dishonest appropriation. This class is the natural result of our perverted distribution of social products. It is one of the many weak spots of the Want theory that an absence of the essentials of life, instead of promoting industry, often produces more direct and injurious methods of transfer. Quite the larger part of our legal machinery is devoted to the maintenance of the local congestion of wealth on the one hand, and to the prevention of the breaking-down of the social tissues under pressure of that congestion on the other. Given a surplus of wealth in some places and a deficit in others, and the fabric of human nature breaks down in a given proportion.

Want makes men steal quite as naturally as it makes them work, indeed more so, as being the earlier custom. Our political economics founded on the Want theory should give half their pages to a study of the proportionate relation between Want, Theft, and Wealth, after the learned discussion of Want, Work, and Wealth. One is as legitimate a fact in economics as the other.

That normal distribution of social products which would provide the growing individual with all that he needed to bring out his best powers, and which would teach him clearly where and how to use those powers in return, would drop out of the world completely this class of sins. The supply coming *first*, the child growing up to measure his conduct as a return for what has been given him; taught from infancy to see in the world, behind and around him, the endless Giver, and himself as the product of it all and owing his output to those now alive, and more especially those to come—that child, that man, will have no comprehension of theft, major or minor. In a word: All illegitimate acquisition of property rests on the illegitimate retention of property. Remove the cause, and you remove the effect.

What remains? Sins against the person. Part of these are based on property also,—all murder and violence done "with interested motives," or in revenge for previous injury to property, or denial of property. A large majority of the sins against the person would go, too, when we establish right distribution.

There remain the sins based on the sex relation. The right economic position for women will remove the greater part of these. When women no longer make their living out of their loving, the prostitute, and that more successful specialist, the mercenary wife, will leave the world. The reduction of sex-attraction from its present fever-height to a normal level, and the perfect freedom for true marriage resultant upon right distribution of property, will take away the cruder and more violent forms of sexual sin, and gives us pure monogamy at last.

I do not say that *all* sin would leave the world upon our assuming right economic relations; nor even that this great mass would disappear in a night; but the cause of the disease being removed, the healthy social currents would flow calmly on and we should soon outgrow these evils too long endured. Social disease will eliminate itself by right living as does physical disease.

"Sins" are always phenomena of defective social relation—they are not individual matters at all, an individual can no more do wrong than he can do right. The beasts have no morals because they have no Society. Human conduct is all interrelative; and right or wrong *as it affects the others*. Given any wrong relation in Society, and a certain proportion of sin works out among its members, now here, now there, according to the nature of the diseased relation.

The despot breeds the sycophant, the liar, the assassin; the rich man breeds the thief; the woman who makes her living by marriage, the prostitute. And these sins cannot be checked in the point of expression, the individual, any more than you can cure scarlet fever with salve.

We are good, or *We* are bad,—with remarkable disconnection of personal circumstance. The thieving produced by the clot of wealth may not break out in the immediately surrounding tissue if that is pretty healthy, but creeps along the line of least resistance, and appears through the brain least able to resist it.

No man liveth to himself, and no man dieth to himself, again.

If, then, this great field of evil, and a thousand as evil concomitants, may be cleared off the world by the adoption of more healthy social processes; if those healthy social processes consist in each person's being in his right place, and doing his right work in Society; if, too, it clearly appears that to the individual consciousness this right place and right work represent Happiness,—Happiness such as we have never been able to conceive in our little ego-stunted brains; then human duty looms up large and clear.

To find your right place, to do your right work, here is the basis of all virtue, joy, and growth. Here is a steady improvement of every human product, things better and more beautiful, things made more easily and more plentifully; and every human being, better nourished physically and socially, pouring forth the ever-rising tide in harmonious social growth through work. It means a lifting from the heart of man, first, of Care. All that life-long terror of the Wolf, the dragging weight that follows from the young father's anxiety over his first-born—can he provide for it?—to the dying man's anxiety over his growing children and wife left behind—can he provide for them? This crippling terror—(which we have solemnly affirmed was an incentive to labour!)—being removed for ever by the mutual insurance of a civilised society; man can lift his head and work with a light heart and a free hand.

It means lifting from the heart of man, second, Sin. Just to see that Sin is *Ours*, not mine and thine, means instant relief and illumination. Then to see where it comes from, to remove its causes, to watch its shadow recede slowly from the glad, bright face of man, like the passing of an eclipse; that will leave us free to work indeed.

It means lifting from the body of man nearly all his load of disease; his diseases being as clearly traceable to social disorder as his sins. There is no difference, save that one is manifested in physical relations, and the other in social. That the human animal should not be as clean and healthy as other animals is due to his false social relations. When they are right, he maintains all the animal's physical purity and vigour, and adds to it the yet unsounded depths of social vigour.

With a prospect like this before us, what prevents a sweeping and instant change? Nothing prevents a sweeping and instant change in the minds of some of us; a recognition of the nature of human life and human work which sees it all natural, all healthful, all good, in itself; and the bad only an evanescent mistake, easily to be avoided in future; but to spread that recognition in the minds of all of us means time and effort, and cannot become general at once.

Meanwhile, it is open to us, without waiting for all to see alike these patent truths, to go to work on such changes in economic condition as shall soonest check the decay in social tissues so dangerously apparent at both ends of our present "Society," and to bring up, as soon as may be, those whose growth has been arrested for ages.

The world is full of aborted people, aborted by the crushing pressure of these old lies in economics; people crippled in mind, people crippled in body, people swollen and distorted from being oversupplied and underworked; people shrunken and distorted from being overworked and undersupplied. These can be helped at once by those of us who see the wisdom of improving the race without waiting for them to understand and accept the principles on which the change in condition rests. We did not wait for all the citizens of America to believe in the principles involved, before giving them the public school and public library. Many do not, when questioned, even now believe in those principles. But they are not reluctant to avail themselves of the provision made; and the advantageous results of that provision are apparent in our citizens, whether they understand why or not.

There are some most comforting facts, meanwhile, in our social relationship, which enable us to attack the concrete problems of our time with courage and patience. Seeing that our gain is social, and not individual, and that it is rapidly transmissible as far as the brain is open to transmission, we have but to develop the brain of our laggard members to bring them into possession of the whole great field of social advance. The wealth of Society, steadily augmented as it is by the very individuals who need so much more social return than they have ever had, is quite equal to any drain which may be necessary to pay up our arrears of debt to the worker. A conscientious and aroused society, seeing how unjustly neglected have been its most valuable constituents, cannot do too much to bring to them, and to their children, all the social nourishment they can absorb; *i. e.*, to provide the best possible educational environment for the children who need it most.

Here arises a question, based on previous social studies and conclusions. If Society provides generously for its most needy members, will not that injure the world by multiplying the least desirable class? Will it not put a premium on deficiency, instead of efficiency? This idea rests not only on the Want theory and the Ego concept, but on the Malthusian doctrine. It is believed that human beings tend to multiply in a certain ratio; that the advantage to the race lies in the development of better individuals, not in mere numbers; and that better individuals are developed by personal competition, by the "struggle for existence" and "the survival of the fittest."

As soon as we see the organic unity of Society, this "struggle for existence" idea must change its terms. What we are now concerned with is the development of ever better social organs and functions, and that development does not take place in a direct combat between individuals, but in a superior process supplanting an inferior process, with no essential injury to the constituents.

The introduction of machinery, for instance, was a legitimate social progress. The injury to working men which we allowed to accompany it, was not in any way essential to social progress, but militated against it. Interdependent organs do not fight with one another. Their change in form and value is gradual, and involves no immediate destruction to constituent cells. Society improves by the development of its component parts, not by a destructive conflict of parts. If you are seeking to improve a family of children or a breed of fowls, you do not do it by pitting them against one another and cheerfully retaining the "survivors" as the "most fit." The egg-laying capacity of the hen, the milk-giving capacity of the cow, is not developed by combat between hens, or between cows (or their respective cocks and bulls)! To this it will be eagerly replied, "Ah, yes, but we do it by *selection*—by carefully choosing the ones best suited, and breeding from them. They do not survive from natural selection, but from artificial selection. Now if we were free to practice *that* on Society, if we could choose the best types and breed from them only, then we could indeed improve the race."

That this is one process of improvement is not denied. But it is not the only, nor by any means the most valuable process in the social organism. The swiftest and broadest medium of social improvement lies in that great common sensorium of ours, the brain. By social contact and example, by social transmission, the more advanced members of Society can lift the less advanced at a rate immeasurably faster than the slow current of heredity. We have all seen this in families of very low-grade people, obtaining sudden access to social advantages by present methods, and changing in mind and body to a marked degree, even in one generation. This gain is of course incorporated in the family through heredity, but the effect of ten years' access to the social stores of knowledge, culture, and refinement changes an individual to a very great degree. This immense power of education, using the word in its very widest sense, can be turned on to every child of the race, if we so choose, with a speedy result of race improvement which would laugh to scorn the fumbling, wasteful processes of natural selection, and the one-step-better methods of artificial selection. It is by transmission that we raise the social level most rapidly; a free and general transmission of the product of the special worker to the hands and minds of all.

For Society to bestow the same care and provision on all its children that the wisest parent now seeks to bestow on his would develop the race faster than anything conceivable. That this method would at once improve the individual, the race, and the productivity of both, is clear. That it would "pauperise" has been shown to be an erroneous deduction from the Want theory; under which we are indeed all potential, and some actual, paupers. The further claim that it would tend to a too rapid increase of population, especially among the least fit, should be carefully examined.

The Malthusian error is in assuming that a given rate of reproduction is fixed and final. If Malthus had studied the subject more deeply, he would have found that the rate of reproduction varies widely, not only in the "animal kingdom" but the man. This variation is relative to other conditions; and has been thus formulated by Spencer, "Reproduction is in inverse proportion to individuation." The lower the efficiency of the individual, the more young ones it has.

Progressive specialisation, bringing a higher degree of individual efficiency, carries with it a decrease in the rate of reproduction. The myriad eggs of the fish or insect are followed as species develop by the lesser litters of high-grade quadrupeds, till we reach one at a birth. A fish that only laid one egg at a time would not have a very tall family tree. In man we have the general rule of one at a time; but we have it more times in some cases than in others. The human birth rate varies widely, too; and the action of the same law, a higher development of the individual, higher specialisation, leads to a lower birth rate.

There are also artificial variants, as so painfully shown in the dwindling of France's population; but quite apart from any morbid processes of stirpiculture lies this broad and beautiful law,—the higher specialisation of the individual tends to reduce the birth rate. This is shown with clearness through all the turbid cross-currents of our mistaken behaviour; the most developed kind of people have the least children, and the least developed kind of people have the most children. Even in folk lore we see it indicated—"there was once a King and a Queen who were perfectly happy, except that they had no children," and on the other hand, "The poor man hath his quiver full."

The capacity of the world to support humanity in health and comfort has a limit; it is not near enough to frighten us, but it is there. If human beings are left to struggle on alone in unnatural individualism, their arrested development fills up the world, too, with numerous, but inefficient people. But as a conscious and intelligent society hastens to spread its gains among all its parts; to make the progress of the race the rich possession of all its members; so fully to educate and develop every child as to promote the higher specialisation of the individual, at a rate unconscious natural processes never dreamed of, then we see a steady diminution of this threatening birth rate. By this means we work steadily toward a far higher average of social efficiency, with a permanent balance of birth and death, involving no arbitrary personal tampering with natural processes, but a recognition of the working of natural law.

It would seem needless to say that the individuation of woman is the most prominent necessity here, as her rate of fecundity is the determining factor in the case, not the man's; yet there are still some who ignore even so patent a fact as this.

See, then, how swiftly and surely an awakened society can right its wrongs, cure and outgrow its diseases, understand, pity, and leave far behind its sins. The highest human duty for the individual is to enter upon his or her special work in the world—that is vital, that is first, that underlies all. There is no right life for any human creature who is not taking part in the organic processes of Society. And if, in our present blurred and jumbled condition, we have not the sure guide of a "calling," a special inborn preference and power; why, that only leaves us freer to take hold anywhere of the thousand things that need doing; paid, or unpaid—that is immaterial. The point is *to do the work* and to do it for the service of Society. No matter for the past account, for arrears of social pampering or social neglect; we are all responsible for both. No malicious crowd of despots, masters, owners, and employers has conspired to injuriously deprive the angelic workingman of his rights. We have *all* believed in these economic falsehoods, the inevitable action of which was to produce the conditions we now suffer from. We must all lay them aside; wasting no time or energy on remorse, and simply set to work to make things right.

From that class of people who "do not have to work"—that is, who have been paid and overpaid in advance—there is an overwhelming debt of honour due the world. In that great field of action where there is no pay, nor even thanks as yet; in the efforts necessary to teach the right things, and to provide the right things for the world's little children, there is ample room for the most helplessly rich. Also in the work of spreading the social supplies where they belong—among the whole people—there is work there, much work, not only unpaid and unthanked, but heartily resisted.

There was never a time in history when more splendid opportunities were open to those who would serve society. Thousands of us are at it already, organised and unorganised; a rising flood of love and service, toiling manfully, and womanfully, at the mighty task. But the economic darkness makes it blind work at best.

Most of our conscious "social service" to-day is directed, naturally enough, to ministering to the social diseases. Now, if a man is sick, there are two ways to re-establish his health—both necessary. One is to restore normal conditions to his body, trusting that a normal body will urge to normal action, and so keep him well. The other is to induce normal action, trusting to that to restore right conditions in the body. Each is a good thing, each tends to produce the desired result; but both are incomparably better than either. Our sick Society needs this double treatment. The first condition of normal action we have here reviewed at length; consciously to assume true place in the organic industries of human life. If all of us do that, the currents of right action will assuredly build us a healthy social body. But we can greatly hasten that good end by rearranging the social body too. Here the law of interaction between spirit and form comes to our aid, and makes possible an incredible rate of progress.

Take, for instance, an advanced case in social pathology—a city slum. Now there are two ways for a conscious society to focus its forces on the diseased part and regenerate it. One is by dealing with the spirit of the slum, the people themselves; by so educating the children, so stimulating the adult, so providing proper opportunity for right social service for all, that the people will change in character, and, reacting, soon make the slum a fair, clean, healthful part of the city.

The other is to deal with the body of the slum, the houses, streets, and shops; and so to reconstruct them that they shall steadily react on the people and change their character. Both can be done, both are being done, but so feebly and partially, in such tiny spots of change, under such heavy opposition and heavier indifference, that the gain is heart-breakingly slow. While one playground is being made, while one new method of education is being introduced, a thousand babies die, a thousand children become criminals, a thousand wretched men and women sink to the hopeless grade, are lost to society, become diseased tissue, and are miserably sloughed off through asylum, prison, and hospital.

The cause of the delay is this: We are treating social disease by local application. We find, as it were, a tubercle or boil upon the body politic, we apply all manner of treatment-the poultice, the counter-irritant, the excising knife of capital punishment; but we forget, or do not know, that this local trouble, however poignantly conspicuous, is on a living body, and is caused and maintained by diseased conditions in that body, far beyond the material boundaries of that location.

We must, of course, use prompt and strong measures in these most painful spots; but the treatment necessary to prevent the formation of these conspicuously evil places must be applied to all of us. It is as necessary for the right education and stimulus to be applied to the rich and well-to-do as to the poor, to the isolated farmer in the field as well as the crowded sweater in the shop; and not only those methods touching the people's character, but the other, the prompter ones, touching their physical conditions.

There are certain physical conditions in the social body, brick and mortar conditions, which are affecting us all for evil, and which can be readily changed. There are, also, certain economic relations in that body, affecting us all for evil, that can equally be changed. We need to see these in their true importance; as affecting not only the immediate individuals concerned, but as so affecting the whole structure of Society as to inexorably produce the conspicuous evils with which we are so painfully familiar. Once recognised, our duty is clear—a glad, swift, forward movement bringing joy and gain to all.

What are these general conditions?

One is the economic position of woman, which involves false sex relations, including all forms of prostitution; maintains primitive individual instincts and checks social ones, and is largely responsible for the morbid action of social economics. Another is the maintenance of domestic industry; which, as I have shown in another book, prevents the development of the home, the progress of woman, the right education of the child, and the normal progress of man.

Combined, these two conditions find material form in that hotbed of primitive egoism, the cumbrous, expensive, inadequate dwelling house of our time, or rather, of past time, of the most remote and barbarous time, most injuriously preserved in this. It is true that each human being needs a wholly private and personal room to rest in; that solitude, pure individual solitude, is a social necessity. It is also true that the great primal group, the family, needs its group of rooms, its private home. But the point of divergence is in the Work involved.

Work is social, it does not belong to the person nor, in any advanced degree, to the family. That so much human work is at present performed in and for the separate family is an enormous condition of social evil. It maintains, beyond all the efforts of religion and science to combat, the selfishness of the primeval Pig.

Social consciousness and its great currents of love and enthusiasm, of power and pride, cannot find room in brains continually cramped by application to the most ignominiously personal concerns.

It is not only that the family could have a far simpler, purer, and more private life if they would but take advantage of our immense social facilities, but so could the individual men and women; born and reared in families, to be sure, but born and reared as members of Society, active and responsible factors in social progress.

These men and women, if the families they grew up in were in true social relation, instead of each one keeping up a little down-drawing whirlpool of antediluvian individualism, would be a thousand times more valuable citizens. While the minds of our women are exercised only, or mainly, in impression and expression of a purely personal nature, they and their stunted children and heavily handicapped men cannot properly receive and discharge the vivifying currents of social consciousness.

That consciousness forces itself out here and there through specially sensitive individuals, usually at great personal sacrifice. These special individuals, heavily charged with the social spirit, push and struggle, work and fight, suffer and die, trying to stir to equal life the great ego-bound mass of unawakened Society. Much work has been accomplished, great good has been done, the world is incomparably better off for the presence of these better developed members, but our gain is as nothing to what it would be if the progress was shared by all.

If we *were* still savages, still beasts, still mere individuals, this book and its many brothers might as well wait for weary thousands of years more, but we are not. We are, in patent fact, highly specialised members of a highly advanced Society; but our eyes are holden, our minds are darkened by piously preserved collections of old concepts long found false. We can lay aside these erroneous ideas at a moment's recognition of the true. We can incorporate the true into the make-up of our minds by acting upon them. We can put ourselves in touch with the heart of the world, sharing its splendid pulses, its tireless energy, its flood of common human love, by simply doing our right work. We can break up forever the old false tendencies of thought and feeling by rearranging our material conditions in line with true social forces.

"Better housing for the poor" is necessary, but so it is for the rich, for all of us. Truer housing; housing suitable to the age we live in; housing proper to the human soul. We build "the house of God," bringing to it the highest love and power and aspiration; and that house uplifts the soul of the beholder. What prevents our building the houses of Man with that high love and power and aspiration—that splendid beauty, ennobling space, and tender ornament? Only that ancient, shrivelled, artificially preserved mummy, the Ego concept, prevents.

You cannot build right houses for modern humanity on the basis of a kitchen, on the service of the belly of a beast. Rightly to nourish all people makes the feeding of humanity as noble a form of work as any other work broad and beautiful and true, to be devoutly entered upon and grandly fulfilled; to cater only to the bodily desires of one's own family is proper to the level of meanest savagery.

A rearrangement of ideas and their consequent feelings, from the process false to the process true, is possible to any sane mind, is the duty of every last one of us. A rearrangement of the external conditions follows logically and helps materially. This we can do in the mind at once, in the body not so promptly, but still swiftly in our age of mechanical wonders. And why should we? What will it mean to us? We should, for underlying cause, because it is in the line of social evolution; a race duty. Because in doing it we further the divine purpose, we fulfil ultimate law. But if the so-long-stunted soul demands its pay, there is reason more than enough.

Are men so happy now, each trying to take care of himself and his family, that they should dread the peace and ease given by society's vast resources in full circulation? Are women so happy now, either the squaw or the parasite, that they should dread becoming full human beings, active, conscious members of society? What this change will mean to us no one can fully measure, but those who know anything of the real heart of humanity, those who can interpret the gleams of light that break through all religions, those who ever felt the soul lift and light and swell with power and joy, under the influence of music, or painting, or speech, or any form of human work, can tell us something of it.

We have been taught, in tattered remnants of worn-out faiths, to despise human nature. We, forsooth, mere worms and weaklings, "as prone to evil as the sparks are to fly upward," we were born in iniquity, conceived in sin, doomed to suffer here, and likely to suffer forever, important worms that we were!

We have been taught in later days, by half-seeing students of science, that we were but beasts, and must fight it out as they did, our progress lying in the slow and painful process of survival.

What a change in thought, in feeling, in action, when we see that we are the crowning form of created life, we, collectively, though never so much "worms" taken personally. That Humanity is the one fact we should realise, and that in it we find free scope and full satisfaction for all the vague aspirations which have haunted the individual. That in that organic social life we are all held together by our mutual service, by our work, and that in our work and only in our work lies growth, lies peace, lies the highest human duty, lies happiness.

Happiness, for a human being, is in full, true, conscious, social relation:

To feel the world's life, unbroken in its steady pour, from the inchoate nebulæ, through age on age of changing orders, into the spreading growth of an organised democracy. To feel our own historic family, the immense racial pride of the long ascent, the conquest of elements, of plants, of animals, the unquenchable fire of progress, the vast and rapid increase of the race: To feel the extending light of common consciousness as Society comes alive!—the tingling "I" that reaches wider and wider in every age, that is sweeping through the world to-day like an electric current, that lifts and lights and enlarges the human soul in kindling majesty: To feel the power! the endless power! Not only the ceaseless stream of the universal Godness, but our interminable array of batteries, full charged; the stored energy of all time embodied in poem and story, in picture and statue, in music and architecture, in every tool, utensil, and giant machine wherein the human brain and the human hand have made force incarnate:

And, so feeling, to Do:

To Do, as only Human beings can; not in the paltry processes of the individual, mere servant of his stomach, but in the fascinating complexity and rhythmic splendour of the march of social activities; to take part in that huge, thrilling, organic life in which the individual thrives unconscious—of which the soul is lodged in each of us:

And in the ceaseless development of that measureless vitality, this vast, ever-increasing Social Life, to feel, now and again,—always oftener,—the distant music of the universe grow clearer—that is Happiness.

THE END

Printed by Libri Plureos GmbH in Hamburg,
Germany